THE CULTURAL BOND
Sport, Empire, Society

THE
CULTURAL BOND
Sport, Empire, Society

Edited by
J. A. MANGAN

FRANK CASS

First published in 1992 in Great Britain by
FRANK CASS & CO. LTD.
Gainsborough House, Gainsborough Road,
London E11 1RS, England

and in the United States of America by
FRANK CASS
c/o International Specialized Book Services, Inc.
5602 N.E. Hassalo Street, Portland, Oregon 97213

British Library Cataloguing in Publication Data
The cultural bond : sport, empire, society
1. Sports, Social life
I. Mangan, J.A. (James Anthony) *1939–*
306.48309171241

ISBN 0-7146-3398-4
ISBN 0-7146-4075-1 pbk

1750811

Library of Congress Cataloging-in-Publication Data
The Cultural bond : sport, empire, society / edited by J.A. Mangan.
   p. cm.
   Includes bibliographical references and index.
   ISBN 0-7146-3398-4. – ISBN 0-71146-4075-1 (pbk.)
   1. Sports–Social aspects–Great Britain–History. 2. Sports–
–Social aspects–Great Britain–Colonies–History. I. Mangan, J.A.
GV605.C86   1992
306.4'83'0941–dc20   91-10190
                                     CIP

Chapters 1, 5, 8, 9, 10 and the Epilogue originally appeared in
The International Journal of the History of Sport, Vol. 6, No. 2 (September 1989);
Chapters 2, 3, 4, 6 and 7 originally appeared in Vol. 7, No. 1 (May 1990)
of the same journal.

Typeset by Regent Typesetting, London
Printed in Great Britain by BPCC Wheatons Ltd, Exeter

CONTENTS

NOTES ON CONTRIBUTORS

J.A. Mangan is Head of Education at Jordanhill College, Glasgow. A Fellow of the Royal Historical Society, the Royal Anthropological Institute and the American Academy of Physical Education (corresponding), he is the founder and Senior Editor of *The International Journal of the History of Sport*, and founder and series editor of Manchester University Press's International Studies in the History of Sport. He is the author of *Athleticism in the Victorian and Edwardian Public School: The Emergence and Consolidation of an Educational Ideology* (1981) and *The Games Ethic and Imperialism: Aspects of the Diffusion of an Ideal* (1986), editor of *Pleasure, Profit, Proselytism: British Culture and Sport at Home and Abroad, 1700–1914* (1988) and *Making Imperial Mentalities: Socialisation and British Imperialism* (1990), and co-editor of *Manliness and Morality: Images of the Male in the Old and New World* (1987) and *From 'Fair Sex' to Feminism: Sport and the Socialization of Women in the Industrial and Post-Industrial Eras* (1987).

Malcolm Tozer is Headmaster of Northamptonshire Grammar School. He has researched the overlapping histories of education, sport and imperialism in the Victorian and Edwardian eras, and has published his findings in a series of books and essays including *Physical Education at Thring's Uppingham* (1976).

James Bradley has completed a doctoral dissertation at Edinburgh University on the theme of imperialism, sport and society.

Ray Jenkins is Senior Lecturer at Staffordshire Polytechnic. Following his contribution to *Studies in West African Islamic History* (1979), his doctoral and post-doctoral research has focused upon the history of the urban communities of the Gold Coast littoral, including the continuities in their post-1807 links with the Caribbean, Brazil and Britain. He has produced numerous papers on Ghanaian coastal history and historiography.

Janice N. Brownfoot is a research consultant, lecturer and writer with a special interest in Southeast Asia. Her research has concentrated on women in parts of the British Empire, and her publications include *The Unequal Half: A History of Women in Australia* (1977).

Gillian Hibbins is a Victorian historian who has researched the origins of Australian Rules Football in England and Melbourne.

Richard Cashman is Senior Lecturer in History at the University of New South Wales. He has edited two volumes on sports history and published two books on Australian cricket crowds and one on Indian cricket. *The*

Demon Spofforth: Australia's First Cricket Hero, appeared in 1990, and *Wicket Women: Cricket and Women in Australia* in 1991. He also edited *Early Cricket in Sydney, 1803 to 1856* (1991).

Tony Mason is Senior Lecturer at the Centre for the Study of Social History, University of Warwick. His publications include *Association Football and English Society 1863–1915* (1980) and as editor, *Sport in Britain: A Social History* (1989).

Gerald Redmond is a Professor in the Faculty of Physical Education and Recreation at the University of Alberta. He served as President of the International Association of the History of Sport and Physical Education (HISPA) from 1981 to 1984; and was appointed Fellow of the British Society for Sports History in 1985, and Fellow of the American Academy of Physical Education (corresponding) in 1986.

Anthony Kirk-Greene, Lecturer in the Modern History of Africa and Fellow of St. Antony's College, Oxford, is a former district officer in Northern Nigeria and professor at Ahmadu Bello University. He has published *The Principles of Native Administration in Nigeria, 1900–1947* (1965), *Crisis and Conflict in Nigeria* (1971), *A Biographical Dictionary of the British Colonial Governors in Africa* (1980) and, with Douglas Rimmer, *Nigeria since 1970* (1981). He edited *The Transfer of Power in Africa: The Colonial Administrator in the Age of Decolonization* (1979), and is working on a history of British colonial administrators in Africa.

Katharine Moore is a post-doctoral research fellow at the University of Queensland. Her main area of research is the relationship between sport and the British Empire before 1930, with particular interest in the significance of the British Empire Games in the social history of the Empire.

Harold Perkin is Professor of History at Northwestern University, Chicago, and the author of many distinguished and internationally acclaimed publications, including *Origins of Modern English Society 1780–1880* (1969), and *Rise of Professional Society: England since 1880* (1989).

ILLUSTRATIONS

ACKNOWLEDGEMENTS

Acknowledgements are gratefully made to the Methodist Church Overseas Division for permission to reproduce plate 4; to the British Library for plate 5; the *Rotherham Advertiser* (plate 6). Plate 7 appeared in the Centenary History of Preston North End F.C. and is reproduced with the kind co-operation of the Club's Secretary, Mr E. Griffith. Acknowledgements are also made to the Australian Gallery of Sport, Melbourne (plate 8); the La Trobe Collection, State Library of Victoria (plate 9); *Vanity Fair* (plate 10); the *Sydney Mail* (plate 11); the Public Archives of Canada (plates 12, 13, 14, and 15); the Royal Commonwealth Society (plate 16); the Malaysian National Archives (plate 17). Plate 19 is reproduced by courtesy of the Hamilton Public Library, Canada, and plates 20, 21, and 22, all from the 1934 British Empire Games Canadian Trials Programme, are reproduced by courtesy of the State Library of New South Wales, Sydney, Australia.

Thanks are also due to the Humanities Department of Staffordshire Polytechnic for photographic assistance to Dr Jenkins.

THE IMPERIAL AND
POST-IMPERIAL BOND

This robust, sport-loving society cradled in peace behind the shield of the Royal Navy.

Edward Grierson, *The Death of the Imperial Dream:*
The British Commonwealth and Empire 1795–1969 (1972)

Sport remains the great unofficial department which permeates the Empire. Whoever can define 'sport' can define the English.

Shane Leslie, *The End of a Chapter* (1922)

Sport was to be after all the Empire's most successful export, played in one form or another wherever Englishmen had set foot.

Valerie Pakenham, *The Noonday Sun:*
Edwardians in the Tropics (1985)

The British took their games with them wherever they went. Sport was their chief spiritual export, and was to prove among their more resilient memorials.

James Morris, *Pax Britannica: The Climax of an Empire* (1968)

The organizational drive for sport had come from Britain. It was from Britain that cricket, and soccer more than cricket, had spread as nothing international had ever spread for centuries before. ... I read and thought and read and unearthed a grievous scandal. This was that not a single English scholar, historian or social analyst of repute had deemed it worth his while to pay even the most cursory attention to these remarkable events in which his own country played so central, in fact the central, role.

C.L.R. James, *Beyond a Boundary* (1964), pp. 157–8.

Britain's Chief Spiritual Export: Imperial Sport as Moral Metaphor, Political Symbol and Cultural Bond

J. A. MANGAN

In a now famous discussion of 'culture' A. L. Kroeber and C. Kluckhohn suggested that its core consisted of historically derived and selected ideas *and* their attached values. Cultural systems, they added, were products of social action and determinants of further social action. In short, culture is essentially a set of potent and dynamic normative ideas, beliefs and actions.[1]

More recently, in the foreword to his innovatory series Studies in Imperialism, John M. MacKenzie asserted that in the era of European world supremacy British imperialism was as much a dominant idea with intellectual, cultural and technical facets[2] as it was a set of economic, political and military imperatives. And with equal relevance Patrick Brantlinger argued a little earlier that, just as it is impossible to write an adequate history of British culture without considering its social and political ramifications in country and city, so it is impossible to understand that culture without embracing colony and dominion.[3]

It is time that it was more widely recognized that by the late nineteenth century sport lay close to the heart of Britain imperial culture. It formed a distinct, persistent and significant cluster of cultural traits isolated in time and space, possessing a coherent structure and definite purpose. While it had many cultural functions, it had certainly become a means of propagating imperial sentiments.[4]

Arguably, the *genus Britannicus*, to differ slightly from C. L. R. James, was more than a fine batsman; he was a committed sportsman. And more often than not his was a moral commitment and an integral part of his imperial 'civilizing' purpose. Sport was the more pleasant part of this melioristic purpose and as real to him as a 'civilizing' medium as British law, religion and education. In his imperial role of man of firm duty, confident ambition, moral intention *and* applied athletics he might appropriately be labelled *homo ludens imperiosus!* To a great extent, of course, the English games field had provided, through the medium of the public-school system and ancient universities, 'a meeting place for the moral outlook of the dissenting middle classes and the athletic instincts of the aristocracy'.[5] Much more than this, however, the middle classes with a strong tendency to serious ethical commitment 'colonized' the upper classes. Late Victorian society witnessed *in reverse* a deliberate and purposeful hegemonic effort. Games, especially cricket, were elevated by the middle classes to the status of a moral discipline. C. L. R. James is correct. The Victorians did make the game compulsory for their children and all the evidence points to the fact that 'they valued competence in it and respect for what it came to signify more than they did intellectual accomplishment of any kind'.[6] Eventually cricket became the symbol *par excellence* of imperial solidarity and superiority epitomizing a set of consolidatory moral imperatives that both exemplified and explained imperial ambition and achievement. It became a political metaphor as much as an imperial game:

> The greatest game in the world is played wherever the Union Jack is unfurled, and it has no small place in cementing the ties that bond together every part of the Empire ... On the cricket grounds of the Empire is fostered the spirit of never knowing when you are beaten, of playing for your side and not for yourself, and of never giving up a game as lost. This is as invaluable in Imperial matters as cricket.[7]

And, of course, for the imperialist adventurers the cricket bat in exotic settings had the further advantage of curing, or rather distracting from, almost every moral disease including that of enforced domination over others. Sport, when necessary, could prove a relaxing couch for conscience.[8]

In John H. Field's *Toward a Programme of Imperial Life: The British Empire at the Turn of the Century*, 'character', both in late Victorian usage *and* in analytical perspective, is the organizing principle. 'Character', he notes, 'was a highly charged term of portentous significance for the late Victorians.'[9] The historian of this period is struck by the high incidence of the term and its frequent use in explicitly imperial contexts. Lord Rosebery, for example, once introduced a school textbook with the dictum: 'Influence is based on character, and it is on the character of each child that grows into manhood ... that the future of our Empire rests.'[10] Caught in this brief assertion, Field suggests, is the ethical preoccupation of late Victorian society. At another level, Field's study is an attempt to locate a connection between Victorian conventional wisdom involving assumptions about individual, social, national and racial values and the ground swell of popular support for empire. A concern with 'character' stimulated enthusiasm for the idea of empire.[11] Late Victorians were committed to the Empire *primarily* because of the close association that it came to have with the inculcation, demonstration and transmission of valued 'Anglo-Saxon' qualities embodied in the concept of 'character'.

This volume adds specificity to Field's assertion. The inculcation of these 'Anglo-Saxon' qualities was attempted substantially on metropolitan and colonial playing fields. Sport was a major medium for the

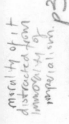

attempted development of 'character' particularly among those who by virtue of their position in elite society were destined to be the Empire's leaders. Of course, this is an assertion now well rehearsed elsewhere. A potent education ideology known as athleticism[12] evolved in response to a late Victorian obsession with character and imperialism. The significance of this ideology in the context of the British Empire should never be underestimated, and it is questionable whether it has as yet been sufficiently appreciated. It is a vital element of British imperialism. The contributors to this volume, like Field, are concerned less with expansionist ambitions and anxieties, crises over the interference or encroachment of other powers, maintenance of economic interests and the organizational structure of imperial control than with the moral associations, symbolic interpretations and emotional meanings associated with the idea of empire in the late nineteenth and early twentieth centuries, and to a certain extent, with subsequent consequences in the modern post-imperial period. They are concerned therefore with the axiology of imperialism. It remains simply to state that in imperial historiography, this dimension of imperialism is no less significant than others despite its relative neglect by historians. Here we are dealing, in Keith Fieldhouse's perceptive phrase, with imperialism as 'a sociological phenomenon with roots in political facts',[13] and this in turn, shifts the focus of imperial study, at least momentarily, from the decisions and policies of proponents and opponents of empire to general social values and to processes of imperial socialization.[14]

Late Victorian, Edwardian and later imperialism now becomes a matter of English social history,[15] and in turn the task within a historical, anthropological and sociological framework becomes that of developing hypotheses about imperialism in relation to cultural ideals and processes. Consequently it also becomes an ethnological inquiry. Another way of setting out this task is to agree with Weber that 'man is an animal suspended in webs of significance he himself has spun' and to search interpretively for their meaning[16] – in this instance within the wide 'web' of empire.

The cultural preoccupations of *homo ludens imperiosus* not only reflected an obsession with 'character' but also served as significant ritual manifestations of association, licensed and approved, banishing both difference and distance and manifesting commonness.[17]

> Only in rites
> Can we renounce our oddities
> And be truly entired.[18]

His culture was an instrument of imperial bonding. To effect bonding, of necessity, all cultures contain in their repertoire of myth, symbol and ritual certain compelling images, narratives, actions and models which social actors, especially their chosen charismatic figures acting as culture heroes, re-enact again and again precisely because of the 'aura effect' of mythic, symbolic and ritual patterns.[19] Throughout the Empire sports-

men, and to a far lesser extent sportswomen, and sports fields were
acknowledged agents and agencies respectively of this bonding process. Through this process by virtue of domination, control and contact
cultural. links were established between Great Britain, dominion and
colony which affected irrevocably the nature of indigenous cultures,
political relationships, and subordinates' perceptions of superiors and
vice versa.

The task of analysing the nature of the purposes, processes and significance of sport as a form of cultural association is a complex one, and this
volume merely initiates it. The phenomenon itself was complex. It took
many forms: intentional and unintentional, direct and indirect, acci-
dental and incidental, formal and informal. Malcolm Tozer, James
Bradley, Richard Cashman, Gerald Redmond and Katharine Moore
provide evidence of formal and informal attempts to use sport, wittthhh
varrying degrees off success and thoroughness, to achieve intentional and
purposeful bonding. Ray Jenkins, Janice N. Brownfoot and Tony Mason
offer examples of indirect and unintentional bonding brought about
respectively in defiance of orthodox ideological priorities, as the unsought
outcome of early 'feminist' idealism and as the by-product of simple
recreational enthusiasm; Gillian Hibbins and Anthony Kirk-Greene, for
their part, discuss sport as informal and incidental means of cultural
association in the imperial and post-imperial worlds respectively; while
Harold Perkin concludes that as part of its post-imperial legacy sport
has had a significant and benign influence ensuring goodwill and good
relations between Commonwealth nations. Collectively and cumulative-
ly the contributors to this volume make the point that sport was a
significant part of imperial culture, and an important instrument of
imperial cultural association and subsequent cultural change, promoting
at various times in various localities imperial union, national identity,
social reform, recreational development and post-imperial goodwill.
These imperial and post-imperial outcomes of sport constitute a missing
dimension of the historiography of imperialism.

In the late Victorian period the unifying force of sport, for the privileged of the Empire, was seldom in question. And compelling incanta-
tions of imperial solidarity through sport were recited endlessly by the
young and the old, but more especially by the old to the young. Some of
these enthusiasts of sport in the imperial design of things demonstrate
below the strength of their fervour, reveal the certainty of their convictions and indicate their full subscription to a belief in sport as the
social cement of empire. Better illustrations of Semmel's 'rhetorical
imperialism' would be hard to find: their purpose to transmit a sense of
commitment to the uninitiated, unaware or indifferent all but leaps out of
the quotations.[20]

From *Greater Britain* in 1891:

    While Britons retain their national interest in sport the subjects which divide them into arid sects must necessarily be of only momentary concern. There will never be more than a formal disintegration of the Empire while we are subject to the bond of a common interest in arts which spring directly from the instincts of the national character. The common love of the chase in any of its forms, the common joy in a well-fought maul in the football field, satisfied our optimistic observers that, whatever may betide us in politics, our British spirit is a thing of permanence.[21]

From the *Cambridge University Magazine* in 1886:

Politicians work out grand schemes with treaties and conventions to bind us and our colonies ... but ... we may also venture to say that a visit of a Canadian crew to Henley ... will bind us and our cousins of the tongue far more closely than any amount of diplomacy and trade conventions.[22]

And these are the words of Sir Theodore Cook in *Character and Sportsmanship*:

English cricketers are playing against Parsees and Mohammedans at Karachi while a team of Maoris are testing the best of our Rugby footballers at home. By such threads are the best bonds of union woven. For the constitution of the British Empire, unexpressed and inexpressible, does not depend on force and cannot by the sword alone be guarded. It is the visible, intangible impersonation of spiritual sympathies and associations. It lives because the blood that is its life is pulsing from its heart in England through every tissue of the body politic in every quarter of the globe.[23]

There is no ambivalence here to confuse the reader. These voices were mostly those of a vociferous upper-middle-class chorus giving song to Lord Rosebery's 'greater pride in Empire which is called imperialism and which is a larger patriotism'.[24] They uttered with confident resonance reverberating ideological statements: motivational, moralistic and emotional.

In his discussion of the development of imperialism in the second half of the nineteenth century Field states that when 'the general population began to identify itself with the wielding and witnessing of international power by the governing elite, the significance of the emotional element would be increased a hundred fold ... It was no vacuum in which the rationality of the Colonial Office worked'.[25] The shibboleths from *Greater Britain*, *Cambridge University Magazine* and *Character and Sportsmanship*, quoted above, heavy with metaphors of imperial conviction, helped transform 'sentiment into significance' and made ideological ambition widely available. Their purpose was to create imperial stability, integration and unity by means of shared enthusiasms. The sports these writers praised constituted a cultural symbol system offering 'institutionalised guides for behaviour'. They were sociological and psychological 'road maps' permitting chosen inhabitants of empire to develop and maintain emotional ties within an ordered, secure environment.

Imperial sport in large measure comprised esemplastic symbolic actions representing in turn allegiance to a set of self-assumed responsibilities arising out of a particular view of social control founded in turn on an unshakeable belief in racial supremacy and an associated moral superiority. Sport was part of a grand stewardship 'to carry peace and order over the world that others may enter and enjoy'.[26] There was more than wishful jocularity in these lines by Norman Gale:

> There will be a perfect planet
>   Only when the Game shall enter
> Every country, teaching millions
>   How to ask for Leg or Centre.
> Closely heed a level-headed
>   Sportsman far too grave to banter:
> When the cricket bags are opened
>   Doves of Peace fly forth instanter![27]

The imperial system of sport was a template 'for the organisation of social and psychological processes much as genetic systems provide such a template for the organisation of organic processes'.[28] And in this way it was an instrument of what the anthropologist would call segmentation. It sustained solidarity as it successfully enlarged the social group. Social historians neglect to study the social meanings, purposes and consequences of sport at their professional peril. They should certainly make every effort in the period of the New Imperialism and after to make contact with a period attitude and to recover a past world that reveals sport as far more than an 'intellectually insignificant' recreational pleasure. It was seen by many Victorians and Edwardians as an imperial umbilical cord. And in this role, arguably, it was far more meaningful at home and abroad than literature, music, art or religion.

The central popularity of cricket throughout the Empire, it has been suggested, brought in its wake illusions of social unity which implied that the game transcended normal divisions of class, colour and status while clearly and carefully maintaining social distance within imperial social structures.[29] This is a point of substance. It puts proper stress on a complex reality. Not merely cricket but imperial sport, predominantly but not exclusively, was a cultural bond of a white imperial fraternity. Within imperial sport racism, sexism and imperialism were as valid a Trinity as athleticism, militarism and imperialism. To a considerable extent imperial sport was a favoured means of creating, maintaining and ensuring the survival of dominant male elites. Athletic proselytism was a statement of masculine cultural superiority as much as a gesture of general benevolent altruism. It is absolutely true that 'even interventions which were of direct and unambiguous benefit ... almost always carried a broader cultural burden and ... were linked with ways of extending control and creating or redefining groups and boundaries in a manner consistent with colonial order and hierarchy'.[30] C. L. R. James, for one, had no doubt that cricket in the English-speaking Caribbean was a major bulwark against social and political change.[31] At the same time he viewed it as a reflection on the pitch of a wider manifestation – the stylized epitome of a moral order and the metaphoric essence of a cultured civilization.

With James' remark about imperial bulwarks against change in mind it must be made clear that it is impossible in this volume to explore all the subtleties of the relationship between imperial proselytizer and proselytized,[32] yet there is an attempt in these pages to investigate several of the complexities of this relationship and to explore modifications to, re-interpretations of, resistance to and rejection of some or even all of the culture of *homo ludens imperiosus*. The trick is to weave a complex pattern while not losing individual threads. While we should fully recognize that dominant elites in empire did seek 'in purposive fashion to engineer the conformity of subordinate groups'[33] through sport, we should also recognize that sport was an area of negotiation. The tensions inherent in all hegemonic relations should not be overlooked.[34] We should also be wary of carelessly patronizing indigenous cultures and at least attempt to avoid 'the enormous condescension of posterity'[35] as well as attempt to be sensitive to the dangers of stereotyping, reductionism and global generalization. Above all, we should be prepared to confront fully the possible disparities between ideological assertion, intention and realization. And in the imperial cultural setting of sport we should certainly appreciate the independent, creative capacities of politically inferior societies and individuals, while at the same time recognizing the effectiveness, by virtue of the ideological and institutional advantages possessed by imperial agents and agencies, of hegemonic control.[36]

Finally, on this matter of analytical subtlety in response to cultural complexities, Richard Cashman has raised several pertinent questions in the specific context of imperial cricket that have equal pertinence in the wider context of imperial sport:

> Where does the promoting hand of the colonial master stop and where does the adapting and assimilating indigenous tradition start? Is it merely adaptation and domestication or does it go beyond that to constitute resistance and even subversion? And how far can the colonial acceptance of cricket be seen as superior colonial salesmanship or a successful exercise of social control using the highly developed and subtle ideology of games and colonialism? Or was it that many colonial subjects chose to pursue a game, because of the ideology, or even in spite of it, because it suited them to take up cricket for their own reasons? Or was the ideology of colonialism the starting point for the adoption of cricket

but once the game was launched other factors came to bear which
led to its spread and consolidation?[37]

It is wise to appreciate that there was no culturally monolithic response to
attempts to utilize sport as an imperial bond. A major problem that the
analyst of ideological proselytism and its cultural consequences should
confront is the nature of interpretation, assimilation and adaptation and
the extent of resistance and rejection by the proselytized – in a phrase,
the extent and form of ideological implementation. Any analyst worth
his salt should be aware of cultural discontinuities as well as continuities.
The unanticipated consequences of stated intentions are neither unusual
nor unreal. This state of affairs has been described rather well by Clifford
Geetz:

> a group of primitives sets out, in all honesty, to pray for rain and
> ends by strengthening its social solidarity; a ward politician sets out
> to get or remain near the trough and ends by mediating between
> unassimilated immigrant groups and an impersonal governmental
> bureaucracy; an ideologist sets out to air his grievances and finds
> himself contributing, through the very diversionary power of his
> illusions, to the viability of the very system that grieves him.[38]

The inclusion within our consideration of the nature of sport as an
imperial bond of cultural encounters between dominant and subordinate
groups certainly provides the opportunity 'to place the grand and theatri-
cal discourses of colonial knowledge and control in the context of their
often partial and ironic realisations'.[39] Once again C. L. R. James pointed
the way, providing a superb illustration of this process in action. Of his
Caribbean school modelled on English public-school lines he wrote:

> It was only long years after that I understood the limitation on
> spirit, vision and self-respect which was imposed on us by the fact
> that our masters, our curriculum, our core of morals, *everything*
> began from the basis that Britain was the source of all light and
> leading, and our business was to admire, wonder, imitate, learn;
> our criterion of success was to have succeeded in approaching that
> distant ideal – to attain it was, of course, impossible.[40]

In this volume Janice N. Brownfoot offers a no less striking example of
the partial and ironic realization of imperial 'valued knowledge', which in
this instance worked against the interests of the imperialist, in her
description of the emancipatory uses of 'the games ethic' in the education
of girls in Malaya. It is hoped that this set of essays will advance, at least a
little, the task, which Cashman rightly discerns has only recently begun,
of analysing the colonial 'domestication' of British sport and determining
how far the process represented cultural assimilation, adaptation and
resistance, or indeed a mixture of all three elements.[41]

It has been claimed that cultural analysis 'breaks up into a disconnected yet coherent sequence of bolder and bolder sorties'[42] with studies building on other studies, not in the sense that they take up where others leave off but in the sense that, stimulated by earlier stumbling, better informed and better conceptualized, they penetrate deeper into the same things. Rather than standing on the shoulders of earlier studies they run by their side – challenging and improving these earlier efforts.[42] This book is an early attempt to locate modern sport near to the centre of British imperial culture. Further and better attempts will be awaited by those involved in this propaedeutic effort with eagerness and satisfaction.

NOTES

1. A. L. Kroeber and C. Kluckhohn, 'Culture: A Critical Review of Concepts and Definitions', *Papers of the Peabody Museum of American Archeology and Ethnology*, 70 (1952), 227.
2. See General Editor's Foreword in Jeffrey Richards (ed.), *Imperialism and Juvenile Literature* (Manchester, 1989), p. vii.
3. Patrick Brantlinger, *Rites of Darkness: British Literature and Imperialism* (Ithaca, 1988), p. 15.
4. See J. A. Mangan, *The Games Ethic and Imperialism: Aspects of the Diffusion of an Ideal* (Harmondsworth, 1987) especially Chs. One and Two.
5. C. L. R. James, *Beyond a Boundary* (London, 1969), p. 164.
6. Ibid.
7. Ric Sissons and Brian Stoddart, *Cricket and Empire* (London, 1984), p. 34.
8. Brantlinger, *Rites of Darkness*, p. 11.
9. H. John Field, *Toward a Programme of Imperial Life: the British Empire at the Turn of the Century* (Oxford, 1983), p. 26.
10. Quoted in ibid., p. 30.
11. Ibid., p. 26.
12. See J. A. Mangan, *Athleticism in the Victorian and Edwardian Public School: The Emergence and Consolidation of an Educational Ideology* (Cambridge, 1981), *passim*.
13. Quoted in Field, *Toward a Programme of Imperial Life*, p. 2.
14. See J. A. Mangan, *Making Imperial Mentalities* (Manchester, 1990), Introduction and *passim*.
15. Field, *Toward a Programme of Imperial Life*, p. 20.
16. See Clifford Geetz, *The Interpretation of Cultures* (New York, 1973), p. 5.
17. Bernice Martin, *A Sociology of Contemporary Cultural Change* (Oxford, 1981), p. 49.
18. Quoted in ibid., p. 49.
19. Ibid., p. 50.
20. Field, *Toward a Programme of Imperial Life*, p. 22.
21. *Greater Britain*, 15 August 1891, 507.
22. *Cambridge University Magazine*, 20 June 1886, 21.
23. Sir Theodore Cook, *Character and Sportsmanship* (London, 1927), p. 321.
24. Field, *Toward a Programme of Imperial Life*, p. 5.
25. Ibid., p. 15.
26. From Charles H. Pearson, *National Life and Character* (London, 1893), quoted in Field, *Toward a Programme of Imperial Life*, p. 49.
27. Norman Gale, 'Pax Britannica' in *Messrs. Bat and Ball* (Tudby, 1930), p. 4.
28. Geetz, *Interpretation of Cultures*, p. 218.
29. Brian Stoddart, 'Cricket and Colonialism in the English-Speaking Caribbean to 1914: Towards a Cultural Analysis' in J. A. Mangan (ed.), *Pleasure, Profit, Proselytism: British Culture and Sport at Home and Abroad, 1700–1914* (London, 1988), p. 326.

30. Nicholas Thomas, 'Hunting Heads: Colonialism as Culture', *The Age Monthly Review* (Dec/Jan, 1989), 31.
31. Stoddart, 'Cricket and Colonialism', p. 250.
32. For an interesting discussion of this issue see Richard Cashman, 'Cricket and Colonialism: Colonial Hegemony and Indigenous Subversion' in Mangan (ed.), *Pleasure, Profit, Proselytism*, pp. 258–63.
33. Peter Bailey, 'Leisure, Culture and the Historian: Reviewing the First Generation of Leisure Historiography in Britain', *Leisure Studies* 8, (1989), 114.
34. Ibid.
35. Ibid.
36. Ibid.
37. Cashman, 'Cricket and Colonialism: Colonial Hegemony and Indigenous Subversion', p. 261.
38. Geetz, *Interpretation of Cultures*, p. 206.
39. Thomas, 'Hunting Heads', 31.
40. James, *Beyond a Boundary*, pp. 38–9.
41. Cashman, 'Cricket and Colonialism', p. 271.
42. Geetz, *Interpretation of Cultures*, p. 25.

CHAPTER ONE

A Sacred Trinity – Cricket, School, Empire: E.W. Hornung and his Young Guard

MALCOLM TOZER

The year is 1909; the setting a school chapel. It is a Sunday in November, with the whole school assembled for evensong. As the hymn draws to a close, the preacher mounts the steps to the pulpit, places his prepared address on the lectern, and finally looks out at the congregation of boys and masters. But this week there are no yawns of anticipation, no games of sermon-cricket have been prepared, and no thoughts drift off into day-dreams – for this is a favourite preacher. He is a famous old boy of the school; not a bishop, nor a politician, nor a soldier, nor a colonial admini-strator – but a popular novelist, and much read by the boys of the school. His annual sermon at his old school is awaited with interest, for it is always a winner: this year his theme is 'The Old School List'.[1]

Now, 80 years on, it is hard to imagine the impact of a public-school sermon. The modern schoolboy is bombarded with information, opinion and exhortation by television and radio, at the cinema and the theatre, and through newspapers and magazines, so the effect of the preacher's words is lost in a welter of propaganda. Of these, only the printed word was available to his Edwardian predecessors, yet even that was likely to have been censored by the school authorities. These same authorities, however, recognized the force of the spoken word and, ever since the 1830s when Thomas Arnold seized for headmasters the power of the pulpit, the weekly chapel sermon became the main organ of the school's policy and principles. Today we might marvel at the boys' endurance, though a ten-minute sermon was far shorter than the hours of oratory reserved for the annual speech day, and wonder at their patience. Yet the evidence suggests that the sermon was listened to and the message was heeded: manuscript sermons were treasured by their grateful recipients; popular sermons would be printed the following week and then circulated among boys and parents; and headmasters would publish volumes of their collected sermons – to serve as a school prospectus, to assure current parents that all was well in the school, and to remind old boys of their lessons of the past. Headmasters and their assistants, all usually in holy orders, dominated the pulpit in the Victorian years, but as the number of lay staff increased in the new century, so the invitation to the pulpit was extended to the visiting preacher.

This visiting preacher was E.W. Hornung, Old Uppinghamian, cricket-ing enthusiast, author of the best-selling Raffles tales, brother-in-law of Sir Arthur Conan Doyle, and ardent imperialist. Willie Hornung was one of many speakers and preachers who visited the public and preparatory schools at this time to press home the imperial message. All ideals need propagandists, and heroes of the Boer War, politicians of the patriotic movements, and eminent men of letters toured the schools to spread the imperial word. The soldiers and politicians generally spoke as representa-tives of the National Service League or the Navy League, and under the guise of lecturing on military history, inspecting the cadet corps, or opening new gymnasia, they sought to promote the ideal of national conscription. Other visitors, like Hornung, were more altruistic, seeking to awaken the ideal of imperialism in the new generation of public schoolboys: an examination of the message plied by this visiting preacher and minor poet evokes the spirit of the imperial heyday, when the sportsman ideal ruled wherever the map was red.

In the years before 1880 a quiet imperial idealism had been based on a federation of the English-speaking white races, and of service to the back-ward peoples of Asia and Africa – it was an imperial extension of the brotherhood of the Christian Socialists. Then came a noisier strain. As a consequence of the new power of the united Germany and the industrial might of the emerging United States, Britain in the late 1880s was seen to lose some of its lead over other world powers. This, together with episodes like Gordon's martyrdom in Khartoum and the subsequent denting of British pride, led directly to an era of aggressive acquisition of territory in the scramble for colonies. Africa became the main attraction, and under a cover of doctrines on national destiny and civilizing mission married to policies on materialistic need, the continent was carved up by the world powers. Soon the Far East and the Pacific brought new acquisitions to the British Empire, and by 1899 the total global area under the British flag was equivalent to four Europes, had a population of some 400,000,000, and provided half the world's seaborne trade. Back at home the Empire was the paychest for many, and a colonial caste of former planters, merchants, adventurers and soldiers became a powerful influence. Many of these returning expatriates developed strong links with public schools: some retired to the spa towns where many schools were sited; others helped in the foundation of new imperially-minded institutions; and many as parents selected for their sons schools that flew imperial colours. At Victoria's accession to the throne in 1837 hardly a thought was given to the Empire; at the Golden Jubilee the emphasis was on civilizing mission and duty; but the Diamond Jubilee of 1897 became an orgy of self-congratulation and national assertion. Crude, rumbustious, imperial fever intoxicated the nation in the last years of the century, carrying all shades of political and religious opinion in its wake. Whether trumpeted by the newly founded *Daily Mail*, imbibed in the verses of Newbolt and Kipling, or sung in such patriotic songs as *Another Little Patch of Red* or *Soldiers of the Queen*, the hysteria of imperialism swept the country. An expanding empire needed not only administrators and merchants to tap its wealth, but also an army and navy to keep what was held and to conquer what could be gained: then, in the new century, came the threat from Germany. It is against this background that Hornung plied his message.

Hornung had three interests as a writer – the Empire, cricket, and public schools – and these intertwining threads twist through all his yarns. His writings also have a strong autobiographical flavour, for his own personality and interests, together with episodes from his schooldays and his travels, figure in them prominently. Hornung's background thus colours his tales, and since his father was an émigré Hungarian it is likely that the passion of the new convert for everything English was imbibed at an early age; and what enthusiasms could be more English than the Empire, cricket and public schools? In this autobiographical vein, many of Hornung's heroes share the villainous asthma that was to dog him all his life; as youngsters they and he saw countless medical specialists, smoked curious cigarettes to relieve the spasms, and were allowed to miss early morning school after a night of bad attacks.[2] Together they go to public school (always Uppingham in the 1880s) but, ill-served by the combined hereditary afflictions of asthma and poor eyesight, they cannot join their contemporaries at play. They compensate, however, by becoming armchair cricket experts, learning every aspect of cricket lore and every statistic of the exploits of the famous. The asthma fails to respond to treatment, so heroes and author alike reluctantly accept the advice of the doctors, to leave school at the early age of 17 and take the long sea-voyage to Australia in search of bracing breezes and a healthier climate.[3] Hornung's own epic voyage under sail on the *Loch Torridon* from Glasgow to Melbourne round the Cape of Good Hope took 77 days, with the time spent continuing his school reading, playing 'the buffoon of the saloon' in the weekly concerts, and getting up a journal of the voyage.[4] Hornung had earlier contributed to the *Uppingham School Magazine*; now this literary effort was printed in Australia for the subscribing passengers; and numerous incidents from the voyage were to find their way into his stories.[5]

Hornung spent nearly two years working on a sheep station in the colony of New South Wales, where the hot, dry climate worked its magic on his asthma. During this period he continued to write, collecting images and episodes that were to be used later in his Australian tales. In March 1886 the now healthier 20-year-old Hornung left the colony, and once back in the home country began work in London as a journalist.[6] Here he had the good fortune to join Arthur Conan Doyle's literary set in the years when the adventures of Sherlock Holmes and Dr. Watson were thrilling the nation. Hornung and Conan Doyle were to become lifelong friends, a relationship cemented in 1893 when Hornung married Constance Doyle, the famous author's young sister. Hornung now had his introduction to the London literary agents and publishers, and his 30-year career as a popular novelist began.

The life on the stations of the young Australian colonies was turned to account in his earliest fiction, and then formed the setting of half his twentieth-century stories.[7] It cannot be said that his Australian novels have lasted well: the first, *A Bride from the Bush*, turns on the gaucheness of an Australian girl in English society: her final offence is to call in the outback yodel, 'Coo-ee', to a compatriot in Rotten Row, a crime that apparently had the same electrifying effect as Eliza Doolittle's famous expletive.[8] Hornung had, however, touched a rich vein and his late-Victorian readers were intrigued by the manners and parlance of colonial life; homesteaders, swagmen, bushrangers and jackeroos brought new colour to the language; even the colonials reckoned that his tales faithfully recorded their Australian life.[9] The outback was described in the style of a down-under western; and never more so than in the best of his Australian writing, *Stingaree*. The eponymous hero is a dandy outlaw: he sports a monocle, totes two long-barrelled revolvers, and mounts a white mare; and he robs the mail stage to secure the latest copies of *Punch* where he can catch the reviews of the newest success from Gilbert and Sullivan.

In all his Australian tales Hornung played the role of the imperial recruiting sergeant, seeking Young Guard to follow the Colours. Life in the colonies was better than in the 'old country': there was plenty of room for all; the climate was perfect; and there was little poverty or ill-health – 'Australia is becoming the crack place to be'.[10] It was also the land of opportunities, whether for the weak to gain strength, the disinherited to seek a fortune, or the disgraced to build a new name. Such was the background of many of Hornung's heroes: public-school failures, army rejects, even Stingaree was an Oxford man fallen on hard times.[11] The colonies also provided great challenges: there the manners may have been brash and the customs quaint, but young men could overcome these rude welcomes and go on to lead the emerging nation into the modern era, one in which faster sea travel brought the antipodes closer to the Western world. Australia was not hampered by outmoded traditions, for wealth, breeding and academic triumph counted for little: it was men of action who would forge Australia's future.

Cricket, the game played by those men of action, was Hornung's second passion. In part cricket was just a game – school matches, country house games, backyard tip-and-run for the invalid, and playing-card cricket for the rainy day, provided episodes and scenery in many of his tales; but in fact it was more than just a game, more 'the quintessence and epitome of life'.[12] In this high Victorian era the game implied wealth, exclusivity and an aura of 'good form', and high standards of honour, loyalty and morality were expected from its players. This tone is explicit in 'Kenyon's Innings' from the short-story collection *Some Persons Unknown*; 'My dear fellow, it was only a game – yet it was life! We live our lives as we play our games; and we *must* be sportsmen, and bide by the umpire's decision, and go out grinning when it is against us'.[13] Despite his asthma and his thick pebble-lensed glasses, Hornung played the game throughout his adolescent and adult life. He was never as proficient as his literary heroes, but he played with his brother-in-law in J.M. Barrie's XI, the Allah-Akbarries; amazed

1. E.W. Hornung at work in his study at 7 Hornton Street, Kensington

2. 'Trusty and well beloved …': Oscar Hornung, the writer's only son, killed in action in 1915

3. An advertisement for *The Young Guard*, Hornung's collected poems of the First World War, published in 1919

all who saw him stand up behind the wicket to the fastest bowlers; and was elected a member of the MCC in 1907. In his dreams he no doubt scored centuries, and once he made his dream come true – but only in fiction![14]

And Raffles was a cricketer! In all Hornung wrote nearly thirty books, but only the Raffles stories of the 'Amateur Cracksman' have passed the test of time. Although it is fairly common to meet people who have not read about Raffles, it is comparatively rare to come across someone who has never heard of him, or to whom the name does not suggest a man about town who was also a burglar. Three of the four volumes of stories are still on the publisher's list, and in recent years the hero's adventures have been dramatized for both television and radio.[15]

Raffles is an early clubland hero, and with his accomplice Bunny forms an inversion of Holmes and Watson. The first volume of stories was indeed dedicated to Holmes's creator, but he was supposedly shocked at Hornung's lack of taste in making the criminal the hero.[16] At school Raffles had been 'captain of the eleven, the fastest man of the fifteen, athletic champion, and ornament of the Upper Sixth';[17] now he is 'a dangerous bat, a brilliant field, and perhaps the finest slow bowler of his decade'.[18] Raffles plays for Middlesex, the Gentlemen of England, and his country, and it is his prowess at the game that is so indispensable both socially and financially for the hero's well-being. The cricket, however, does not provide challenge and thrill enough; he turns from taking a man's wicket to relieving him of his silver, so finding 'the one game he knew that was always exciting, always full of danger and of drama'.[19] Raffles possesses a healthy, athletic approach to crime – even making one snatch as rain provides an interval in his Test Match innings – and the only violence encountered is reserved for his opponent's stump. Cricket actually led him into crime, for it is on a tour of Australia that he becomes penniless, impersonates a bank manager of the same surname, and makes off with the funds.[20]

The first adventures of Raffles were published in 1899, and are set in the years before the Boer War; the third and fourth volumes were written much later, but span the same period; whereas the second volume was written just after this war and has one episode set in it.[21] Raffles and Bunny now go to war. The last years of Victoria's reign were far from quiet for the Empire as trouble had brewed in the Sudan and the Boer War brought the Home Country to its biggest test for nearly a century. Hornung determined that Raffles would 'do his bit'; overtures of loyalty to the old Queen were not enough; old school-fellows had already fallen; Raffles must join the Young Guard.[22] Raffles and Bunny make their own way to South Africa and, in disguise, enlist in a volunteer regiment. The inevitable happens, for he is first recognized and arrested, and then shot dead by a sniper's bullet – but not before he honours his debt to the Empire by unmasking an enemy spy.

Hornung's third love was the public schools, for here was the agent and medium that could link cricket and the Empire. Uppingham is always the setting of the public school in his stories, although never mentioned by name: the author does, however, provide clues in abundance.[23] The young hero in *The Camera Fiend* begins his adventures there; Raffles and Bunny return to 'The Field of Philippi' to honour the school's founder; but it is in *Fathers of Men* that the public school plays the crucible, transmuting ordinary, average chaps into Hornung's imperial Young Guard.[24] Jan Rutter is Hornung's base metal – bad accent, worse manners, and a stable boy. His grandfather had been a rural dean, but the wayward daughter had run off with the coachman, and only returned to the family fold on the death of her husband. 'Has the gentle blood', asks Jan's housemaster, 'been hopelessly poisoned by the stink of the stables, or is it going to triumph and run clean and sweet?'[25] The story charts the progress of this unconventional boy – his struggle to keep up with the work; his friendship with the bronchial Chips, yet another embryo Hornung; his strivings at cricket, where he is a slow bowler with a most ungainly action; and the lessons he learns on truth, honour and loyalty. The combined efforts of housemaster, headmaster and games-master – the last eventually leaving for a headship in Australia – carry him through his various trials and see him to triumph at the Old Boys' Match. Here the cricket is well handled, and every ball is lovingly and expertly described; for a terrible moment the reader fears that Hornung is going to sink to the luxury of letting his schoolboy hero take all ten wickets, but he recovers at the last moment and allows him only nine.

Hornung was a great believer in the English public school system, and always protested how much it could make even of unpromising material. The writing of *Fathers of Men* became a mission, and the result of his whole-hearted labours was his finest book since the creation of Raffles 13 years earlier. As he wrestled with the tale's climax and message Hornung wrote ecstatically to a friend: 'I have never loved writing anything so much as those closing chapters. I *know* they are good. But they do keep me awake at nights .... It is the one thing of mine that might not only succeed, but *live*'.[26] In these closing chapters Jan proves his worth, selflessly saving the son of his dead father's former employer from shame, and shows that a public school can transmute the base metal of a stable boy into the solid silver of a gentleman. When Jan's housemaster comes to assess the chemical process he gives full credit to the role games have played in teaching the unacademic average boy how to manage men. And where better can such skills be put to good use than in the Empire? If Jan had the private means then he would have joined his cricketing uncle soldiering in India; but without such advantages Jan determines to go to Australia and work for another uncle on a sheep station. Yet another ordinary chap joins the imperial Young Guard.

Fathers of Men is the synthesis of Hornung's passions for Australia, cricket and public schools, and it was the most prolix of all his sermons. But it was a novel about boys for men, and so he recognized that he must do more to ensure that the call of the Empire reached the youth of the nation. Throughout the years of his own son Oscar's schooling, Hornung made it his duty to 'do his bit' at several public and preparatory schools. The sermon was his preferred medium, and the Game of Life was a favourite theme. In July 1914, less than a month before the start of the Great War, Hornung chose 'The Game of Life' as the title for one of his last school sermons.[27] He told his young listeners that it was a very old comparison that likens Life to a Game, so old indeed that there was little that could not be expressed in terms of games, and particularly, of course, in terms of cricket. 'When you want someone to try hard at something, you tell him to "play up"; when you find it hard to do the right thing, you tell yourself "I must play the game" – because, you may add, because what I'm tempted to do is "not cricket". If it is a case of doing our share in some way to help another, we call that "keeping our end up"; and if only one good word could be said for us by our friends, and by the world, we would love to be known above all else as "sportsmen". Being "a sport", as we use it among ourselves, has come to signify every virtue which is dearest to our hearts: courage, honesty, unselfishness, chivalry, you cannot have a sportsman without all these; and if you have all these, you must be a good man.'

Here Hornung broke off to include some lines from Henry Newbolt's '*Vitaï Lampada*', with its refrain 'Play up! play up! and play the game!'[28] together with some lines of verse from *Punch*:

> He kept a rule, if a thing seemed right –
> I hope I may do the same –
> To go and do it with all his might,
> And hardly a thought of fame.
> For it isn't the winning that makes a man,
> But it's playing the game on the good old plan,
> As hard and straight as a mortal can –
> In fact it is playing the game.

'Life', he continued, 'was the most glorious game of all, right up to the end – in a game we know when we are doing well, but in Life we never do. You cannot keep your own score in the Game of Life, and if you try you will make mistakes. God keeps our score, and He does not tell us what we have made until we are out. It is better not to think what we are making, better just to try to play the game.

'Try as we can, we cannot tell the score, for we see so dimly: so dimly that sometimes we can hardly see to play; but never so dimly that we think to appeal against the light, for we must glory in the very difficulties that we have to overcome. Who wants an easy victory? Who wants a life full of pitches to leg? Do you think the Great Scorer is going to give you four runs every time for those? No – for in this splendidly difficult Game of Life these cheap and easy triumphs will be written in water on the scoresheet. And the way we played for our side, in the bad light, on the difficult pitch, the way we backed up and ran the other man's runs; our courage and unselfishness, not our skill or our success; our brave failures, our hidden disappointments, the will to bear our friend's infirmities, and the grit to fight our own: surely, surely, it is these things above all other that will count, when the innings is over, in the Pavilion of Heaven.'

This, then, was the message of Hornung's sermons: games were a training ground for life; and service to the Empire was the ultimate test of that training. It was a message that was well received at his old school, Uppingham, where Edward Selwyn was the headmaster.[29] The school's reputation at games was high, and a series of very fine cricket elevens had brought national renown. The cadet corps steadily grew in importance, and in the first months of the new century Selwyn announced to the school that all boys, whether in the corps or not, were required to pass a shooting test, and that no boy would be allowed to take part in any inter-house athletic or sporting contest, nor could he gain a school prize, until he had passed that test.[30] In February 1900 C.H. Jones, the commanding officer, left for active service in the Boer War, and his adventures in South Africa were reported in the School Magazine in gory detail: 'We hear that Mr. Jones has killed five Boers single-handed. We congratulate him heartily on the exploit and hope that he will dispose of many more'.[31] In the early years of the new century about half the school was in the corps, and by 1905 over a thousand cadets had passed Uppingham's 'Recruit Drill and Fire Exercise'. To Selwyn the corps was 'one of the glories of the school'; to the visiting Lord Roberts – Commander-in-Chief in the Boer War – who came to open the school's South African War Memorial – a gymnasium – Uppingham's lead in military matters was an example to set before all public schools.[32] And other schools followed: later that year Edmond Warre, the headmaster of Eton, persuaded a committee of the Headmasters' Conference to pass a unanimous resolution that 'all persons in *statu pupillari* at the Universities or the Public Schools above fifteen years of age, able to bear arms, should be enrolled for the purposes of drill and manoeuvre and the use of arms'.[33] Eighty-three of the 102 schools represented agreed to take action immediately; old corps were revived and enlarged and, where there was none, new corps were founded. Field days, reviews and war games proliferated. Conan Doyle was active too after his own spell of service in South Africa, calling for every able-bodied youth and man in the Kingdom to learn to shoot a rifle: the rifle was to be the new long-bow, and the Young Guard were the men of Agincourt sprung to life.[34]

When war was declared on Germany in August 1914 it was almost as if Providence had given a test by which the public schools might prove their worth. War, with its call to self-sacrifice, to duty and to honour, was seen by many as the realization of a hope. The schools' answer to the call was swift: young masters and senior boys set to return for the autumn term said quick farewells to their schools and volunteered almost to a man for the front; while in the schools themselves the cadet corps became compulsory overnight, often through direct action on the boys' part.[35] Corps parades were suddenly meaningful and war exercises full of realism – all too soon these cadets would be joining their seniors in the crusade against Germany. At the front the public-school subalterns did well, remarkably so when we remember that they had only a few weeks' training in England before embarking for France. Their concern for their men, their outward determination to succeed no matter what their innermost feelings, and their hardiness amid all the deprivations of war soon won the respect of the professional soldiers under their command, and to such a degree that it is almost impossible now to realize just how young and how inexperienced these subalterns were. The price paid was enormous, for a generation of public-school boys died in the four years of war. The Uppingham roll of honour numbered 436: almost every other name in the *Uppingham School Roll* for the years 1907 to 1909 is followed by the words 'killed in action'.

Hornung captured the spirit of the public-school sportsmen as they changed out of their cricket whites to don army khaki, and transferred their allegiance from house and school to king and country. Though his literary reputation rested on his work as a novelist, he was also a competent poet and he wrote much patriotic and propagandist verse in similar vein to his friends Newbolt and Kipling. It is his 'Lord's Leave' of 1915 that the sporting rhetoric is captured at its most innocent:

> No Lord's this year: no silken lawn on which
> A dignified and dainty throng meanders,
> The Schools take guard upon a fierier pitch
> Somewhere in Flanders.
>
> Bigger the cricket here; yet some who tried
> In vain to win a colour while at Eton
> Have found a place upon an England side
> That can't be beaten!
> ...
> Sinks a torpedoed Phoebus from our sight,
> Over the field of play see darkness stealing;
> Only in this one game, against the light
> There's no appealing.
> Now for their flares ... and now at last the stars ...
> Only the stars now, in their heavenly million,
> Glisten and blink for pity on our scars
> From the Pavilion.[36]

So resound the late-Victorian and Edwardian ideals of athletic and imperial manliness, where war was to be fought in a Homeric atmosphere. The war to end all wars would be won by the public-school heroes playing 'The Game of Life'. Hornung's connection with the Eton and Harrow cricket match at Lord's comes about because his only child, Oscar, went to Eton and not to Uppingham. Oscar did not inherit his father's afflictions and was able to become the games player his father had always wanted to be, capping his school career by being elected Captain of Games. He had left Eton in July 1914 at the age of 19 to go up to Cambridge, but on the outbreak of hostilities he joined the Essex Regiment as a subaltern. From his training camp he wrote to his parents that he wanted 'to have a plug at those blighters over the water'; and to his godfather, Conan Doyle, 'I am waiting to go off any night now – I am longing to go – it *is* a chance for us chaps, isn't it? It is the one good thing the war has done – to give public-school fellows a chance – they are the one class who are enjoying themselves in this war'.[37]

Throughout the autumn of 1914, when the war was only going to last a few months, the idealism of Oscar and his fellow subalterns was high. His letters to his parents were always 'merry and bright', and were littered with sporting phrases that match his father's. 'Topping' and 'ripping' were favourite adjectives; life in the trenches was hard to bear at first, but he stuck to it, likening it 'to putting your left leg to the ball at cricket'; and he compared '*this* game to the old House Ties – only the odds aren't so against us here and we've more to back us up!'.[38] It was just like being back at Eton: letters came regularly from his parents; occasional hampers of food arrived from Fortnum and Mason's; leave was given for officers to go back to England, as if on exeat; his housemaster was still consulted; and he wrote poetry, as if for the school magazine.[39] The athletic ethos came from the schools to the front: the battle for the Belgian sea-ports quickly gained the tag 'The Race to the Sea'; the German use of chlorine gas was seen as 'illustrative of the Prussian idea of playing the game'; and a craze developed for kicking footballs towards the enemy line during an attack.[40] In the late spring of 1915 Oscar was appointed to command a bombing patrol equipped 'with *new Hand-bombs* – glorious things, *just* the size and weight of a *Cricket Ball*!'. Using an action 'just like throwing in from cover' he aimed to 'beat the Teuton Batsman' and then 'haste back to the Pavilion' before rain created a 'sticky wicket' and darkness meant there was 'a case of appealing against the light'.[41]

Shortly after the summer of 'Lord's Leave' Oscar was killed at the front, leading his platoon from the fore. The distraught father sought comfort in the compilation of a privately printed memorial to Oscar, titled *Trusty and Well Beloved*, and in the composition of a tribute in verse.[42] 'The Last Post' refers not only to the military rite but also to the contents of Oscar's last letter which, like all his letters from the front, arrived by the last post of the day. Many of the words and phrases are taken straight from those letters home.

Last summer, centuries ago,
I watched the postman's lantern glow,
As night by night on leaden feet
He twinkled down our darkened street.

So welcome on his beaten track,
The bent man with the bulging sack!
But dread of every sleepless couch,
A whistling imp with leathern pouch!

And now I meet him in the way,
And earth is Heaven, night is Day,
For oh! there shines before his lamp
An envelope without a stamp!

Address in pencil; overhead,
The Censor's triangle in red.
Indoors and up the stair I bound:
'One from the boy, still safe, still sound!

'Still merry in a dubious trench
They've taken over from the French
Still making light of duty done;
Still full of Tommy, Fritz, and fun!

'Still finding war of games the cream,
And his platoon a priceless team –
Still running it by sportsman rule,

Just as he ran his house at school.
'Still wild about the bombing stunt
He makes his hobby at the front.
Still trustful of his wondrous luck –
Prepared to take on old man Kluck!'
  . . .
He said those weeks of blood and tears
Were worth his score of radiant years.
He said he had not lived before –
Our boy who never dreamt of War!

He gave us of his own dear glow,
Last summer, centuries ago.
Bronzed leaves still cling to every bough.
I don't waylay the postman now.

Doubtless upon his nightly beat
He still comes twinkling down our street.
I am not there with straining eye –
A whistling imp could tell you why.[43]

While the war was fought in this Homeric atmosphere so the athletic-imperial ideal of manliness sustained the Young Guard – and the propagandists of patriotic prose and poetry – but the arrival of entrenchment saw the start of its demise. The enemy became invisible: there was nothing chivalrous about chlorine gas; there was nothing heroic in dying under bombardment; and there was nothing idealistic in inhuman mechanistic warfare. As the mode of warfare moved from the nineteenth to the twentieth century, so the public-school officer met his limit and the ideal of the Young Guard met its end. The young subalterns still led as well, still fought as bravely – and bore all with a stoical reticence that could turn the worst disaster into something that was merely darned unpleasant. Now, however, the shortcomings of their military training were becoming evident and, more importantly, the war had moved away from a level where individual action was vital to one where the individual was lost in an army of millions.

In 1916 Hornung went to France with the YMCA, and helped to organize a library and a rest hut for the troops. He was determined once again 'to do his bit' and the action brought him solace in his grief – mercifully his asthma behaved. He was present at the German bombardment of Arras in 1918, experiencing at a mature age warfare already described in imagination.[44] He maintained his belief in the Young Guard – thrilling to the jauntiness of the Australian troops; enjoying a reunion at the front with three other Old Uppinghamians; and delighting in his meeting with an exemplar, the much-decorated former Blue who

> stood for the generation which has been wiped out almost to a boy, as I knew it; he stood for his brothers, and for all our sons who made their sacrifice at once; he stood for the English games, and for those who had seemed to live for games, but who jumped into the King's uniform quicker than they ever changed into flannels in their lives.... I should like to know which [class of men] was quite as valuable when the war was in its infancy? In each and every country, by one means or the other, the men were to be had: only our Public Schools could have furnished off-hand an army of natural officers, trained to lead, old in responsibility, and afraid of nothing in the world but fear itself.[45]

In February 1918, after much searching, he eventually discovered Oscar's grave at the front, and around its wooden cross planted flowers from an English garden – narcissus, primroses and pinks, phlox and saxifrage, and a young rose-tree.[46] His 'Wooden Crosses', first printed in *The Times*, evoked an immediate and wide response:

> 'Go live the world wide over – but when you come to die,
> A quiet English churchyard is the only place to lie!' –
> I held it half a lifetime, until through war's mischance
> I saw the wooden crosses that fret the fields of France.
> ...
> So stand the still battalions: alert, austere, serene;
> Each with his just allowance of brown earth shot with green;
> None better than his neighbour in pomp or circumstance –
> All beads upon the rosary that turned the fate of France!
> ...
> The brightest gems of Valour in the Army's diadem
> Are the V.C. and the D.S.O., M.C. and D.C.M.
> But those who live to wear them will tell you they are dross
> Beside the Final Honour of a simple Wooden Cross.[47]

   Throughout the years since his return from Australia Hornung had kept in contact with schools, and with Uppingham in particular. The old boy reunion at the front continued the tradition of the annual London dinners, where Hornung was occasionally an honoured guest, and in 1913 he had composed 'Uppingham Song' to celebrate the fiftieth anniversary of the School Magazine.[48] 'The Old Boys' of 1917 sees the Young Guard who can returning to the old school – and those who cannot handing the torch to the new generation:

'Who is the one with the empty sleeve?'
'Some sport who was in the swim.'
'And the one with the ribbon who's home on leave?'
'Good Lord! I remember him!
A hulking fool, low down in the school,
And no good at games was he –
All fingers and thumbs – and very few chums.
(I wish he'd shake hands with me!)'

'Who is the one with the heavy stick,
Who seems to walk from the shoulder?'
'Why, many's the goal you have watched him kick!'
'He's looking a lifetime older.
Who is the one that's so full of fun –
I never beheld a blither –
Yet his eyes are fixt as the furrow betwixt?'
'He cannot see out of either.'

'Who are the ones that *we* cannot see,
Though we feel them as near as near?
In Chapel one felt them bend the knee,
At the match one felt them cheer.
In the deep still shade of the Colonnade,
In the ringing quad's full light,
They are laughing here, they are chaffing there,
Yet never in sound or sight.'

'Oh, those are the ones who never shall leave,
As they once were afraid they would!
They marched away from the school at eve,
But at dawn came back for good,
With deathless blooms from uncoffin'd tombs
To lay at our Founder's shrine.
As many are they as ourselves to-day,
And their place is yours and mine.'

'But who are the ones they can help or harm?'
'Each small boy, never so new,
Has an Elder Brother to take his arm,
And show him the thing to do –
And the thing to resist with a doubled fist,
If he'd be nor knave nor fool –
And the Game to play if he'd tread the way
Of the School behind the school.'[49]

Hornung was thrilled when his 'dear Uppingham' asked him to help with the creation of its 1914–18 War Memorial, and he promised that 'they would not regret giving [him] a hand in it'.[50] The memorial took two forms – the building of an assembly hall, and the erection of panels of names in an alcove in the chapel. The visiting old boy of Hornung's 1909 sermon on 'The Old School List' found a handful of names on the South African War Memorial; his successor of 1929, on being shown the Great War Memorial, would find seven panels of names, three columns in each panel, and beneath the panels are inscribed seven texts from the Bible, Hornung's seven chosen Watchwords.[51] Hornung never saw them, for he died suddenly of influenza in March 1921, at St. Jean de Luz, in his fifty-fifth year. Now he was buried in the same country as his beloved son.

From the safe vantage of a distant – and more cynical – age, it is easy to scoff at Hornung, and to mock all that he stood for. Hornung's working life coincides with the rise and fall of athletic-military imperialism, and his words and actions must be judged by the temper of the times. That much personified by Hornung fell out of favour in the 1920s is not in doubt, but there is no point in speculating whether in the wake of the war he would have changed his views or still held to them. Before 1914 the link between sport, the public schools and the Empire was not seriously questioned; and that the games hero would become the valiant warrior was rarely doubted. And Hornung was straightforward; there was no guile or subtlety about him, his enthusiasms were clear and his motives transparent. In his love for cricket, the public schools and the Empire, he was typical of many whose background was the public school and the professions, and his writings merely expressed the unspoken words in many hearts. Today he might be labelled a militarist or a warmonger, but this did not happen in his own time, and he would have been horrified if it had. He did not create the ethos of the Edwardian years, though he echoed it sympathetically in his work; he did not form Britain's imperial policy, though he was keen to diffuse its message; and he did not advocate military might, though when Kitchener called his answer was immediate. Hornung is the articulate voice of the middle-class opinion of his time.

NOTES

1. The full sermon, delivered on 14 November 1909, is printed in Shane R. Chichester, *E.W. Hornung and his Young Guard* (Berkshire, 1941), pp.14–19.
2. For example, Kenyon of 'Kenyon's Innings' in *Some Persons Unknown* (London, 1898), pp.8–9, and Upton in *The Camera Fiend* (London, 1911/1916), pp.8–9.
3. Upton nearly goes to Australia (*The Camera Fiend*, p.40), while Tahourdin does ('The Jackeroo of G. Block' in *Old Offenders* (London, 1923), p.140).
4. Hornung's manuscript account of the voyage is in the possession of his great-niece, Mrs. Elizabeth Stanton. A copy is held in the Uppingham School Archives.
5. For example, 'The Star of the "Grasmere"' in *Some Persons Unknown*, and *Denis Dent* (London, 1903).
6. Several letters from Hornung in Australia to his mother in England are in the possession of Mrs. Stanton. Copies are held in the Uppingham School Archives.
7. Short stories with an Australian setting can be found in *Under Two Skies* (London, 1892), *Some Persons Unknown*, *The Amateur Cracksman* (London, 1899), and *Old Offenders*; while the following novels have Australian settings; *A Bride from the Bush* (London, 1890), *Tiny Luttrell* (London, 1893), *The Boss of Taroomba* (London, 1894), *The Unbidden Guest* (London, 1894), *Irralie's Bushranger* (London, 1896), *The Belle of Toorak* (London, 1900),

   Denis Dent, and *Stingaree* (London, 1905).
 8. *The Bride from the Bush*, pp. 184–5.
 9. See the review of *Under Two Skies* from the *Melbourne Argus*, reprinted in the end-papers of *Tiny Luttrell*.
10. *The Bride from the Bush*, pp. 297, 301.
11. For example, Jim of 'Jim-of-the-Whim' and some young overseers in 'Strong-minded Miss Methuen' in *Under Two Skies*; Harry Manister in *Tiny Luttrell*; Stingaree, first appearing in *Irralie's Bushranger* and then in *Stingaree*; 'The Beetle' in 'After the Fact' and 'Hell-fire Jim' in 'The Magic Cigar' both from *Some Persons Unknown*.
12. *Mr. Justice Raffles* (London, 1909), p. 122.
13. These words are spoken by the schoolmaster-cricketer Forrester; *Some Persons Unknown*, pp. 18–19. He regularly preaches his messages too, and at his old school – just like Hornung.
14. 'Chrystal's Century' in *Old Offenders*. This posthumous collection of short stories brings together otherwise unpublished material. Three of the stories have cricketing themes, and it would seem that Hornung had plans to complete a book of such stories under the title *Old Scores*.
15. *The Collected Raffles* (London, 1985) brings together the three volumes of short stories (*The Amateur Cracksman*, *The Black Mask* and *A Thief in the Night*) but omits the full-length novel (*Mr. Justice Raffles*). Raffles was played by Gerald du Maurier on the London stage during the Great War, and by John Barrymore, Ronald Colman and David Niven on film in later years. A trial run of the Raffles character, but called Nettleship, can be found in 'Nettleship's Score' in *Under Two Skies*.
16. Arthur Conan Doyle, *Memories and Adventures* (Londdon, 1923), p.101.
17. *Mr. Justice Raffles*, p. 70.
18. *The Amateur Cracksman*, p. 49.
19. *A Thief in the Night* (London, 1905), p. 161.
20. 'Le Premier Pas' in *The Amateur Cracksman*.
21. The second volume of the adventures of Raffles is *The Black Mask* (London, 1901); and the Boer War story is 'The Knees of the Gods'. Earlier in the same volume, Raffles and Bunny arrange 'A Jubilee Present' for the Queen.
22. *The Black Mask*, p. 275.
23. In the Raffles tale 'The Field of Philippi' from *A Thief in the Night* 'The Upper' and 'The Middle' playing-fields keep their real names, whereas nearby Wardley and Stockerston are altered slightly to Warfield and Stockley; while in *The Camera Fiend* the description of the uniform and the boys' studies makes the identification simple.
24. *Fathers of Men* (London, 1912).
25. Ibid., p. 6.
26. Letter from Hornung to Shane Chichester, dated 11 August 1911. A copy of some extracts from it is held in the Uppingham School Archives.
27. The full sermon, delivered on 5 July 1914, is printed in Shane R. Chichester, *E.W. Hornung and his Young Guard*, pp. 31–7.
28. 'Vitaï Lampada' was first published in Henry Newbolt's collection, *Clifton Chapel* (London, 1908). Hornung gave a first edition as a Christmas present to one of his family; it is now in the possession of Mrs. Stanton.
29. The efforts of some headmasters to diffuse imperial ideals to their pupils are detailed in J.A Mangan, *The Games Ethic and Imperialism* (London, 1985), pp. 21–70.
30. *Uppingham School Magazine* (February 1900), 1.
31. *Uppingham School Magazine* (September 1900), 265. The editorial of the subsequent issue began: 'First we must apologize for the scandalous paragraph in the last editorial referring to Mr. Jones. We entirely exonerate ourselves from any blame in the matter, which rests with our publisher'. *Uppingham School Magazine* (November 1900), 313.
32. *Uppingham School Magazine* (April 1905), pp. 41–51.
33. C.R.L. Fletcher, *Edmond Warre* (London, 1922), p. 267.
34. John Dickson Carr, *The Life of Sir Arthur Conan Doyle* (London, 1949), p. 166.
35. Guy Kendall, *A Headmaster Remembers* (London, 1933), p. 246.
36. Hornung's poems were originally published in various magazines, newspapers and

journals, and were later collected together as *The Young Guard* (London, 1919). 'Lord's Leave' is to be found on pp. 2–3 of this collection.

37. Extracts from many of Oscar's war letters are published in Hornung's privately printed memorial to his son, *Trusty and Well Beloved* (1915). The letter from Oscar to Conan Doyle is to be found on p. 1. A copy of this memorial volume is in the possession of Mrs. Stanton.

38. Letters from Oscar to his parents, 23 May 1915 and 15 June 1915: *Trusty and Well Beloved*, p. 13, 37. For more on the language used by young subalterns, see Paul Fussell, *The Great War and Modern Memory* (New York, 1975), *passim*.

39. Letter from Oscar to his parents, 22 May 1915: *Trusty and Well Beloved*, p. 19. Oscar includes many quotations from Kipling in his letters.

40. Fussell, op. cit. pp. 9, 27.

41. Letters from Oscar to his parents, 12 June 1915, 14 June 1915 and 19 June 1915: *Trusty and Well Beloved*, pp. 28, 32, 39.

42. The title is taken from the opening words of the King's Commission to all serving officers. Oscar's commission finally arrived at his parents' home on 6 July 1915, on the same day that the telegram came bringing news of his death.

43. *The Young Guard*, pp. 4–6. Hornung regularly waylaid the postman in the street as he delivered the last post of the day: *Trusty and Well Beloved*, p. 49.

44. Hornung's experiences at the front are logged in *Notes of a Camp-follower on the Western Front* (London, 1919).

45. Ibid., p. 233.

46. Ibid. pp. 121–37. Hornung does not tell the reader that it is Oscar's grave, but he does provide plenty of clues to make the idenfication simple.

47. *The Young Guard*, pp. 45–7.

48. Hornung devoted his speech at the 1901 London Dinner to the work of Old Uppinghamians serving the Empire: *Uppingham School Magazine* (February 1901), p. 9. 'Uppingham Song' can be found in *The Young Guard*, pp. 42–4.

49. *The Young Guard*, pp. 7–8.

50. Letter from Hornung to a relative, 20 December 1919. The letter is in the possession of Mrs. Stanton. A copy is held in the Uppingham School archives.

51. His Watchwords were: 1. What are these which are arrayed in white robes? 2. A people that jeoparded their lives unto the death in the high places of the field. 3. They were a wall unto us both by night and day. 4. Their sound went out into all the earth. 5. Therefore they shall be mine, said the Lord of Hosts, in the day when I make up my jewels. 6. Thine, O Lord, is the greatness, and the power, and the glory and the victory. 7. Make them to be numbered with Thy Saints in glory everlasting .... They are the epitaph for Hornung's imperial Young Guard.

CHAPTER TWO

The MCC, Society and Empire: A Portrait of Cricket's Ruling Body, 1860–1914

JAMES BRADLEY

In 1987 the Marylebone Cricket Club celebrated its bicentenary and to mark the occasion the ex-Glamorgan and England captain Tony Lewis published an official history of the club in a glossy table-top edition. On the back of the dust-jacket, underneath a slightly abstract painting of the famous weathervane Old Father Time taking the bails off the stumps, in bold black print is the simple motif 'THE STORY OF THE MCC IS THE HISTORY OF CRICKET'. This is hyperbolic, and is akin to saying that the story of the English monarchy is the history of its people. Lewis' book is establishment history; it is cricket history from the top with the MCC as the elite.

To define what the MCC once was is a hard task. In the 1990s it seems to be a semi-mythical body, with its traditions and history concerning its power in the cricketing world shrouded in the mists of antiquity, having shed all its powers, save that of guardian of the laws, to the Test and County Cricket Board, the National Cricket Association, the Cricket Council and the International Cricket Conference.[1] Yet in the early years of this century it was perceived to be the Vatican of cricket, the very power-house of the game, controlling and arbitrating for Britain and its Empire. In the latter it had a symbolic value, and there must be some truth in the statement of the eminent Lord Harris that it was 'perhaps the most venerated institution in the British Empire'.[2] Similarly, Lord Hawke made the trite observation that the MCC 'had become the Parliament House of cricket, not only of Great Britain but of overseas Dominions'.[3] Yet this makes even more remarkable the fact that the club steadfastly ignored imperial cricket until the 1890s.

If the MCC was the Vatican of cricket, the committee was the conclave. It was this body, through the work of its meetings and various subcommittees, that sought to rule the world of cricket. This article begins by examining the structure of that committee and the way in which it attempted to enforce its rule, and then looks at the implication of this for imperial cricket. Using a detailed examination of all those who served on the committee of the MCC over the period 1860–1914, and evidence obtained from the archives of the club itself, I intend to challenge some of the assumptions that have been made by and for the MCC as regards its relationship with cricket in the mother country and the colonies. In doing so I hope to demonstrate that like any other formally constituted body of people the committee of the MCC was a product of its own time and thus was bound by the beliefs of the society in which it existed.

I

The committee was the apex of the club and its structure remained markedly similarly for the whole of this period. However, there were two major changes. First, in 1865 new rules increased the numbers on the committee from 16 to 24 with the approval of the general meeting of the club.[4] This meant that the committee now consisted of a president, secretary, treasurer, and up to five trustees (all of whom were ex-officio members of the committee), the general committee making up the rest of the numbers. The second major change occurred in 1898, with the appointment of F.E. Lacey as secretary. At this point the secretary ceased to have an executive role on the committee. However, his power remained relatively undiminished as he retained an influential advisory role.

The pinnacle of the MCC and its figurehead was the president, who held office for one year and one year only. By the rules of the club the president nominated his successor, and on only one occasion during this period did the committee make a recommendation, when in 1879 William Nicholson was nominated as a gesture of thanks for his generosity in lending the club £18,000 for the purchase of the ground. The importance to the club of the president is debatable. Lewis says 'the president was originally an aristocratic figurehead, a good name to have on the letterhead and in the chair at the anniversary dinner'.[5] But in reality the presidency was what the incumbent made it. The fifth Earl of Cadogan described the position as the 'Woolsack of cricket',[6] which suggests that considerable power could be wielded (although Cadogan himself was forced to miss many meetings owing to the illness and death of his father). Likewise, Lord Hawke, never one to underestimate a job, claimed that he turned down the offer of the presidency in 1900 because he 'had not the time to obey the calls such a post must make of its holder'.[7] Some presidents were assiduous in their attention and actions, notably V.E. Walker (1891), W.E. Denison (1892), and Lord Harris (1895), while most fulfilled their role enthusiastically enough, but slightly more sporadically. On the whole, as the MCC became more organized so did the role of the president. He was expected to serve on the financial and other sub-committees, as well as fulfilling his role as figurehead and mouthpiece of the club. Thus, in 1890, the twenty-second Baron Willoughby de Eresby was nominated to sit on the Finance, Tennis and Building Committees. Others, like Lord Harris, were able to dominate all the actions of the club, but most notably the important Cricket and Selection sub-committee.

There are many reasons why the presidency should not be regarded as a mere figurehead job. First, by representing the club, presidents reflected and symbolized the whole tenor and atmosphere of the MCC. Thus, even if they did very little, they were still a flesh and blood symbol of the club. But more significantly many of the presidents were extremely active in the MCC before, during or after their term of office. If we take, for example, the year 1880, we find that the president, Sir William Hart-Dyke, had previously served on the committee in 1868–71 and 1873–76. There were also three future presidents on that year's committee (Hon. R. Grimston; the fifth Baron Lyttelton; and V. E. Walker) and three past presidents (all three of whom were trustees of the club: the fourth Earl of Sefton; the first Earl of Dudley; and William Nicholson). This situation was ensured partially by the unwritten rule that the retiring president was automatically elected to the committee for at least the following year.

The secretary and treasurer were on the next rung down the ladder but either could dominate the club. There were only three secretaries of note during this period. The first, R. A. Fitzgerald, was responsible for transforming the fortunes of the club after its influence had been seriously weakened by several cricketing controversies, including the infamous debates over the question of whether the ball should be bowled round-arm, under-arm, or over-arm. His successor was Henry Perkins, an untidy yet forceful character, who was capable but occasionally troublesome. During his term of office (1876–97), his position was eclipsed by that of the treasurer, Sir Spencer Ponsonby-Fane, who ruled the finances from 1879 to 1916. Ponsonby-Fane was a born aristocrat and a long-standing member. His presence at committee meetings, often in the chair, was a constant feature, and it is his signature which most frequently ratifies the minutes of each meeting. But by the late 1890s he was an old man, having been born in 1824, and when Perkins retired it was F. E. Lacey who organized and all but ran the club. When Lacey arrived as secretary in 1898 the club's internal workings were in drastic need of reform and overhaul. He remodelled the sub-committees, a feature of the club's organization that seems to have evolved along the same lines as English Common Law, and put club business on a more formal basis. Lacey stamped his character on the post-Perkins MCC, and his influence on the wider sphere of cricket administration was not inconsiderable, demonstrating that even without serving on the committee, the secretary was a potentially powerful person.

The trustees were also another important section of the committee as they fulfilled the role of elder statesmen. Once made trustees they held that position until death. This was significant because the trustees represented a static core in a changing committee, so much so that William Nicholson and R. J. P. Broughton served for most of the 1860–1914 period. The trusteeship also enabled the Earl of Sefton to serve for 35 years and V. E. Walker for 39 years. This has implications for the way in which the club was run and the policies which it implemented. It certainly gave the committee a leavening of conservatism.

The rank and file of the committee also had their significance. Lord Hawke commented on the Ordinary Committee that:

> [It consisted] of sixteen members, four of whom annually retire for re-election for one year. The retiring president always fills one of the four vacancies, and the candidates for the other three are proposed and seconded by members of the committee. It would be open to any member of the club to nominate a candidate for the committee, but this has never been done, and probably would be regarded as tantamount to proposing a vote of censure.[8]

This reveals that the committee was, in a way, self-perpetuating. They chose whom they wanted and, like all autocratic bodies, they got whom they wanted. Usually the committee would put up four members for election, including the retiring president, who was elected as a matter of courtesy by the Annual Meeting, but sometimes they would give the members a slightly wider choice. The general committee member was free to initiate business and put forward his own particular concerns. But committee members were also important because they formed the hard core of the sub-committees, which effectively controlled the running of Lord's and cricket.

The committee had its own formal hierarchy, but it must be remembered that the MCC was a private club, and all clubs have their own cliques. The MCC was no exception, and on reading the minutes it becomes very clear that this was how the club was run. As we will see, the social background of this clique was extremly important to the MCC's involvement in imperial cricket. Not surprisingly, the ruling clique was centred on the permanent ex-officio officers of the club. Between 1860 and 1869 it had among its members the Hon. F. Ponsonby (later the sixth Earl Bessborough), T. Burgoyne (treasurer) and William Nicholson. After Burgoyne's death in 1869, Sir Spencer Ponsonby-Fane was added to the ranks of the clique. It remained stable until the 1890s, gathering around it the members of the Walker family and the Hon. R. Grimston. In the mid-1890s Lord Harris became the dominant figure at Lord's and he gathered around himself Lord Hawke, P.F. Warner and others.

To summarize, the structure of the committee was hierarchical, with a backbone of ex-officio members. Its membership was self-perpetuating through the nomination of its own replacements, but it was dominated by a limited number of individuals who could and did determine the policy of the MCC.

II

This study comprises an examination of the 145 members of the committee who served between 1860 and 1914.[9] Of the 145, insignificant information was found on only four people. It is attempted here to determine a composite picture of the committee: their place, as a body, within British society. To achieve this it was necessary to discover what schools they had attended, whether they went to university and what they did professionally or otherwise. I was also interested in the political affiliations of the committee. Overall, the results were generally clear and interpretable, although there was a lack of information on the political beliefs of the majority of the committee.

The presidency had an aristocratic image and indeed the majority of presidents were, if not actual earls or lords, the brothers or sons of peers, knights and baronets. There were obvious exceptions. In 1879, William Nicholson, whose money was made in gin-distilling and whose family were usually MPs, was president, while in 1891 V. E. Walker was another non-aristocratic incumbent of the office. There were several more who were extremely high-ranking barristers but certainly not peers of the realm, including Sir Henry James, the Attorney General at the time that he was president (1889), and A. L. Smith, Lord Justice of Appeal during his year of office (1899). But all those who were not aristocrats certainly moved with ease in that milieu.

The majority of presidents, not surprisingly, went to Eton (52 per cent), while a significant minority attended Harrow (30 per cent). It was more common for presidents after 1900 to have attended other schools, which reflects the growth of public-school education after 1850. But it must be noted that in numerical terms only nine out of a total of 54 did not attend either Eton or Harrow, which demonstrates the extent to which the presidents were chosen from the elite section of British society. Indeed, if more emphasis is needed, generally those who were not titled had been at one of the two schools and had therefore been integrated into the upper echelons of society.

This pattern of education is reinforced by the numbers attending either Oxford or Cambridge (77 per cent), with Oxford being the more popular (44 per cent) and Cambridge a few points behind (33 per cent). The most likely college at which they would matriculate was Christ Church (67 per cent of total) if at Oxford, or Trinity (89 per cent of total) if at Cambridge. This, of course, did not mean that they all obtained degrees. Many followed the traditional pattern of 'going up' to university for a term or two, and then 'coming down' without graduating. Others gained their higher education in the army, which they left after a while.

In adult life it is harder to gauge what some of them did because not a few, one must suspect, were gentlemen of leisure. However, some resorted to their land, doing little else save live a squirearchical life, and getting involved in cricket (V. E. Walker was a non-aristocratic example of this). Many had business connections in the form of directorships both of the active and passive kind (46 per cent), a factor that becomes increasingly more important after 1885. Other presidents were among the great landowners of Britain, including the sixth Duke of Buccleuch, who owned 460,000 acres worth about £217,000 per annum in 1883. Others still were among the great landed industrialists of their day, including the Earl of Dudley, who owned mines, and the sixth Earl of Dartmouth, whose estates included huge coal deposits. But the most commonly identifiable profession among the presidents was the Law, and, in particular, the Bar (13 per cent), while colonial administration and politics were also recognizable areas of involvement. In administration we see the second Baron Wenlock (Governor of Madras 1891–95), Lord Harris (India Office and Governor of Bombay 1890–95), and the seventh Earl of Jersey (Governor-General of New South Wales 1890–93). In politics there were the significant figures of the Honourable Alfred Lyttelton, the famous Liberal Unionist and Colonial Secretary, and W.H. Long, the Conservative statesman.

The pattern of political beliefs is the most interesting and significant aspect of the presidency during this period. From 1860 to 1914 57 per cent were Conservative, while 37 per cent were Liberal or Liberal Unionist (after 1885 very few of those who were Liberal remained loyal to Gladstone). However, between 1860 and 1885 there were more Liberals than Conservatives. The Conservative majority only becomes apparent after the Home Rule crisis. This reflects the typical pattern of upper-class beliefs during this period, when political polarizations became more decided after 1885. This has significance for beliefs about Empire and will be discussed in due course.

The presidents of the MCC were members of an exclusive British elite and this is seen in their whole set of values: belief in the ideals of political service, the obligations of the land-owner, and the rightness of the hierarchical nature of society. Their wealth and prestige would lend credence to the figurehead theory of the presidency, if one did not realize that many of them were dedicated to the MCC and to the game of cricket.

The social and political background of the general committee reveals a slightly wider spectrum of schools attended and professions followed. Indeed, the whole ambience of the general committee was more upper-middle class than aristocratic. Eton was still the most popular of the public schools (34 per cent), with Harrow a long way behind in second place (15 per cent). But there was a much wider range of schools in evidence, including Uppingham, Lancing, Loretto, Edinburgh Academy, Rossall, Marlborough, Malvern and Wellington, as well as the more established Rugby, Winchester and Charterhouse. Equally, fewer of the general committee attended Oxford or Cambridge (34 per cent and 23 per cent respectively), and those who did went to a broader selection of colleges. Likewise, there was a wider range of professions, but like the presidents, the most overwhelmingly popular was Barrister-at-Law (28 per cent), while that of solicitor also proved a fairly common choice (9 per cent). The only other significant minority was the Armed Forces (13 per cent); otherwise we see a large variety of jobs, including those related to business (stockbrokers, merchants, company directors), while there were also schoolmasters, an artist, a surgeon, a priest, and at least one person who classified himself as having 'no profession'.

The bond which held these people together was cricket. At no time during this period did the number of first-class cricketers on the committee, playing and retired, drop below 45 per cent. At most times it was considerably higher. Even those who could not be classified as first-class were keen players or spectators. On this basis the committee was at least qualified to discuss cricketing matters, if not actually to rule the game.

Unfortunately, it is considerably harder to gauge the political convictions of general committee members. For example, throughout this period at least half of every committee has unknown political affiliations. It is interesting to note, for example, that the figure for Conservative support in 1914 is at least 45 per cent of the whole committee, by far the highest figure of the whole period. But, these figures do tend to fluctuate, owing to the high proportion of unknowns, making any statement highly debatable. But given the fact that the presidency increasingly becomes a Conservative reversion during the later years of this period, it may not be unreasonable to assume that the committee was also becoming more Conservative politically.

Statistics, especially averages, can be extremely misleading, and it would be unfair and unrealistic just to take the aggregate of all those who served on the committee over this period. These 54 years were ones of considerable social, economic and political change. Some of those who are included in the statistics were merely on the committee in the early years of the 1860s, while others appear only at the very tail-end of this period. It was therefore necessary to reconstruct each committee year by year and to make a detailed breakdown, in social terms, of one committee every five years. On the whole there was little fixed pattern to be observed. However, there are three points that are worth considering.

First, the average age of the committee rises gradually but consistently from 36 to 56 years old. This is also reflected in the age of successive presidents (before 1885 the average age is 42 years, while afterwards it is nearly 51). Part of the reason for this is that several of the ex-officio members of the committee were getting extremely old in the post-1900 period. But this is not the whole reason. One has to assume that either older people were being elected to the committee, or that more members were serving longer terms. It is, in reality, a combination of both these factors, added, perhaps, to the belief that age lends authority.

Secondly, and more importantly, those who attended schools other than Eton or Harrow show a marked increase after 1880, which demonstrates the growing strength of the more broadly based public-school system, and at the same time the slightly wider social base of the club. As the club took in more members so it took in more from upper-middle-class society, and this inevitably percolated through to the committee, to the extent that in the years 1900, 1905, 1910 and 1914, the figures for those not attending either of these schools were respectively: 41 per cent, 45 per cent, 36 per cent and 59 per cent.

Thirdly, and in some ways running counter to the last point, during this period the titled and aristocratic element of the committee stays relatively static. In 1860, 44 per cent of the committee belonged to the immediate family of a peer, while 6 per cent were baronets. In 1905, the figures are 32 per cent and 5 per cent, while in 1914 50 per cent of the committee had aristocratic origins. Therefore, while the committee was becoming less socially exclusive, there was still a very strong aristocratic involvement. This must have undoubtedly defined the image and atmosphere of the club and might point to the way in which the upper-middle and professional classes were being assimilated into the highest ranks of society.

Of course, figures do not tell the whole story and tend to depersonalize. There are unseen ties that can never be revealed by statistics. However, the study of the committee has identified that it was drawn from those sections of society that tended to be socially and politically conservative.

III

The first group which truly controlled the MCC during these years consisted of the aforementioned Sir Spencer Ponsonby-Fane, the Hon. F. Ponsonby (later the sixth Earl of Bessborough), the Hon. R. Grimston, W. Nicholson, R.J.P. Broughton, and those who surrounded them including the Walkers of Southgate and A.J. Webbe. It was rare that more than one of these was not present at committee meetings in the years between 1860 and 1895, and they inhabited Lord's on match days during the summer.

The major figures of this group had two things in common. First, they were all born in the pre-Victorian era (the oldest of them, Fred Ponsonby, was born in the same year as the battle of Waterloo). Secondly, they were all Harrovians, and often loyal to the point of obsession. Ponsonby and Grimston were remembered for many years with affection as the coaches of the Harrow School XI. Nicholson purchased playing fields for the school in the 1890s for the promotion of games. They were all friends whose major bond was their school. This was cemented by their love of cricket and its values, their membership of the MCC and the cricket club that they themselves founded, I Zingari. While they shared mixed political beliefs, they were definitely upholders of the establishment and absolute social conservatives.

Their satellites were generally younger but shared many similarities. The most famous of these were the Walkers, who lived as country squires at Southgate in Middlesex. They were cricket socialites, founders of Middlesex County Cricket Club, and admired throughout the cricketing world. The two most famous of the seven brothers were V.E. and I.D. V.E. was one of the greatest all-rounders of his day while I.D. was yet another pillar of Harrow School. He succeeded Ponsonby and Grimston as coach of the eleven, and he ran, for many years, the prestigious old boys' club, the Harrow Wanderers. When he died in 1898 he was eulogized by the *Harrovian* and his tombstone was inscribed with an epitaph composed by the Harrow master E.E. Bowen.[10]

A friend of I.D. and constant companion was the Middlesex cricketer A.J. Webbe, another Harrovian, who was described as having 'no profession' in the *Harrow School Register*. He too was part of the clique and he served on the MCC committee for twenty years all told during these years.

This group represented attitudes which were early Victorian and unconnected with the beliefs of the New Imperialists of the late nineteenth century. Although many of them were involved in a diverse range of activities, from law and government administration, to business and brewing, they all adhered to a central but parochial view of cricket which looked more to the green and insular fields of Lord's, rather than to the outside and the Empire.

There was a sharp sea-change in the 1890s. By this time Lords Harris and Hawke had matured and were the controlling voices of Lord's. They too were surrounded by a group of younger men including P.F. Warner, H.D.G. Leveson-Gower and the Hon.F.S. Jackson.

Lord Harris is now revered as one of the men who shaped the MCC. A Conservative and an imperialist, Harris saw cricket as having a wider significance than that of a mere game. He himself came from an imperial background, having been born in Trinidad, where his father was governor. His family had a remarkable record of service in the Indian Army and administration, and this was continued by Harris, who served as Under-Secretary for India (1885–86) and Governor of Bombay (1890–95). Harris always believed firmly in the civilizing mission of cricket. He saw it as a game which had the power to unite classes and colonies and uplift the native races of India. Thus he said of games, but more in particular of cricket:

> Pastimes serve good purpose in causing the young noblemen and gentlemen of England to rub shoulders with those who are lower than themselves in the social scale, but in the republic of the playground are, perhaps, their superiors, and so force upon the minds of the former a respect for industry, honesty, sobriety, and any other of the qualities that are necessary to produce an efficient athlete.[11]

But Harris extended his ideas even beyond Britain and the white Empire. Before he left for his appointment in Bombay, he attended a number of celebrations given in his honour. At all these he echoed the sentiments shown above. But he also embraced the ideal of the improving mission of Empire:

> England in her supreme confidence, in an admiration for her own free institutions, had undertaken to educate oriental people on western lines, to imbue them with western modes of thought, and

to encourage them to admire and to strive at western systems of
government.[12]

Undoubtedly part of Harris's 'systems of belief' was the inculcation of
cricket and its ethic. At a dinner attended by many members of the MCC
he said that 'he had done his best to promote the interests of the noble
game in this country, and he hoped not unsuccessfully, and that he
intended to extend his patronage to the promotion of cricket in India so
far as lay in his power'.[13]

In fact, promotion of cricket was one of the few noteworthy things that
Harris achieved in office, although it did nothing to aid his popularity,
which was particularly low with the nascent Congress Party, which vilified
him for spending his time playing cricket to the detriment of more
important issues.[14] But despite this Harris continued to reiterate his belief
in the power of cricket and its importance to the Empire throughout this
period and beyond.

Harris was the regular chairman of the Cricket and Selection sub-
committee, whose duty it was to decide upon the laws of cricket, to make
selection of the MCC and other teams playing at Lord's (excepting those
of Middlesex County Cricket Club which had a playing arrangement with
the club), and other cricketing matters. He was regularly assisted in his
duties by Lord Hawke, the bluff and abrasive Yorkshireman. Hawke
shared a fairly similar background to that of Harris. He was an ardent
cricketer and an Old Etonian. But, like Harris, he was also a conservative
of the new school believing, more or less, in the imperial dream. He
firmly believed in the class system, but he also ascribed to the 'republic of
the playground' ideal to the extent that he treated the Yorkshire professionals with a protective and patronizing cordiality, as if the pros were
special children, and thus he displayed all the characteristics of the good
squire. He would always fight for 'his boys', as he called them, but woe
betide any who misbehaved. As a result he was able to say 'I believe I
have done more than anyone to raise the standard and self-respect of the
splendid paid section of first-class cricketers'.[15] And to a degree he was
right, although modesty was not one of Hawke's characteristics. However, he was quite capable of being insufferably overbearing, and he
prevented two of 'his boys' from touring Australia in 1901–02 with a
private side, thus depriving them of a lucrative winter. His motive for this
was that the side was not officially sanctioned, although it is equally
possible that he wanted to keep the two men fresh for the county
championship. In fairness to Hawke he was able to get Yorkshire to
recompense them.

Hawke also shared Harris's belief in the important role that cricket had
to play in the Empire, although his methods of taking cricket's message
overseas were somewhat less altruistic. Hawke was responsible for sending out touring teams across the Empire. He himself accompanied G. F.
Vernon's teams to Australia (1887–88), and India and Ceylon (1888–89).
This gave the noble lord a taste for travel, which he continued to indulge

with the organization of his own touring teams to India (1892–93), South Africa (1895–96 and 1899–1900), the West Indies (1896–97), Australia and New Zealand (1902–3), and with the captaincy of an MCC team to Argentina (1912–13).

It is hard to judge the extent to which these tours were designed to encourage cricket in the Empire and how much they were for the benefit of a group of amateur gentlemen, acting as intrepid adventurers abroad, who had nothing else to do in the winter except play cricket. Hawke was in no doubt that the former was a powerful motive. On his trip to South Africa in 1896 he commented that his 'object was to develop and meet South African cricketers',[16] and it cannot be denied that this may have been true. His tours certainly had a beneficial effect for the cricket of the countries he visited. However, Hawke's main testament of faith was his memoirs written in the early 1920s, and it is possible that he was attributing too much to himself. Certainly a reading of this work does make one suspicious of Hawke because it is excessively egotistical.

Nevertheless Hawke was a man of the British Empire. Touring South Africa in 1896, he did his bit for the old country when he dutifully took the opportunity to visit Farrer, Rhodes, Fitzpatrick and Phillips in gaol after the disastrous Jameson Raid. He took great delight in dining with them and relieving them of large sums of money in a game of cards.[17] He also refused to visit President Kruger on principle, although two of his team members went and vainly tried to persuade him to come and see Hawke's team play.[18]

Hawke was quite capable of waxing lyrical about India, which obviously moved him the same way it did other imperialists. He even published in his memoirs a dreadful poem, which, one must suspect, he wrote in one of his weaker moments. It drips sentiment:

A land that we've conquered and have to hold
Though it costs us millions of lives and gold,
Shall we call her the jewel of England's fame?
Or throw our curse at her vampire name?
But whether we bless her, or damn her, or deride her,
We are bound by our honour to stand fast beside her,
The Empire's India.[19]

Around Hawke and Harris were ranged some slightly younger men who carried the same set of values. Notable among these were the Hon. F.S. Jackson, H.D.G. Leveson-Gower, and P.F. 'Plum' Warner. They were all of a similar background and were all Conservatives. They attended a variety of schools (Eton, Winchester and Rugby respectively) and were definitely more representative of the late nineteenth century than of an earlier date. Jackson was a brilliant cricketer and a Yorkshire compatriot of Hawke. He was also director of his own tanning business in Leeds. After 1914 he became involved in politics as a Conservative MP and then as an imperial administrator, when he was made Governor of Bengal in 1927. Leveson-Gower was a stockbroker, although he seemed to spend much more of his time playing cricket. He was a noted administrator of the game in his later life, a connection that dates back to this period. Warner, on the other hand, was a barrister, but he too spent much of his time playing and administering the game. He was to become a cricket journalist, a stock-broker, and, eventually, as important a figure in the MCC as Lord Harris himself. All three were particular friends of Hawke. They all toured, at one time or another, with him and Jackson played alongside him during the summer. Hawke was best man at Warner's wedding, while Leveson-Gower was affectionately referred to as 'Shrimp' throughout Hawke's memoirs.

Of all three during this period Warner was by far the most imperially minded, and he donned the mantle of Hawke by taking several teams abroad. In other ways he was the natural successor to Harris, as he too was born in the West Indies where his father was Attorney-General of Trinidad. He was also the first to captain an MCC side in Australia (1903–4) and followed this with trips for the club to South Africa (1905–6) and Australia again (1911–12). Warner was a travelling cricket diplomat and there is little doubt that he was genuinely inspired by the idea of cricket and Empire, and he used his oratorical skills whenever he was required to make a speech on the significance of cricket in some farflung outpost of Empire. On the 1905–6 MCC tour of South Africa he quoted himself, on his departure from that country, as saying:

> The games which could produce such fine sporting spirit, and had done so much for British manhood should be encouraged. By encouraging the principle of fair play they would show to the loser as to the winner the same hearty good fellowship which has charac-terised the feeling which animated the great crowds at Newlands and Johannesburg.[20]

His writing on this tour was dominated by the recent Boer War, and throughout Warner is at pains to demonstrate that reconciliation could come through cricket, as this anecdote demonstrates:

> We had the pleasure of meeting Mr P. de Villiers, a Boer Comman-dant in the early battles on the Natal side . . . and a courteous gentleman with the wildest enthusiasm for cricket. De Villiers was taken prisoner. At the time he happened to be wearing an old cricket sweater and trousers. A Tommy shouted, 'look here lads we've got a cricketer', to which de Villiers replied, 'yes you have . . .'. He made no secret of the fact that he liked Englishmen, and hinted that South Africa would settle down rapidly and that there would be no distinction between Briton and Boer, all would be South Africans – if only, he added, 'the newspapers would stop talking'.[21]

Warner wrote many books about his tours abroad and all of them have an underlying imperial purpose. In the preface to *Cricket In Many Climes* Warner wrote that cricket was:

> extending its influence wherever the English Language is spoken, and it is even said by diplomats and politicians that its friendly intercourse does much to strengthen the amity of nations, and to make for international understanding. . .Cricket, indeed knits together many interests, and the crown of its influence is the good-fellowship which accompanies it.[22]

This is the feeling that he and many others brought to the cricket fields of the Empire and it was a feeling which would have been acknowledged by not a few of the inhabitants of the colonies and dominions.

Warner was just one of the lieutenants of Harris and Hawke, the two men who dominated MCC after 1895, and it was a reflection of their views when Warner wrote:

> Cricket has become more than a game. It is an institution, a passion, one might say a religion. It has got into the blood of the nation, and wherever British men and women are gathered together there will the stumps be pitched. North, South, East and West throughout the British Empire, from Lord's to Sydney, from Hong Kong to the Spanish Main, cricket flourishes. It is the policy of the MCC to encourage the love of cricket in every possible way. . .And in these days when cricket has become the interest of the whole Empire, whither should the Empire turn for guidance but to the club which has grown up with the game which has fostered it, and which has endeavoured to preserve its best traditions? And it is the wish of every true cricketer that the MCC should so continue to conduct its affairs that it may always remain not only the trustee but the mother of cricket.[23]

The rest of this chapter is devoted to demonstrating the development of the MCC as a body which claimed to be the spirit and guardian of imperial cricket.

IV

The most important area of imperial cricket was believed, both by the British and by the inhabitants of its cricketing Empire, to be the sending of touring teams abroad. It served the twin purpose of giving an opportunity for the hosts to re-affirm their faith in Britain and the Empire, and also of stimulating the game in the colonies by setting an example and a standard to be followed. The private tours, which became another expanding and important part of cricket in the 1890s, were an important aspect of developing this bond, whether this was the intention of their organizers or not. Once the MCC started sending teams abroad this gave them more power than any edict promulgated in conclave at Lord's. Therefore it is not

surprising that Lord Harris should draw our attention to some of these
aspects in a piece written at the very end of this period:

> In these latter days a fresh and important responsibility has been
> undertaken by the MCC, not of its own seeking but in response to
> the solicitation of the cricket Associations of the great Dominions
> and other colonies. They have preferred that cricket elevens visit-
> ing their shores shall do so under the aegis of the MCC, and the club
> therefore has the anxious task of selecting teams in the case of
> Australia and South Africa, as nearly representative of the best of
> English cricket as is possible, and also of arranging the terms upon
> which the cost of these visits shall be defrayed. Teams of lighter
> calibre are also formed to visit other parts of the Empire. . . There
> has resulted a conference of great importance, from a cricket point
> of view, between the representatives of the club and of the great
> Dominions which have, perhaps strengthened the cricket associa-
> tions of the latter, and have certainly served to introduce a spirit of
> harmony which cannot but be of advantage to the game.[24]

The first English team to visit Australia went in 1862. Forty-one years
later the MCC sent out a team under its own auspices. Conversely the
Australian equivalent of the MCC, the Melbourne Cricket Club, had
been sending teams to England since 1886 and had been acting as agents
for English teams visiting Australia from an earlier date. This dis-
crepancy was the cause of complaint of one indignant correspondent to
Cricket magazine in 1882:

> Now turn to our team. No such invitation has been extended to
> them. . . Now that the colonials have shown themselves worthy
> antagonists of the best English elevens. . .have given a very great
> impetus to the noble game throughout the length and breadth of
> England, why should not the MCC, the mother of cricket, invite a
> team of such antagonists over, as we have already done more than
> one English team?[25]

This idea was not acceded to until 1893 when the MCC gave a limited
amount of patronage to the 8th Australian touring team when 'it was
resolved that. . .if the Australasian Cricket Council find it possible to
send over a representative team, it will be welcomed by MCC'.[26] Given as
we have already seen that luminaries like Lords Harris and Hawke were
interested in Empire, and that Harris himself regarded the link between
cricket and Empire as important enough to comment upon in 1885, why
did it take MCC until this date to welcome officially a representative
team from Australia and, more importantly, until 1899 to take tentatively the first steps in organizing an English team for Australia?[27]
Indeed, up to that point the MCC's interest in any part of the Empire had
been expressed simply by entertaining touring teams to dinner and
handing out temporary honorary membership to various Indian princes
who happened to be visiting Britain.

The conclusion must be that the MCC was not interested in the Empire and did not feel that it was its duty to send teams abroad or to establish important contacts with the cricketing colonies. It preferred to leave that to private enterprise and to individuals with a sense of adventure.

This reluctance to get involved officially in imperial cricket led Hawke to say in 1937 that 'it has been possible to set aside a sum of money for the financing of tours in different parts of the Empire for the control of which the MCC at first accepted responsibility with some reluctance'.[28] The sudden change of heart in the MCC's attitudes towards Empire was a direct result of a change in the composition of the committee after 1890. As demonstrated above, it was after this date that the new Conservatives gained the upper hand. Consequently, it was from 1895 onwards that the major developments in international cricket occurred, culminating in the Imperial Cricket Conference of 1909 and the triangular tournament between England, Australia and South Africa in 1912.

V

It is now necessary to examine this change in detail against the background of the new imperialism, which epitomized *la belle époque*. It is impossible to understand the actions of the MCC if we do not comprehend the era in which they operated.

In the MCC minutes for 8 January 1894 there is this entry:

> Re. Astley Cooper's proposed pan-Britannic festival. A letter was read from the Hon. Sec. to Australasian conference (B.J. Parkinson) asking whether the MCC committee had considered the scheme and generally what they proposed to do in the matter: resolved to reply that at present they had seen no scheme but would be prepared to consider the same when submitted.[29]

The 1890s were the great age of social imperialism, which reached its zenith in the Diamond Jubilee celebrations of Queen Victoria in 1897. The Diamond Jubilee was a pageant of imperial splendour and power, the psychological high-watermark of Empire. Since the 1870s a belief in Britain's imperial purpose had been growing, triggered for many people by the Queen's enthronement as Empress of India. The poetry, literature, art and popular culture of this period demonstrated the extent to which imperialism had fired and captured the imagination of the British people. The repercussions were felt in sport and even within the confines of Lord's.

In 1891, John Astley Cooper proposed the establishment of a periodic festival demonstrating the industrial, cultural and athletic prowess of the British race, the purpose of which was to strengthen the bonds of Empire.[30] Very soon the athletic idea came to surpass the others. In the issue of *Greater Britain* dated 15 October 1892, there was a list of the great and the good of the land who were espousing the idea of an 'Anglo-Saxon Olympiad'.[31] This refrain was repeated by a range of daily newspapers and magazines, including *The Times* which commented:

> The proposal for the periodic idea of holding a grand imperial festival may not be as ambitious as an all-embracing scheme of Imperial Federation. But it is superior in one respect, that instead of imposing irksome burdens and fetters, it would foster a taste which the Anglo-Saxon race in all corners of the world cultivates with enthusiasm.[32]

Unfortunately it has proved impossible to discover any direct involvement in the scheme by the MCC, and this quote from the minutes suggests that leading lights of the committee were sceptical about committing themselves to any such grand imperial design. Certainly there is no mention again of Astley Cooper in the minutes.

Astley Cooper's plans only reached a limited fruition in 1930 with the establishment of the Empire Games, but the seed of an idea had been planted and germinated. The MCC itself was about to be dragged along by the overwhelming beliefs of the day, and the time when it could ignore the importance of cricket to the Empire was diminishing rapidly. Elsewhere it was being recognized, not least thanks to the private touring teams of Hawke *et al*.

Wherever these teams went in the Empire they met an imperial reception. Thus in 1896, Priestley's team in the West Indies was bade farewell by this speech made by the Solicitor-General of Barbados:

> Mr. Priestley has referred to the sympathy which the West Indian colonies have shown to them, but it is something more than sympathy that we feel. We feel we are more brothers than friends. [Hear, Hear] This strong filial feeling is only the natural outcome of the relationship which exists between us and the Mother Country. We are sons of Old England.[33]

These sentiments were reiterated Empire-wide and soon the MCC would not be able to ignore them. Equally, stimulus was being given to the game across the Empire by the influx of administrators who had been educated in the public schools, institutions which placed an intensely strong emphasis on the Games Ethic. Some of these men were members of the MCC, and were even past or present members of the committee. I have already discussed Lord Harris, but to his name must be added those of the third Baron Wenlock, who as Governor was keen to promote cricket in Madras; A.W.L. Hemming, Governor of Demerara (1896–97) and of Jamaica (1898–1904); Hon. J.S. Udal, Attorney-General of Fiji from 1889; and the seventh Earl of Jersey, MCC president in 1894 and Governor-General of New South Wales between 1890 and 1893. All of these men encouraged imperial links through cricket and some of them, like Jersey, were prepared to represent the cricketing interests of the colonies in which they had served at Lord's itself. All of them, bar Udal, were able to welcome touring teams from Britain during their terms of office.

Lord Harris returned from Bombay in 1895 and was immediately installed as president of MCC. From this time onwards Australia and South Africa are referred to in the same ways as the counties over law changes. Similarly when every first-class touring team from the Empire was welcomed to dinner at Lord's, as had long been the custom, special guests were now invited, often the Colonial Secretary or someone with imperial interests. Thus the Right Honourable Joseph Chamberlain was invited to meet and dine with the Australians on 6 July 1899.[34] He was also invited to the celebration of the return of the triumphant 1904 MCC side from Australia, along with the Colonial Secretary of the day, G. Hillyard. Unfortunately it has been impossible to discover the contents of many of the speeches made on these occasions, but it is reasonable to believe that they were not materially different from any of the cricket and Empire speeches quoted above.

It was inevitable that the MCC should become caught up in the imperial mood. Once they had concentrated all domestic power at Lord's they were set to become the most powerful body in world cricket. Under their auspices they were able to inaugurate the Imperial Cricket Conference in 1909, although, like many things gone before, it was not originally their idea.

In late 1907 'a letter from Mr. Abe Bailey had been read in which he proposed a scheme for holding an Imperial cricket contest between England, Australia and South Africa, in 1909'.[35] This suggestion was referred to the Advisory County Cricket Committee which endorsed the idea. Abe Bailey was one of the staunchest supporters of cricket and Empire and had welcomed and entertained the MCC team which went to South Africa in 1905–6. It was probably the success of this tour and the return visit of a South African XI the following summer which led Bailey to make this suggestion, although it is also possible that he may have discussed his ideas with someone like Warner before writing to the MCC. However, the Australians were not overwhelmed by the proposal, perhaps because they jealously wanted to guard their position as the number one rivals of the Mother Country. Although the MCC believed the contest to be a good idea, they were not in a position to enforce the participation of the Australians. Finally, not wishing to lose a lucrative Australian tour, they realized that the only solution was to invite the Australians alone, an invitation which was accepted. But as a compromise the Conference was proposed 'to discuss arrangements under which matches between England, Australia and South Africa might be held'.[36] This was duly organized, and by holding it at Lord's, the MCC put its own seal on international cricket. Inevitably Lord Harris was one of the representatives in a series of meetings dominated by the MCC, with the secretary, Lacey, proving extremely important in an organizational capacity.

The result of the first Imperial Conference was the arrangement of a triangular tournament for 1912, and the establishment of the rules under which Test matches would be played in future by the three countries.

When the tournament was held imperial cricket was established on a firm basis and the MCC, which had concentrated all power around the environs of St. John's Wood, now fulfilled the imperial function to which its prestige as the premier cricket club in the Empire seemed to entitle it. Since 1903 when it first sent a team abroad its indulgence in these activities had snowballed. Within the following years the MCC sent teams to South Africa, Australia, New Zealand, the West Indies and Argentina. It received requests and pleas from other areas to do the same. Thus Sir Ernest Birch vainly wondered 'if the MCC will some day send out a team of amateurs to play in Malaya'[37] and suggested that the MCC might consider, for its own good, conferring 'the privilege of wearing the red and yellow ribbon on those in all parts of the world who are aspiring to wear it . . . In British colonies the wearing of the red and yellow ribbon is, and always will be, a much coveted honour'.[38]

The MCC was at last fulfilling some of its claim to being the headquarters of cricket and acknowledging an obligation towards the empire. In the annual report of 1911 it was stated:

> An MCC team under Mr. A. F. Somerset as captain, has recently visited the West Indies at the invitation of cricketers in those islands. Your Committee have reason to think that such visits do much to encourage cricket and establish good fellowship.[39]

The club had moved with the times after frequent goadings from outside. It had been unable to resist the imperial tide or its own obligations to cricket.

VI

The MCC has built itself a myth of such potency that few people question the facade of prestige and power. Yet when all is examined it took the MCC until the end of this era to exercise any real authority over the cricket world. There is a moral in this for all historians and cricket writers: if too much time is spent studying a central organization it might really appear that that body is the only important element. Therefore, it might really appear that the story of the MCC is the history of cricket and vice versa. To arrive at this diagnosis is not unlike staring at a mirage for a prolonged period and eventually believing that it is water. But like a mirage there is very little substance to the claim of MCC omnipotence unless we are looking at the highest echelons of the game. There is a large and marked difference between governing as above, and omnipotence. The MCC had gathered all power around it, but in reality this was of a very limited significance to most cricketers across the Empire.

The history of cricket is a convoluted affair which is inextricably linked to the social and economic history of Britain and its Empire. Indeed, the game served as a symbol of that Empire's ideology. The MCC has little place in these developments. Cricket was encouraged overseas by a disparate band of people. Government administrators, engineers, sol-

diers, sailors, missionaries and teachers all played their part. The spread
of cricket was bound to the imperial movement as a whole. As the
boundaries of the Empire pushed forward, so did the cricket frontier. It
even played its own small part in informal Empire, being played in such
diverse areas as Argentina (a country in which both Lord Hawke and the
MCC invested) and China. The book *Imperial Cricket* is full of exotic
locations and isolated games played with different motivations by different people. The description of cricket in West Africa by Major E.G.
Guggisberg goes some way to capturing the essence and complexities of
cricket in the Empire:

> Three stumps are pitched in a small patch of ground, innocent of
> grass, rolled hard and fairly smooth by the roller . . . That roller
> . . . is worth examining – it is an extempore one, roughly cast of
> cement, with a rusty piece of waterpipe as an axle . . . A poor-
> looking thing as rollers go, but a fine witness to the keenness on
> cricket of the maker – that sunburned man in the dungaree breeches
> . . . who is standing at the wicket, padless and gloveless, and with a
> much scarred, much bound bat in his hand. He is a 'Sheffield Blade'
> . . . and learnt his cricket after his day's toil in the great engineering
> works where he was employed. One of the two individuals bowling
> to him – the short man clad in a similar kit – is an old soldier and the
> overseer of the mine gangs. The other – the possessor of real
> flannelled cricket trousers, you will notice – was once a by-no-
> means inconspicuous figure in a great public school eleven a few
> years ago. . . . A curious trio drawn together by the love of the
> game. . .they are cricket missionaries these three, propagating the
> game, for look at the half-dozen other players from the native
> clerk. . .to the brown, more or less clad, natives fielding with the
> greatest of keenness.[40]

The spirit of imperial cricket was diverse in its extremes, but it was
deliberately compacted into this piece of writing. In it, nowhere can one
find the influence of the MCC. This is a game alien to Lord's and
thousands of miles from the serenity of St. John's Wood. One institution
cannot govern and cannot represent the actions and ideals of the whole
Empire. By concentrating on the central body one ignores the myriad
experiences outside it.

NOTES

1. A. Lewis, *Double Century. The Story of MCC and Cricket* (London, 1987), p. 11.
2. G.R.C. Harris and F.S. Ashley-Cooper, *Lord's And The MCC* (London, 1914),
   p. 209.
3. M.B. Hawke, 7th Lord, *Recollections and Remniscences* (London, 1924), p. 260.
4. *Minutes of MCC*, 3 May 1865, p. 478.
5. Lewis, *Double Century*, p. 15.
6. Harris and Ashley-Cooper, *Lord's and the MCC*, p. 229.

7. Hawke, *Recollections and Remniscences*, p.260.
8. Ibid.
9. This section was written with the aid of a multitude of secondary printed sources and reference works. These ranged from *Who Was Who* to *The Dictionary of National Biography* and beyond. I also had recourse to old school registers and the Alumni lists of those who attended Oxford or Cambridge.
10. W.A. Bettesworth, *The Walkers of Southgate* (London, 1900), pp.89–92.
11. *Cricket*, Vol. 4 (1885), p.454.
12. A. Haygarth, *Scores and Biographies* (London, 1908), Vol. 14, p.lxxiii.
13. Ibid., p.lxxii.
14. R. Cashman, *Patrons, Players and the Crowd. The Phenomenon of Indian Cricket* (India, 1980), pp.4–13.
15. Hawke, *Recollections and Remniscences*, p.82.
16. Ibid., p.155.
17. Ibid., p.151, 'I never partook of a merrier meal', said the noble Lord of his visit, high praise from one who was a member of the gluttonous and uproarious gentleman's dining club, the Beefsteak.
18. Ibid., p.158.
19. Ibid., pp.274–5. I suppose that it is remotely possible that this is an unpublished Austin, but the reason I believe that this was penned by Hawke was his introduction to the poem: 'Here is an unpublished poem which all these years has been in my scrapbook and is too beautiful not to see the light of print. . .'.
20. P.F. Warner, *The MCC in South Africa* (London, 1906), p.218.
21. Ibid., pp.29–30.
22. P.F. Warner, *Cricket in Many Climes* (London, 1900), p.vii.
23. P.F. Warner, *England v. Australia* (London, 1912), pp.17–19.
24. Harris and Ashley-Cooper, *Lord's and the MCC*, pp.209–11.
25. *Cricket*, Vol. 1 (1882) p.142.
26. *Minutes of MCC*, 14 Nov 1892, p.1292.
27. Ibid., 26 June 1899, p.1564.
28. *The Times* (ed.), *MCC, 1787–1937* (London, 1937), p.13.
29. *Minutes of MCC*, 8 Jan. 1894, p.1320.
30. Katharine Moore, 'Sport, Politics and Imperialism. The Evolution of the Concept of the British Games', in The British Society of Sport History, *Sport and Imperialism, The Proceedings of the Fourth Annual Conference of the BSSH*, pp.47–9.
31. J.A. Mangan, *The Games Ethic And Imperialism* (London, 1986), p.52.
32. Ibid., p.54.
33. C.P. Bowen, *English Cricketers in the West Indies* (Bridgetown, Barbados, 1896), p.24.
34. *Minutes of MCC*, 15 May 1899, p.1551.
35. Ibid., 16 Dec. 1907, p.1938.
36. Ibid., 29 July 1908, p.1971.
37. P.F. Warner (ed.), *Imperial Cricket* (London, 1912), p.38.
38. Ibid., p.390.
39. *Minutes of MCC*, 3 May 1911, p.2039.
40. Warner (ed.), *Imperial Cricket*, pp.330–31.

CHAPTER THREE

Salvation for the Fittest? A West African Sportsman in the Age of the New Imperialism

RAY JENKINS

> The feature of the racing at the Amateur Athletics Championships on Saturday July 3rd was the fine running of Arthur Wharton, a young gentleman of colour, who is a student of Darlington College. He won the 100 yards Race in the wonderful time of 10 sec., which as it is fully authenticated by the timekeepers, may be accepted as establishing a best on record for that distance.
>
> *The Sporting Chronicle*, 5 July 1886

Arthur Wharton achieved national prominence in Britain when he became the first athlete to run 100 yards in ten seconds in both the heats and the final at the Amateur Athletic Association's annual meeting at Stamford Bridge in London on 3 July 1886.[1] For the next three months, the new champion competed before large crowds at athletics meetings in the north of England and the Midlands as a member of Darlington Cricket and Football Club (CFC) and Birchfield Harriers, respectively.[2] In September, at the start of the association football season, he was signed by Preston North End FC for the duration of that ambitious club's challenge in the Football Association Cup competition. When Preston's challenge ended in the semi-final on 5 March 1887, their new goalkeeper had conceded only four goals in six cup ties. A week later, he again played for Preston against the Corinthians in the Festival of Football, which was staged at Kennington Oval before the Prince of Wales to celebrate the Queen-Empress's Golden Jubilee.[3] The rapid rise of Arthur Wharton, from unknown student in Darlington to record-breaking amateur athlete, Birchfield Harrier and goalkeeper with one of British football's elite clubs, had been accomplished in the nine months from July 1886 to March 1887.

For the next ten years, Wharton seems to have become one of the most visible and, at times, controversial of Britain's sporting personalities. The rapid nature of his rise to national prominence helps to explain why he began and continued to attract the attention of journalists and sports officials and entrepreneurs and, by implication, their paying customers:

the readers and spectators. There were, however, several extra dimensions to the person and personality of Wharton. Together, these served
to enhance his profile in the press, to augment the drawing-power of his
presence on the field of play and to produce his reputation for controversy.

I

For two years before his rise to national prominence, Wharton's reputation as a sportsman had steadily grown in the West Midlands, the North
East and the North in general. In South Staffordshire his contributions to
cricket and associaton football were 'much missed' after 1884;[4] in the
North East there followed competition for his services as a goalkeeper at
local club and regional representative levels[5] and his potential as a future
champion sprinter was soon recognized by local athletics *aficionados* and
journalists, particularly after his successful and lucrative season on the
Northern circuit in 1885 when he achieved a notable but 'handicapped'
victory over the American runner, L. E. Myers. His success at Stamford
Bridge in the heartland of the South was regarded in the North and the
West Midlands, therefore, as a regional triumph.[6] A song, 'Wharton of
Darlington', was composed and sung in his honour at a dinner in a
Darlington hotel, as Wharton 'stood half-dazed before the reiterated
volleys of the guests'.[7]

The rise of this local and regional hero was the result of the considerable talents which he displayed and continued to display across a wide
range of winter and summer sports: athletics, cricket (as an all-rounder),
football (as a goalkeeper and winger), swimming, rugby football (albeit
briefly, as a wing three-quarter) and, probably, cycling. Moreover, his
versatile performances were enhanced by astonishing bursts of speed and
feats of athleticism, enlivened by his apparent use of unorthodox styles
and eccentric techniques, and attributed by Wharton to the skill of his
coaches and his own dedication to fitness.[8]

His versatility off the running track and the games field also contributed to the growth, if not the improvement, of his reputation. Wharton seems to have crossed the murky boundaries between amateur and
professional sport, which incurred charges of illegal payments, the 'fix-
ing' of races and other misdemeanours associated with the 'sport' of
gambling.[9] Not only did he transgress or appear to transgress the amateur
code in the late 1880s, he also 'sold' his services for prize-money or
expenses to several clubs at the same time between 1886 and 1888 or
within a short space of time after turning professional in 1889.[10] In
keeping with some of his fellow professionals, Wharton also extended his
role as a sports entrepreneur by becoming a licensed victualler and a
football club shareholder in the 1890s.[11]

His tendency to indulge in what may be described in modern sporting

parlance as 'displays of temperament' also contributed to the making of
Wharton the sports personality – at least, in the columns of the press. At
various times during his career, he disputed decisions of track officials;
responded to insinuations concerning his amateur status by issuing challenges either in person or in print, and registered his contempt for the
organizers of 'open' races and the official keepers of the amateur code by
failing to appear at meetings or disciplinary hearings. In one of his rare
press interviews, he was described as

> a most sociable fellow when you know him, but 'you have to know
> him first'. Arthur has a bit of a temper when he's crossed, but taken
> all round he is a straightforward, good-natured chap.[12]

Not surprisingly, perhaps, Wharton's displays of 'good nature', in which
local friendships and loyalties were remembered and repaid by personal
appearances for charity or in aid of Wakes Week events, were not
accorded the same publicity.[13]

Finally, Wharton was distinguishable from his fellow sportsmen
because he was black. Indeed even though he could raise his fists in
response to racial taunts,[14] by avoiding (or transcending) the old
association of black athletes with boxing, Wharton became the first of
Britain's 'modern' black sportsmen and sporting personalities. As a
pioneer, therefore, his displays of bad and good temper and his apparent
reluctance to entertain all but a few, mainly local, journalists may be
interpreted, either partially or wholly, as reactions to what he perceived
as attitudes of colour prejudice or colour blindness. It was only after his
success in London in July 1886 that Wharton was variously described and
defined as a 'gentleman of colour', a 'brunette of pronounced complexion' and by 'no means a representative Englishman in appearance'
by national athletics journalists, for whom his origins became a source of
imaginative speculation. Thereafter, he was usually referred to as
'Darkie', 'Darkey' or 'Duskey' Wharton, whose birthplace was located
almost exclusively but erroneously in the 'Caribbean'.[15] Even today,
when Wharton's achievements are recalled, exceptionally, in athletics
and local football club histories, he is usually described as a 'Jamaican' or
'Trinidadian'. In fact, Wharton was born and raised in the Gold Coast
(now the Republic of Ghana) in West Africa.[16]

Did Wharton's Gold Coast origins and early experiences contribute to
the making of Wharton the black British sportsman and sports
personality? From the insights which prevail in the historiography of the
connections between British imperialism and sport, it is tempting to
conclude that his exploits of the 1880s may be attributed to the dynamic
sporting component of the 'civilizing mission' in West Africa. Did his
successes represent, therefore, triumphs for the doctrine of 'salvation for
the fittest', the credo of those builders and caretakers of empire, who, as
amateur sportsmen *par excellence*, took their games and diffused the
'games ethic' wherever they went?[17]

An affirmative answer to this question would be difficult to sustain for two reasons. First, there are features of Wharton's sporting biography which suggest that his exploits and experiences may be attributed to the failure, rather than the success, of British imperialist ideology in action. His 'unsporting' behaviour, his apparent 'shamateurism' and his ultimate defection to professionalism, on the one hand, and the racial insults which he clearly experienced, on the other, do not seem to square easily with the perception of Wharton as a product of the sporting 'cultural bond' between the Blues and the Blacks in West Africa. Moreover, the shallow contradictions of the British imperialist enterprise become all too apparent if Wharton's activities on the playing fields of late Victorian Britain – including his roles as regional hero and patron of charitable causes – are viewed against the background of the conquest and occupation of 'inferior' West Africans by the 'superior' Blues. Indeed, from an African perspective, his triumph in a 'struggle of the fittest' against white opponents in the imperial capital, only a year after the European 'scramblers' for Africa met at the Berlin Conference, was not unlike that of Jesse Owens in Berlin, half a century later.[18]

Secondly, if, at this stage, the case for the influence of the Blues in the Wharton story remains unproven, the verdict can only be partially ascribed to those 'tensions' between subject and context which usually plague the study of biography. It is also a reflection on the shortcomings of the arguments in favour of the imperial case. Even though the geographical range of interest in imperial sport history has been recently extended to include anglophone Africa to the north of the Limpopo, research into the diffusion of British forms of sport within the West African region remains underdeveloped.[19] For Wharton's Gold Coast, therefore, hard evidence is lacking. In addition, there has been a strong tendency to equate the diffusion of Britain's 'chief spiritual export' with outflows of expatriates and their activities and aspirations as outsiders within the context of 'formal' (rather than 'informal') empire.[20] As a consequence and with a few notable exceptions,[21] little is yet known or understood about the nature of the responses of the imperialized – from the 'inside out' rather than the 'outside in' – to the presentation or imposition of the rules, rituals and values of alien sport as elements of British 'cultural imperialism'.[22]

On the basis of recent research into European (British, Danish, Dutch, Swiss-German) 'cultural imperialisms' in the nineteenth-century Gold Coast, from the 'inside out', it may be suggested that local responses to British forms of sport hinged upon three sets of inter-related influences.[23] These may be tabulated as follows:

1. the nature of the 'cultural' relationships (commercial, confessional, educational, linguistic, familial) which particular communities developed with Britain and the British (as opposed to the Swiss-Germans of the Basel Mission, for example) during the phases of 'informal' and 'formal' imperialism and the period of transition between the two.

2. the ethnic or social origins, the occupational concerns and the ideological orientations of the agent (local African and Afro-Caribbean as
   well as British) of a particular sport.
3. the perceived advantages or disadvantages that co-operation or non-
   co-operation seemed to present to individuals or groups within a local
   community, at particular moments in time.

In an attempt to identify those elements from the imperial 'cultural
baggage' which Wharton carried with him from the Gold Coast in 1882,
and to assess, rather tentatively, their significance in the making of
Wharton the black British sports personality, his origins and early years
are examined in the context of these three sets of influences. While the
main aim of this study is to determine whether Wharton was a product of
the doctrine of 'salvation for the fittest', its additional purpose is to throw
some light upon the creation of the sporting 'cultural bond' in the Gold
Coast of West Africa.

II

Apart from a brief six-month visit to England in 1870, Arthur Wharton's
first 16 years were spent in the Gold Coast, the name which was given by
the Portuguese to that 300-mile stretch of the West African littoral
between the rivers Tano and Volta.[24] He was born in 1866, the eighth of
ten children of the Rev. Henry and Mrs Annie Florence Wharton. His
birthplace was most probably the Wesleyan Mission House, which was
situated in the English castle-township, called James Town or 'English
Accra'.[25] James Town took its name from Fort James, one of the some 30
castles and forts, which European gold and slave traders constructed in
the 200 years after 1480 and which, at the time of Wharton's birth, still
'clung like leeches' to the Gold Coast littoral.[26]
    Wharton's early childhood was spent in James Town until May 1870.
The following eight months were passed in the company of his parents,
sister and youngest brother, either on board ship, sailing to and from
Liverpool, or in Islington, north London. On the family's return to Accra,
the Rev. Wharton was transferred to Anomabo and then to Cape Coast,
the administrative 'capital' of the Wesleyan Missionary Society in the
Gold Coast and southern Nigeria and the headquarters of British political, commercial and military-naval interests along with Gold Coast littoral.[27] It was an inauspicious moment to be promoted to the General
Superintendency of the Mission. Three years of tension and sporadic
warfare in the locality culminated in the invasion of Fanteland and the
siege of Cape Coast by the Asante army, early in 1873. As a consequence
of the prolonged disruption of trade and farming and the large influx of
refugees from the rural hinterland, starvation and disease reached crisis
proportions before Gladstone's government decided to despatch inadequate supplies of food 'relief' and a task-force to relieve the castle-

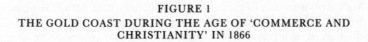

FIGURE 1
THE GOLD COAST DURING THE AGE OF 'COMMERCE AND
CHRISTIANITY' IN 1866

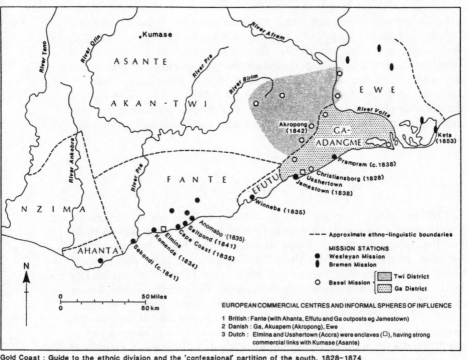

Gold Coast : Guide to the ethnic division and the 'confessional' partition of the south, 1828–1874

© R.G. Jenkins

township.[28] In these circumstances, it is not surprising that the health of
the Rev. Wharton (and members of his family) deteriorated. In addition
to the strains of the two-year leadership of the Mission, which had proved
to be both difficult and dangerous, he was appointed chaplain to the
Methodist troops in the British military task-force. While *en route* for
Britain, the ailing Rev. Wharton died and was buried at Funchal in the
Madeiras in October, 1873. He was 54 years of age and had served the
Mission for 28 years.[29]

After the British defeat of Asante and their annexation of the southern
Gold Coast in 1874, Mrs Wharton settled in her 'home' town, Cape
Coast, with her three surviving children, Charles, Arthur and William.[30]
She was a senior daughter of one of the township's most influential
trading families, the Grants, and she soon followed the family's entre-
preneurial tradition by entering the retail and hotel trades.[31] Her eldest

son, Charles, re-entered the colonial civil service in 1877 as assistant pay
and quartermaster in the Gold Coast constabulary.[32] With the sudden
death of the Rev. Wharton, however, it is very probable that his brother-
in-law, F.C. Grant, the head of the Grant family, began to exert a real
influence over the affairs of the Whartons.[33] From the early 1870s until his
death in 1894, Grant was one of the wealthiest of the Gold Coast's
'merchant princes'. With his interests in the retailing of imported European goods and the export of palm oil and the 'boom' commodities,
rubber and gold, Grant maintained a chain of warehouses and stores
along the coastal littoral and a network of agents and contacts, which
extended from the hinterlands of southern Asante to Europe (including
Manchester) and the Americas. His local social status and political power
were not only derived from the prestige which coastal communities
accorded to business acumen and wealth through trade. He was also a
prominent lay member of the Wesleyan Mission and the head of the Cape
Coast lodge of the Order of Good Templars. As the proprietor of the
Gold Coast Times, he was able to promote his commercial, confessional
and political interests throughout the coastal townships and in Freetown
(Sierra Leone) and Lagos.

As a member of the formidable F.C. Grant's extended family, it would
be surprising if the young Arthur Wharton had not been strongly
encouraged to attend the church which his father had served for so long
and to pursue vigorously – after the interruptions of the years from 1870
to 1874 – his educational studies at the Wesleyan Mission school in Cape
Coast with a view to joining the family business, like his mother, or
entering the professions, like his elder brother, Charles. When the 16-
year-old Wharton sailed from Cape Coast in July 1882, to become a
student at Shoal Hill College, a private Wesleyan school in Cannock,
Staffordshire, he was accompanied by his uncle, F.C. Grant.[34]

At the time of his departure for Britain, therefore, Arthur Wharton's
Gold Coast was confined to a 100-mile strip of the coastal littoral, which
was delimited by the Accra and Cape Coast clusters of townships. Communications between the two were usually effected by sea. Thus, apart
from perhaps the short ten-mile trek, as a child, to his father's farm in the
Accra plains, the young Wharton was less familiar with the Gold Coast
hinterland than with other West African coastal 'capitals', such as Mon-
rovia, Freetown and Bathurst (now Banjul in The Gambia), which
served as regular ports of call *en route* by sea to Liverpool. Indeed, even
though he had had first-hand experience of large numbers of Fante
peasant refugees and Asante prisoners-of-war in the early 1870s and he
must have witnessed the arrivals of the large Asante diplomatic-military
missions in Cape Coast during the tense Asante 'war-scare' of 1881,[35] it is
likely that he had spent more time in Liverpool and Islington than he had
in rural hinterland towns, such as Akropong, some 25 to 30 miles inland.
These early English experiences were reinforced by the long Wharton–
Grant family involvement (since the 1830s) in the development of a
British commercial and confessional sphere of 'informal' imperial

influence in the southern Gold Coast. Both families were products and
agents of the 'trinity of the Cs: Commerce, Christianity and Civilization':
the dominant ideological components of that version of Britain's 'civilization mission', which had underscored the humanitarian and governmental campaigns against the West African slave trade after 1787 and
then 1807.[36] Even though the influence of 'Exeter Hall' humanitarianism
at governmental level declined during the 1850s and 1860s, the shift from
an 'informal' to a 'formal' imperial relationship with the Gold Coast, as
manifested in the conquest of Asante and the annexation of the colony in
1873–74, seemed to signal that the British were now intent upon reinforc-
ing their political and renewing their cultural bonds with the anglicized
business and professional families of the coastal townships, such as the
Grants and the Whartons.

                                        III

In October 1881, Rider Haggard returned to Britain from South Africa;
several months before Wharton's arrival from the Gold Coast. Within
five years, both men had achieved success. Wharton, the African sportsman, acquired a little fame but no fortune on the playing fields of British
cities; Haggard, the English novelist, acquired fame and a substanital
fortune describing the violent antics of sporting English gentlemen on the
'playing fields' of Africa. The images of Africa and Africans, which
Haggard provided for his British readers in his best-sellers of 1885–87,
contrasted sharply with the Africa and the Africans of Wharton's
experience.[37]
    Haggard's was a manufactured rural Africa of the interior: a mys-
terious Dark Continent of plains, hills, rivers and forests, replete with
wild beasts; with dangerous and devious racially mixed pastoralists; with
hidden riches and undiscovered non-African civilizations. His Africans
were noble savages: pristine, pure black peasant-warriors, who were
manly, brave, loyal and honest. For Haggard, and somewhat paradoxically, his Africa and Africans had yet 'to be torn and fought for by
speculators, tourists, politicans and teachers' or subjected to the 'greed,
drunkenness, new diseases, gunpowder and general demoralisation
which chiefly mark the progress of civilisation amongst unsophisticated
peoples'.[38]
    Wharton's real Africa, as we have noted, was essentially the Africa of
the coast rather than the interior; the Africa of the 'modern' towns rather
than the 'traditional' village and the countryside. His Africans were the
Africans of the castle-townships and their local rural environs, who had
experienced 400 years of contact with – or, in Haggardian terms,
contamination by – Europe's merchants, missionaries, administrators
and adventurers-cum-travellers, and who had learned to fear the 'noble
savages' of the hinterland, the peasant-warriors of Asante. It may be
suggested with some confidence, however, that the young Wharton was

already familiar with, and sensitive to, the stereotypes and attitudes associated with the 'good' (preferred) and the 'bad' (unfavoured) African, before his arrival in Britain. Indeed, this ideological duality may be regarded as one of the formative Gold Coast influences, which contributed to the making of Arthur Wharton the African and the black British sports personality. In the following attempt to identify and estimate the significance of such formative influences from the 'inside out', three features of Wharton's Gold Coast will be examined: the emergence of the Euro-African communities of the coastal urban enclaves; the impact of British 'formal' imperial expansion and the growth of imported British recreational pursuits.

IV

Throughout their long history, the castle-townships served as a cultural, as well as an economic, crossroads between Africa, Europe and the Americas. By the 1860s, therefore, they had long become a melting-pot for a variety of ethno-cultural influences and orientations. These included: the Gold Coast African (the Fante and other Akan-speaking communities, such as Asante and Akuapem; the Ga); the West African (Sierra Leonean, Liberian and Nigerian); the European (Portuguese, English, Irish, Scottish, French, Danish, Dutch, German); the Bahian and Caribbean (the influx of repatriates during and after the 1830s). From this complex range of ethno-cultural interactions through time, three are worth noting here. First, influential mulatto families emerged (such as the Brews, Bannermans, Grants, Reindorfs, Lutterodts, Hesses, Bartels), whose patronyms revealed their European ancestry. The senior sons were often educated in Europe to enable them to act as intermediaries between European traders and the political and business elites of the African states of the coast and hinterland. Secondly, with the notable exception of the majority of expatriate missionaries; the European trader-administrators, the West African settlers and the West Indian repatriates were usually assimilated by marriage into local African communities. Through their 'country-wives' and children, they acquired a knowledge of local languages, rituals, beliefs, laws and institutions, and as a result of the complex local systems of matrilineal and patrilineal modes of inheritance, they and their children acquired clan, extended family and other institutional affiliations and responsibilities. Thirdly, and in tandem with, but in opposition to, the process of local acculturation, an active programme of European-oriented assimilation was implemented by the Missions during and after the 1830s.

By the middle decades of the century, the effect of these three developments was the emergence of what I have defined and described, elsewhere as a distinctive ethno-cultural constellation, Gold Coast 'Euro-African Society'.[39] Euro-African communities comprised a network of families, who were inter-related through a dense and complex

maze of marriage alliances. While the 'core' consisted of 'old' mulatto
families; those of local African converts, West African and West Indian
settlers were also incorporated into the network. In the 1850s and 1860s,
however, these communities were differentiated according to their
affiliation to the Missions. In the Wesleyan sphere, Euro-Africans were
English- and usually Fante-speaking teachers, preachers, clerks,
lawyers and traders. The majority were also literate in English and
members of the prominent families had been educated in Britain. In the
Basel Mission sphere, Euro-Africans were locally-educated pastors and
'scholar' farmers and artisans, who were literate and fluent in English
and German or Danish and at least one African language. As the Basel
Mission had its own trading company, few Basel Mission affiliates
became 'merchant princes' in the mould of F.C. Grant. In the Accra
enclave, however, where the Wharton children had spent their early
years, the Euro-African communities were the most cosmopolitan of the
Gold Coast littoral. In addition to having families of British, Dutch and
Danish descent and those of free and freed repatriates from Jamaica and
Bahia, Accra was situated on the boundary of the Wesleyan and Basel
Mission spheres of cultural influence.

V

The three strands in Arthur Wharton's ancestry – the British (Scottish),
the Gold Coast African (Fante), and the West Indian (Afro-Caribbean
creole) – reflect the triangular pattern of trade, which developed between the Gold Coast, Britain and the Caribbean. His father, Henry, was
the son of a Scottish sea captain-trader called Wharton and a free
'coloured' or black woman. Henry was born in 1819 in St. George's, the
main township and port of the island of Grenada. Arthur Wharton's
mother, Annie Florence Grant, was the daughter of a Scottish trader,
John Chapman Grant, and Ama Ejiriba, a Fante royal of the Ekumfie
state.[40]
    The presence of the slave trade and plantation slavery is represented in
Wharton's Caribbean background by his African-born great grandmother,
who was a slave. The fact that his grandmother was a free creole
(Grenadian-born), suggests that his great-grandfather was a slave-holding
white planter. The rise of the Gold Coast Whartons is directly related to the
humanitarian-inspired policy of recruiting West Indian volunteers to
promote Christianity and 'civilization' in West Africa.[41] While strong
emotional commitment to 'righting the wrongs' of the slave trade in the
'land of their forefathers' is evident in the career of West Indian repatriates,
such as Henry Wharton,[42] the racial thinking which inspired their recruitment by European missionary and colonial interests often proved to be
tragically misguided. Blacks from the West Indies proved as susceptible to
West African diseases as whites from Europe. This is particularly true in
the case of the Whartons. After serving in the Gold Coast for 18 years

4. The Rev. Henry Wharton (seated right) at Cape Coast, April 1873

100 Yds. Final.

5. Arthur Wharton's championship victory at Stamford Bridge, London, 3 July 1886

6. Arthur Wharton (back row, centre) goalkeeper for Rotherham Town FC, c. 1892

without a break, Henry Wharton's appearance startled his Wesleyan colleagues, who had known him before his departure for West Africa. On his arrival in England in 1863, he was grey, elderly and his health was broken.[43] He was to endure chronic illness until his premature and sudden death, twelve years later. By this time, however, death had proved to be 'a regular visitor' in the Wharton household. Although Arthur was the eighth of ten children, only four survived by 1873. Five had died in infancy; a sixth, Alfred, died aged about 16 in 1870 (while his family were in England); a seventh, Arthur's youngest brother, William, probably died in the late 1870s.[44]

Despite this tragic dimension to the Whartons' involvement in the 'Exeter Hall' crusade in the Gold Coast, it may also be suggested that the pursuit of the 'holy trinity' – 'legitimate' commerce, Christianity and civilization – left an indelible imprint upon Arthur Wharton's family history.

Apart from the fact that Arthur Wharton had spent his early years in Accra and Cape Coast and had been exposed, as a result, to the trading-entrepreneurial 'culture' of these urban enclaves, trade was the dominant occupation in his family's history. His Scottish grandfathers, Wharton and Grant, his Grenadian creole grandmother and aunt, and his mother's family, the Grants, had been or were involved in trade.[45] His father had worked as a commercial clerk in Grenada in the 1830s and, although his later role as a Wesleyan minister precluded any involvement in trade, it seems clear that Henry Wharton's long service in James Town, Accra, encouraged him to follow the Basel Mission's ideas toward agricultural development and self-reliance. From Burton's description of Wharton's farm in the Accra plain, in 1862, it seems clear that he was growing vegetables for sale in Accra markets. The inclusion of Caribbean 'ground provisions' (food crops) in the Wharton farm suggests that he had collaborated in his horticultural ventures with his Jamaican brethren, who formed the 'core' of the Basel Mission's station in Akropong-Akuapem. In 1871, according to the *Accra Herald*, the Rev. Wharton was a prominent member of the Agricultural Association of the Eastern Districts of the Gold Coast, which offered monetary prizes in the annual exhibition of 'Horto-Agricultural produce'.[46]

The Rev. Henry Wharton and his in-laws, the Grants, were also dedicated to the promotion of Wesleyan Christianity in the southern Gold Coast. Evidence suggests, therefore, that Arthur Wharton was raised in a strict and indeed puritanical household, in which Wesleyan evangelism was suffused with the Basel Mission's pietist tradition of self-discipline and self-reliance. It should be also emphasized that the Rev. Wharton in James Town (the eastern outpost of the anglophone, Wesleyan sphere of interest) and his in-laws, the Grants, in the Cape Coast enclave, were in the vanguard of the commercial and confessional expansion of Britain's 'informal' empire in the Gold Coast. The rise and the interests of both families were intimately connected to the British presence.

By examining Arthur Wharton's ancestry and family ties, it is possible to provide some answers to the question: who was Arthur Wharton? In 1874, this nine-year-old boy belonged to four ethno-cultural 'worlds': the Caribbean; the British; the Gold Coast African; the Gold Coast Euro-African. It is more difficult, however, to suggest answers which the young Arthur Wharton might have provided to the above question in 1874. To which 'world' or 'worlds' did he relate in an emotional sense? Were his emotional bonds with Africa, the Caribbean or Britain, or all three?

If Wharton had any ties with the Caribbean, they were literary, social or sentimental rather than familial. Following his departure for England and the Gold Coast in 1845, the Rev. Wharton never returned to Grenada, nor did he wish to after 1863. In that year, he was informed of 'the death of his dear mother and beloved sister, and that his patrimonial inheritance was involved in ruin [in St. George's].' Henceforth, the Rev. Wharton regarded the Gold Coast as 'the land of his adoption' and Britain as his 'base'.[47] Thus, the Grenadian Whartons had died out before Arthur was born and, with his father's death in 1873, his last direct link with the Caribbean was broken. Apart from the social ties, which he may have forged with the Basel Mission's Jamaican families (the Clerks, the Halls, the Millers and the Rochesters) in the Accra-Akuapem localities, young Wharton's Caribbean connection was, therefore, a sentimental and a literary one: the personal memory of his father, supplemented by Moister's biographical memoir, published in 1875.[48]

As far as the British connection is concerned, there is some circumstantial evidence that suggests Wharton may have had some family ties with England, if not Scotland. Wharton is not a Scottish name and, for the period in question, records in Edinburgh and London reveal that there were comparatively few Whartons in Scotland or England, outside clusters in Durham (Darlington) and South Yorkshire (Sheffield and Rotherham).[49] It is also possible that the Grenadian Whartons had family connections with Liverpool. The Rev. Wharton's sister (Arthur's aunt) had married a planter (or plantation manager) in Grenada called Fairclough. The Faircloughs visited Liverpool, with their daughter, in the 1840s.[50]

In 1874, however, the bond between Arthur Wharton and Britain (his late father's 'base') may be appropriately described as educational or confessional or both. His father, mother, older brothers (Charles and Alfred) and his cousins (the Grants) were all educated in Britain at private schools associated with the Methodist Church – with the exception of the Rev. Wharton, who spent six years at school in Scotland. Arthur's only surviving sister, Clara, had been at school in England since 1870.[51] His father had strong professional and friendship ties with Methodists and Methodism. In addition to his long and close 'father-son' relationship with one of the 'grand old men' of the Wesleyan missionary enterprise, William Moister, during his visits to England in 1863–64 and 1870, he had preached in local chapels and addressed annual conferences in towns and cities in the North and the Midlands, including those where clusters of Whartons were particularly prominent. Arthur did accompany his father to England in 1870, as we have noted earlier. His father did intend to find a place for him in an English school. The family's visit was cut short, however, by the news of Alfred's death in James Town. The seven-year-old Clara was left at an English school; the five-year-old Arthur returned to Accra and the Asante crisis.[52]

It seems reasonable to suggest, therefore, that if Wharton had any secure roots in 1874, they were in the Gold Coast. Through the Fante–Akan matrilineal system, he was related through his mother to the royal family of the Ekumfie and, most probably, the Nkusukum Fante states. In the local African ethno-cultural context, Arthur Wharton was a Fante–royal! As his maternal grandmother was Fante, Arthur, like his mother, would almost certainly have spoken Fante since early childhood. Having spent his early years in the Accra townships, it is likely that he could also speak Ga – not an uncommon ability for Fante residents of Accra. Thus, in addition to speaking English, his father's first language and the preferred language of anglophone Euro-African households, Wharton's local African acculturation took place through the medium of the two main coast languages; Fante and Ga. By 1874, however, his formal educational experience had probably been rather modest. After he had been exposed to the 'four Rs' (religion, reading, writing and arithmetic) through the medium of English (and perhaps Ga[53]) at the Wesleyan elementary school in James Town, his father's failure to place him in an English school in 1870 meant that Arthur returned to Accra and then Cape Coast, where Wesleyan educational provision was severely dislocated by the prolonged Asante crisis in the years, 1870–74. During this insecure period, it seems clear that security for the nine-year-old Wharton lay within the extended Euro-African family of the Grants, through which he had access to the network of Euro-African communities in the Cape Coast and Accra enclaves. Some familiarity with the Euro-African use of the system of wardship indicates that his senior uncle, F.C. Grant, would have become his guardian in the years after his father's death.

The above outline of Wharton's ancestry and family ties reveals that he belonged to the Euro-African and African 'worlds' of the Gold Coast townships, the land in which he, his mother, two brothers and sister had been born and in which six of his brothers and sisters lay buried. Britain was a part of his 'world' only in so far as he was baptised in and attended an English church in the Gold Coast, he spoke the English language and he had briefly visited that faraway country, which sent consumer goods, soldiers, sailors, missionaries and merchants to the Gold Coast and to which his brothers, sister and cousins had been sent to be educated. With Britain's 'formal' annexation of the Gold Coast in 1874, the Whartons and the Grants, like other Euro-Africans would now be more secure in their oft-made claims to British citizenship: a legal nicety which could have fallen only lightly upon the shoulders of a nine-year-old. His ancestral ties with the Caribbean and with Britain had either been broken or remained, at

least at this stage, undiscovered or untapped. Thus, while his elders may
well have laid emphasis upon their and his British cultural connections, for
Wharton as a young boy, his emotional ties were more securely located in
the Euro-African Society of the Gold Coast.[54]

VI

After the hardships of the early 1870s, the advances in British power in
1874 appeared to signal the start of an age of optimism for anglophone
Euro-Africans. As the old trade in palm products revived and new
demands for timber, rubber and gold increased, Pax Britannica raised
the prospect of a reinvigorated Atlantic commercial system, securely
centred on Cape Coast. The township's local leaders of the Wesleyan
Mission, confident that the new overlords would favour a British, rather
than a Swiss or German, based church, now began an aggressive programme of expansion into the Basel Mission sphere of influence. This
confidence also manifested itself in the opening of the new Wesleyan
High School in Cape Coast in 1876, the purpose of which was to produce
a new generation of Euro-African business people and professionals.

By 1882, however, the new optimism had given way to doubt and
pessimism. During and after 1877, the so-called 'great depression' began
to affect the import-export trade and the Asante 'war-scare' of 1881
revived the fears of another invasion from the north. British moves to
establish 'formal' administration over, and to exploit the agricultural and
mineral resources in, the southern Gold Coast were accompanied by
changes, which were detrimental to Euro-Africans and their interests.
First, there was an 'inflow' of British officials and representatives of new
trading firms and freebooting stock companies, engaged in the scramble
for gold, timber and rubber concessions. Secondly, and as a consequence
of the first, the economic and political significance of Cape Coast began
to decline with the growth of Sekondi to the west (gateway to the gold
and timber resources) and Accra to the east (centre of the Basel Mission's commercial agriculture). The decision to move the colonial capital
to Accra in 1877 was a symbolic break in Cape Coast's 200-year association with the British. The effect of these changes was to threaten the
strategic intermediary roles, which anglophone Euro-Africans, with
their Fante allies, had long fulfilled.

Thirdly, these changes were accompanied by pronounced ideological
shifts in the racial ideas and racist attitudes of the new inflows of British
officials. The prodigious spate of publications on Gold Coast and Asante
Africana, which followed the success of the military task-force of 1873–74,
gave vent to the anti-'Exeter Hall' racist propaganda of the 1860s,
associated with the Burton 'school' of ethnology and the Jamaican
'Revolt' of 1865.[55] Captain Henry Brackenbury, an officer of the task-force
and the author of the official history of the Asante War, concluded that:

. . . as soon as the [Gold Coast Fante] boy grows into a man his courage seems to dwindle away, his energy to disappear, and his only remaining idea to be how he can best spare himself all fatigue and danger. [To create a labour force from this] weak, idle and cowardly race . . . Chinese coolies should be imported, who would breed in with the natives and infuse some energy.[56]

Brackenbury's advocacy of a genetic solution to the effeminacy and the cowardliness of the males of the Cape Coast locality may be regarded as a proto-fascist military variation of the theme which Haggard was to popularize a decade later: the dichotomy between the 'good' noble savage of the rural interior and the ignoble, tainted (Europeanized) 'bad' Africans of the coast. These prejudices were reflected in the growing racial tensions of the townships[57] and in the system of legal apartheid, which the British introduced in the Gold Coast between 1878 and 1882. This system differentiated 'natives' from the increasing number of 'Europeans': the former were to be subject to local African customary law, administered by local 'traditional' chiefs and expatriate district commissioners; the latter were subject to English law, administered by the judicial officers of the colonial government in the townships. By 1882, therefore, it seemed from a Euro-African viewpoint that British rule was now based upon the contradiction: all Africans were 'natives'; but not all 'natives (Euro-Africans) were 'real' Africans.

This early impact of British 'formal' occupation elicited a set of complex and seemingly contradictory responses from Euro-African communities. First, for legal (and political and economic reasons), it now became essential for Euro-Africans to demonstrate their 'Africanness'. This pursuit of local roots was manifested in a new genealogical consciousness, especially where chiefly or royal family ties were concerned; a reversion to the use of African names and dress; the Fanteization of Wesleyan church ritual and education; research into local history, laws and institutions. Secondly, in order to compete with in-coming expatriates, it was necessary to demonstrate high levels of anglicization by gaining professional qualifications. From the late 1870s, therefore, the exodus of Euro-Africans to pursue higher education in Sierra Leone and Britain accelerated markedly. Finally Euro-African leaders, such as F.C. Grant, orchestrated skilful campaigns of anti-colonial protest in the Gold Coast, through the press, petitions and the formation of 'patriotic' societies and clubs, and in Britain, by exploiting their traditional links with the old trading firms of Liverpool, London and Manchester and with the Missions and by the activities of a growing minority of Gold Coast Euro-Africans, resident in Britain.

For the younger generations of Euro-Africans, who were born in the 1850s and 1860s before 'formal' control, the contradictory impact of colonial rule produced serious inter-generational clashes and severe crises of loyalty and identity. In the struggle for the salvation and survival of Euro-African society, success hinged upon the production of patriotic leaders with political, business and professional skills. This message, from the older to the younger generation, was stressed in the columns of

the *Gold Coast Times*, the weekly newspaper owned by F.C. Grant. In a
letter to the editor in 1881, an attempt to form a club in Cape Coast was
roundly condemned by an irate correspondent:

> I was told afterwards that the intended club for which the circular
> had been issued [by 'some young Gentlemen recently from
> England'] was nothing more than a football club. A football club
> and nothing else! [It is by] the cultivation of the perceptive faculties
> only [that] we can affirm those powers of conception which are
> essential to our future advancement in life ... our country's
> welfare cannot be served by mere football and cricket clubs. The
> mere dressing gaudily and appearing pompously as is common
> among our young men, and the only thing which seems to be cared
> for by them is on the contrary not what makes the man, but the
> mind when it is well-cultured. [Their time is] only squandered in
> pursuit of idle sports and vicious pleasures.[58]

Imported consumerism and idle pastimes, such as cricket and football,
were denounced in favour of the 'patriotic' virtues of hard work, self-
restraint, thrift and educational achievement.

In the years from 1874 to 1882, therefore, young Euro-Africans of the
castle-townships, such as Arthur Wharton, were faced with the racial
prejudice of British military officials, who believed that they were unfit,
biologically, to succeed at manly or gentlemanly sport, and with the anti-
'games ethic' of their elders, who argued that they should not waste their
time by trying to do so. It was their patriotic duty to seek 'salvation' in the
field of 'the trinity of the Cs', commerce, Christianity and civilized
education, rather than on the games field.

VII

In the Gold Coast–West African context, European recreational
activities may be differentiated into two basic types: 'indoor pursuits',
which were promoted by traders (and denounced by some missionaries)
during the phase of 'informal' seaborne empire, and 'outdoor activities',
which accompanied the expansion of 'formal' empire and the creation of
an expatriate military and civil bureaucracy. The years between 1874 and
1882 represent the start of a transitional stage in which the new 'outdoor
activities' were slowly and tentatively introduced in and around the
coastal townships. It was not until after 1896, however, that this gradual
process of change accelerated to the extent that by 1914, the old 'indoor
pursuits' were either harnessed to or supplanted, but never wholly
subsumed, by the 'outdoor activities' associated with 'formal' conquest
and control.[59]

Although the small number of European expatriates on the coast had
plenty of time and usually enough cash or credit, their opportunities to

engage in recreational activities were severely limited or inhibited.[60] To stray outside the confines of the castles, forts and main streets of the townships was both difficult and dangerous.[61] Local African communities had long resisted any threat to their control over the trade routes from the interior to the coast and European vulnerability to, and perceptions of the causes of, tropical diseases meant that any activity which involved exposure to the sun and the expenditure of energy was avoided. 'Over-heating' led to chills, which resulted in fevers and, ultimately, death or chronic illness.[62] The graveyards of the castle-townships and the ports of the Canaries and the Madeiras served as an equally chilling reminder of the dangers attendant upon over-exposure or over-exertion. Moreover, river estuaries and lagoons and the sea, with its heavy rolling surf, were regarded as evil and dangerous but necessary forms of coastal communication. Outdoor activities, the hunting of game in the forest and plains of the littoral and fresh or sea water fishing and sailing, remained a local African monopoly.

European recreation was restricted to 'indoor pursuits'. These consisted of billiards and cards (with or without gambling), which were preceded and/or followed by wining and dining and, depending upon the amount of alcohol consumed, a range of improvised activities: 'parlour games', which included leapfrog, dancing (without or with women), singing, story-telling and the firing of guns, and womanizing. An expatriate's reputation (and profit-margins) could be built or broken by the quality of his hospitality and the quantity of the entertainment that he provided for fellow expatriates, visiting traders, travellers and sailors, his local Euro-African extended family and friends, and his African clients, the local chiefs or their representatives, for whom hospitality was usually a prerequisite for the successful transaction of business. Not surprisingly, therefore, from as early as 1700, published travellers' tales contained often exaggerated and politically motivated accounts of the debauched and licentious nature of 'indoor pursuits' in the castle-townships of the Gold Coast.[63]

The missions and some expatriate missionaries were antagonistic to the corrupting influences of the expatriate trader-administrators.[64] An examination of the curricula of the Wesleyan and Basel Mission schools reveals, however, that physical education, drill or games were not regarded as a healthy antidote to unhealthy 'indoor pursuits'. Indeed, with the exception of the Basel Mission's inclusion of 'developmental' manual activities, such as farming, gardening and craft skills, there is little evidence for any 'outdoor' activity in Gold Coast schools until 1904, when the new Governor Rodger insisted upon the inclusion of 'suitable physical exercises' and 'military drill for boys' in the Revised Educational Rules. These prescribed the curriculum content of government and government-assisted elementary schools. No payment of grant was allocated for the teaching of these 'subjects', however, and with the phasing out of the system of 'payment by results' in 1909, these became optional, rather than compulsory, 'subjects'.[65]

Until the start of the colonial government-sponsored Achimota College experiment in 1924, post-primary schools were modest in number, expensive to attend and, because of competitive market forces, designed exclusively to provide the children of Euro-African fee-paying parents with an English-style grammar-school education – without physical education and team games.[66]

VIII

The first signs that the British were beginning to contemplate or initiate outside alternatives to 'indoor pursuits' are to be found in the years between 1874 and 1877. The sources are 'literary' and 'historical' and the alternatives reflect the age-old preoccupation of the British hidalgo: hunting, shooting and horse-racing.

In 1876, Chapman and Hall, the publishers of Carlyle and Dickens, presented their British readers with a 'romantic novel' by J. A. Skertchly, entitled *Melinda the Caboceer or Sport in Ashanti. A Tale of the Gold Coast.*[67] The work is of interest for three reasons. First, as one of, if not, the first in this genre, the 'novel' may be described as 'proto-Haggardian', given its preoccupation with the rural African interior and the noble hunter-warriors: Britain's recent enemies, the Asante, who were 'real' Africans.[68] Secondly, the story provides the reader with a 350-page catalogue of violence, depicting the effects of 'modern' military weaponry upon 'traditional' Africa: upon African animals and 'real' Africans. The sequence of violent encounters is punctuated by the reflections of the hero ('a son of a wealthy squire in one of the southern counties'[69]) upon the real value of such sporting adventures for members of the English squirearchy:

> What is more glorious than the sight of these fair heavens spreading out above us, with the twinkling stars peeping at us in place of the damask bed-curtains of civilisation . . . How much more enjoyment to be here in the forests of Africa than stewing along the boulevards of Paris or getting muddled in the biergartens of Germany, as is the fashion of some people . . . Let the advocates of reduction of national expenditure for defence take warning . . . the surest method of preserving peace is to prepare for war.[70]

Thirdly, it was not until 20 years later, in 1896, that Skertchly's heroes, in the form of a British military expedition, returned to Asante. Thus, it was only after the killing of Asante and the conquest and destruction of the Asante state that the hunting of animals, both on foot and on horseback, really began. In the 1920s, it became possible for district officers to ride with the Tamale Hunt.[71]

Skertchly's fictional portrayal of sport in the Gold Coast and Asante bore little relationship to the initiatives taking place in the mid-1870s. In May 1874, a short-lived Rifle Club was formed in Cape Coast by Captain A. W. Baker of the First West India Regiment. Its members included some of

Baker's fellow officers and five leading traders, two of whom were Euro-Africans. The club folded after two months, following Baker's transfer.[72] Three years later, with the decision to move the colonial capital to Accra, a racecourse was laid outside James Town. Although the Colonial Office's decision was, and has since been, attributed to the healthier climate of the plains and hills which surround the Accra enclave, official evidence reveals that the area's potential for recreational activities also influenced the decision to leave Cape Coast.

> The aesthetic appeal of the open country behind Accra as well as the opportunities there for hunting and acquiring equestrian skills was also especially important to the Europeans. The tangle of bush and forest behind many of the coastal towns was an ugly and depressing sight to most European residents.[73]

The move from Cape Coast to Accra provides one indication of the post-Asante war shift from military control to the equally hierarchical pattern of civil administration, associated with the old Crown Colony system of government. By 1883, 43 official senior posts had been created above the clerical class.[74] These included the executive 'core' in Accra (the Governor, his Secretariat and the Departmental Heads) and the range of officials, located along the coast zone (District Commissioners; Customs, Judicial and Police Officers). This creation of the bureaucratic structures of the embryonic colonial state was accompanied by a shift in recruitment patterns. The old pattern, comprising a minority of civilian expatriates and a majority of expatriate military and local Euro-African civilian officers, was reversed. In 1883, only nine of the 43 senior posts were occupied by Euro-Africans. A decade later, the number of senior administrative posts had almost doubled (80). Again, only nine of these were filled by Euro-Africans, who did form, however, the backbone of the lowest echelons of civil establishment.[75]

The gradual emergence of outdoor sporting activities, such as horse-riding, horse-racing, hunting and cricket, may be attributed to the recruitment of an increasing number of civilian expatriates, a significant number of whom (such as William Brandford Griffiths Senior and Junior) had gained their early colonial experience in the West Indies. In August 1881, The *Gold Coast Times* (of Cape Coast) noted that: 'Cricket, the world-famed outdoor sport, has apparently several votaries at Accra'. During this month, the paper included lengthy reports upon three matches, which were played between Accra (James Town and Ussher Town) and Christiansborg (the old Danish Town, whose castle was now the Governor's residence). By the end of that year, the 'votaries' of the 'world-famed' game seem to have extended to Cape Coast itself. Brandford Griffiths Junior, who had acquired a love of the game in Bridgetown, Barbados, was invited to play cricket during a brief visit to the township in December while en route, by ship, to take up his first appointment in the colonial service at Accra.[76] It was also during this period that a gymnasium was provided in Cape Coast for the senior ranks in the Gold Coast police force.[77]

Apart from shooting, cricket, horse-riding and the competition for the Brandford Griffiths Cup during the annual two-day race meeting – all of which were centred mainly or exclusively at Accra – the further diffusion of outdoor activities was very limited until 1896–97. During these two years, the Accra Club was opened in Ussher Town for European residents, who, in addition to horse-riding and cricket, were able to play golf, polo and tennis (as well as cards and billiards) 'from 5 to 6.30 every evening'.[78] The main developmental stage in the history of the diffusion of British outdoor sport took place in the quarter of a century after 1896–97. This period coincided with the end of the 'scramble' for the Gold Coast–Ghana (the southern colony; Asante; the Northern Territories) and the subsequent increase in the number of British civilians, both female and male, as a result of the expansion of 'formal' administration, improvements in medical facilities and the creation of separate European cantonments in the growing urban enclaves. The direct patronage and promotion of outdoor activities may be attributed, however, to the series of appointments of Governors with Malaysian experience (Maxwell, 1895–96; Rodger, 1904–11; Clifford, 1913–19) and the length of W. Brandford Griffiths Junior's service in the Gold Coast administration (1881–88; 1895–1911).

IX

As the living embodiment of the once dominant but now discarded imperial ideology of 'commerce, Christianity and civilization', Euro-African bourgeois, Christian gentlemen, such as F.C. Grant, saw that an over-indulgence in indoor pursuits was not only bound to corrupt the younger generation, but would also confirm, in practice, the tarnished image of Euro-Africans which hostile British writers eagerly sought to present in print.[79] Outdoor activities, on the other hand, encouraged undemeaning and often uncivilized behaviour, which was more appropriate to the 'bush' Africans of the interior, so beloved of Brackenbury, Burton, Skertchly and, later, Haggard. Moreover, such activities were perceived as a waste of valuable time, energy and resources (expensive fashions and equipment) and as being conducive to the formation of incomprehensible attitudes, especially towards animals. The advocacy of outdoor sport, British-style – like the colonial advocacy of a craft-based rather than a literary-oriented education[80] – was calculated to deprive future Euro-African communities of leaders and skilled personnel. A devotion to business training and 'high-class' education was required if Euro-Africans were to demonstrate that they were not racially inferior to Europeans in the fields of trade and finance, administration, the professions and patriotic intellectual pursuits (the research, writing and publication of newspapers and books).[81]

While the foregoing précis of arguments and exhortations does provide insight into Euro-African 'anti-recreationist' ideology, it also tends to obscure the complex and contradictory nature of Euro-African responses to European recreational activities in the 1870s and 1880s. It seems clear, from the frequency and the force of 'anti-recreationist' arguments and exhortations, that the younger generation was attracted to 'indoor pursuits' and outdoor games, such as cricket. Both offered opportunities for social gatherings, involving the display of imported fashions, drinking imported alcohol, playing cards and local African board games, and musical entertainment. In a report of a cricket match in Accra, for example, it was wryly noted that, 'the ground was enlivened by music consisting of a clarionet [sic] and two kettle drums. Young men uninterested in cricket were occupied in dancing and young ladies in watching them'.[82]

Evidence also suggests that Euro-African traders shared responsibility for the promotion of 'indoor pursuits' and that members of the young generation pioneered the introduction of team games, such as cricket and possibly association football. Traders were unable to resist the profits which were to be made from the import and/or retailing of clothing and alcohol (more cosmetics and hair-oils were imported than books and newspapers in the 1890s!) and from the growing hotel business.[83] From the late 1870s, there was an increase in the number of young men who had been introduced to team games while at school in England and who were keen to continue to play and to promote outdoor sport, such as cricket, on their return to the Gold Coast. It was not only the British, therefore, who took British games to the Empire. In the case of the Gold Coast, in the 1870s and 1880s, expatriates were able to create the facilities for cricket, but they were unable to produce the numbers to field two teams. Thus, the majority of players in the Accra matches of 1881 were Euro-Africans (Bannermans, Lutterodts, Richters, Hesses, Hutton-Mills), and, somewhat paradoxically, the outstanding batsman was F.C. Grant Junior, closely followed by his brother, C.F. Grant.[84]

In the 1870s and 1880s, therefore, the 'recreation question' produced debates and divisions between and within generations of Euro-Africans and between the Euro-African communities of the declining Cape Coast enclave – the centre of the anglophone Wesleyan, Fante-oriented business elite – and those of the new colonial capital, the more cosmopolitan and increasingly prosperous Accra. An examination of these debates and divisions reveals that Euro-African responses to recreational activities may be characterized in four ways: rejectionism; reformism; instrumentalism; collaborationism.

1. *Rejectionism.* The Rejectionists were to be found among the mercantile elite and the young intelligentsia (journalists; political activists) of Cape Coast. Their 'anti-recreation' ideology was expounded in the local press, which reported and promoted the ideas and activities of the preferred alternatives: the temperance, improvement and literary societies and clubs. The virtues of thrift, self-restraint, sobriety, intellectual development and gentility were encouraged through lectures and debates and prayer, choral and Sunday School meetings. Political, economic and racial issues were raised through discussions of the history and current affairs of the Gold Coast, West Africa, Britain and Europe.[85]

2. *Reformism.* The Reformists, who were to be found in Cape Coast and Accra, were realists. They acknowledged the social importance and potential economic significance of 'indoor pursuits', but they also recognized their corrupting influence. An example of the reformist position is the Masonic Club. This was launched to provide 'social recreation' for its members, who could play 'chess, draughts and billiards', and, at the same time, gain 'intellectual improvement' through lectures and the use of the club's library of the 'best' newspapers and periodicals. Opportunities would also be created for useful European-Euro-African social (and business) exchanges because the club was also likely to attract European expatriates who were often members of the English or Scottish Orders of the Freemasons.[86]

3. *Instrumentalism.* The Instrumentalists were prepared to endorse or actively engage in those outdoor activities, which were likely to enhance the image and status and to improve the occupational and business opportunities and contacts of the Euro-African communities as a whole. Membership of the Rifle Club, horse-ownership and attendance at the Accra race meetings and selection for the Cape Coast, Accra or Christiansborg cricket teams all involved identification with the ruling caste and entry into the new colonial society, with its marked tendency towards erecting social, economic, institutional and ideological barriers between 'natives' and Europeans – barriers which had not existed in the 'golden years' of the 'informal' empire of 'commerce and Christianity'.[87]

4. *Collaborationism.* The Collaborators were drawn from the ever-increasing ranks of young 'graduates', who experienced a degree of culture-shock upon their return to the Gold Coast after six or nine years at residential private schools in Britain. With their young relatives, who also belonged to that dense network of extended family relationships, they were keen to introduce cricket or association football because of their love of these games and their desire to enhance their own employment prospects and to promote social exchanges between young Euro-Africans and with Europeans, having grown accustomed to inter-racial exchanges in Britain. Lacking the appropriate finance and facilities, however, they were dependent for their success upon the patronage of their elders and their colonial masters. This dependence helps to explain why association football, unlike cricket, failed to emerge in the coastal townships in the late 1870s and early 1880s. While Europeans, even in the early 1900s, regarded association football as an unsuitable sport for the Gold Coast, an attempt to generate interest in the game by young Euro-Africans in Cape Coast was furiously denounced by both rejectionist and reformist factions in the columns of the *Gold Coast Times* in July 1881. The lack of European interest in the game also suggests that Euro-African elders were unwilling or unable to find instrumental reasons to accommodate football.[88]

Before 1897–98 and certainly before 1882, British outdoor sporting activities remained under- or un-developed. The principal agents of the export of British sport – the British expatriate and the Euro-African

'graduates' of English schools and universities – were comparatively few
and their efforts to import 'outdoor' activities were restricted for four
reasons. First, the climate, and the diseases with which it was associated,
acted as a real or imaginary 'brake' upon the indulgence in energetic
activity. Second, the effective zone of British control was limited to the
townships of the coastal littoral, which, with the exception of the Accra
enclave, was unsuitable, topographically, for outdoor sport. Third,
there were strong countervailing forces within this zone of control. The
Gold Coast had long been regarded as an 'informal' market for goods and
souls. Thus, as far as recreation was concerned, the materialist and
potentially immoral 'indoor pursuits' of merchants competed with the
missionaries' chapel-oriented drive for intellectual improvement and
moral regeneration. The interests of both groups were unsympathetic or
antagonistic at this stage towards outdoor recreational activities. Fourth,
Euro-African communities, whose members had been regarded and still
perceived themselves as the main recipients, and the principal agents for
the diffusion, of British culture, did not share the view that sport was
Britain's 'chief spiritual export'. They remained hostile in thought, word
and deed to all recreational activities until or unless they perceived that it
was advantageous to do so. It is not insignificant that in the annals of the
Euro-African biography-history of 1920s and 1930s, whose purpose was
to record the lives and labours (for posterity) of the patriotic ancestors of
the heroic age of struggle in the 40 years after 1874, only two sporting
achievements are listed: those of a fast bowler and the winner of the
Brandford Griffiths Cup at the Accra Races. The real victors in the
struggle for Euro-African salvation and survival were journalists,
lawyers, doctors, teachers, preachers, businessmen and politicians.
Needless to say, the bowler and racehorse owner were included because
of their contributions as lawyer and doctor respectively – not because of
their sporting achievements. Thus, Arthur Wharton remained, or was
rendered, invisible in the ancestral gallery of Euro-African 'Men of
Affairs' or 'celebrities', unlike his contemporaries such as John M.
Sarbah (b.1864) and J. E. Casely Hayford (b.1866). Both, like Wharton,
left the Gold Coast in the early 1880s to seek their educational fortunes.
Both are still remembered by Ghanaians today – unlike Wharton.
Indeed, the memory of his life and labours remained unrecorded and
therefore unknown in the annals of Grant family history until 1985.[89]

                                    X

In 1882, the 16-year-old Wharton became a student at Shoal Hill,
Cannock, where he remained until 1884, when he transferred to
Cleveland College, Darlington. It was two years later, while still a
student at the College, that he achieved his success as a sprinter in the
AAA championships at Stamford Bridge. When this and his subsequent
achievements are viewed in the contexts of British sporting history, with

its penchant for the bare statistical record, they may be described as outstanding. When they are viewed within the context of Gold Coast history, however, they may be more aptly described as remarkable. In 1882, Wharton possessed few, if any, of the prerequisites which may be associated with the making of a successful sportsman, particularly one from the frontiers of Britain's expanding West African empire. Among such prerequisites one may reasonably include: biology, opportunity, access, sporting culture and the British imperial 'bond'.[90]

1. *Biology*. Two sets of biological requisites may be isolated: the one, the possession of good health and a sound medical history, may be regarded as a statement of the obvious; the other, the attribution of 'natural' genetic (including physiological and anatomical) advantages to sportsmen and women of African descent, though popular in sporting circles past and present, is both controversial and untenable, as Cashmore has recently demonstrated.[91] Life in the Gold Coast and in West Africa was not conducive to the production of healthy individuals, whether white or black, male or female, sporting or non-sporting. The high mortality levels and the low rates of progress in tropical medical research are reflected in the tragic catalogue of illness and death, which left its imprint upon Wharton family history. Moreover, and somewhat paradoxically – given Cashmore's critical review of prevailing 'scientific' explanations for the success of black sportsmen and women in the UK and USA – Wharton, as a Euro-African mulatto with strong Fante family connections, was not a 'real' African according to the 'scientific' views of contemporary guardians, and promoters of amateur British sport, such as Brackenbury, Skertchly and Haggard. He was a 'native', biologically unsuited to manly outdoor sporting activities. A peasant-warrior, an Asante for example, would have the 'natural' advantages to run 100 yards in 10 seconds, but not a coastal Euro-African.

2. *Opportunity*. If it may be argued that the opportunities to engage regularly in sporting activities hinge upon the degree of political stability, social harmony and ritualization of conflict and competition, which a community may achieve at particular moments in time, and upon the amount of time and resources which are available to its members, then it may be suggested that Wharton's opportunities were limited. His last three years in the Gold Coast were threatened by the prospect of a return to the intense political conflict and open warfare which had marked his first nine years. During and after 1879, the early moves in the European scramble for West Africa and Africa signalled the start of a period of uncertainty, which was consistently communicated to the readers of the local press. The Asante war-scare of 1881 was accompanied by a series of troop movements to and within the southern Gold Coast and the arrival of a large Asante embassy in Cape Coast and then Accra. Equally, given the increase in racial disharmony, political violence (especially between the rival quarters of the townships) and crime in the growing urban enclaves,[92] the use of sport as a form of institutionalized conflict management could have been counter-productive. From an economic

point of view, such conflict, uncertainty and nervousness were not conducive to the buoyancy of trade, upon which Wharton's access to resources (either his own earnings or those of his family) depended. Even if Wharton had had time and limited resources, it is not certain that he devoted both to the underdeveloped range of outdoor recreational activities.

3. *Access.* The making of a young sportsman in the fields of athletics, swimming or team games depends upon his or her continued access to facilities and equipment and to the patronage of those with appropriate knowledge, skills and enthusiasm. Such access may be provided by educational institutions, local clubs and societies or family and friends. Again, the evidence suggests that Wharton's access to outdoor sport was severely circumscribed. The Wesleyan, Basel Mission and colonial (whether Dutch, Danish or British) school systems had not paid and did not pay any attention to such activities and the existing clubs and societies were established to actively deter Euro-African participation in them. In 1882, the Euro-African Wesleyan business elite of Cape Coast campaigned for the abolition of swimming in the sea on the grounds that nudity and partial nudity were unbecoming and undermined the town's reputation for 'civilization' and gentility.[93] It seems likely, therefore, that Wharton's access to games was restricted to impromptu 'street' cricket or football initiated by his cousins, the Grants, his older brothers, and others who had received their education in Britain. In 1882, it is possible that Wharton may have acquired rudimentary ball skills and the idea that games afforded the participant the chance for social contact and employment.

4. *Sporting culture.* The availability of opportunities for, and the easy access to, sport may be related to the existence of a 'sporting culture' in which the social and economic benefits of participation are readily acknowledged. As a Euro-African, Wharton belonged to a Gold Coast community in which an 'anti-sporting culture' was dominant. The preservation and promotion of status, image-building, character and leadership training and business interests, for the individual and the group, were to be derived from experience and application in the chapel, the marketplace and the classroom. Only when and where 'indoor pursuits', tempered by self-restraint, and outdoor activities could be turned to positive social and economic advantage was participation in sport countenanced. The temptation to deviate from these strict codes of community conduct was strong in the cosmopolitan environment of the coastal townships and increasingly produced inter-generational tensions. Given the underdeveloped nature of outdoor recreation, however, deviance was closely linked to the social evils, which stemmed from the over-indulgence in 'indoor pursuits'. When these conflicting pressures and temptations are applied to the life of the young Arthur Wharton in the years between 1874 and 1882, the outside observer can only attempt to begin to comprehend 'from the inside' the range of 'mental and moral states' with which he was confronted. To have been tempted, as a schoolboy, by the influence of his brother, Charles, and his sister, Clara

(both of whom appear to have over-indulged in 'indoor pursuits')[94] or by the influence of his cricketing cousins, would have incurred the wrath of his guardian, F.C. Grant, the most influential advocate of 'anti-sporting' ideology and the individual who exercised some control over the family finances.

5. *The British Imperial 'Bond'*. An emotional identification with, and the desire to achieve success in, Britain may also be regarded as important ingredients in the making of the sportsman or sportswoman from the frontiers of Empire. In Wharton's case, there is little hard evidence to suggest that he was 'pulled' by Britain in 1882 for emotional reasons or by the promise of a sporting career. At this stage in his life, it seems that his family ties were more firmly planted in the Gold Coast than in Britain and the attitudes of some British expatriates towards 'natives' and 'real' Africans were not always calculated to cement Euro-African emotional ties with the 'Mother-country'. If the Euro-African trend to discover or rediscover local African roots, after the introduction of the discriminatory colonial legal system, presented Wharton with an identity-crisis, it seems likely that he might have adopted his father's Caribbean rather than his grandfathers' British ethno-cultural affiliations – hence, the tendency to describe his origins as Jamaican or Trinidadian in the British sporting press.[95] The weight of evidence indicates, however, that local factors 'pushed' Wharton to leave the Gold Coast and that the choice of Britain, rather than Sierra Leone, was determined by family tradition and facilitated by the family's connections with the Wesleyan Methodist Church and its private schools.

Among the local 'push' factors, four may be suggested here. First, it remained his widowed mother's ambition to provide her last surviving child with a British education which she, her husband, her brother, son and daughter and her nephews and nieces had already acquired. Secondly, in 1882, Mrs Wharton and her brother were both keen to ensure that Arthur escaped from what seemed to be a renewal of local political and military conflict and the untoward influences of his brother, sister, cousins and their friends among the younger generation. Thirdly, as he was already 16, there was an urgent need to enhance his future employment prospects by the acquisition of British academic qualifications and an increased proficiency in the use of English. Finally, the timing of his departure also coincided with a marked increase in the 'educational exodus' to Britain of young Gold Coast Euro-Africans.[96]

The force of this combination of local 'push' factors is confirmed by other evidence. A comparison between the fees of the Wesleyan High School, Cape Coast, and Shoal Hill College, Cannock, reveals that those of the latter were far more expensive. Moreover, the prospectus of the Cannock and Darlington Colleges laid great stress upon the provision of a literary grammar-school type of curriculum and upon their success rate in external examinations for the professions: accountancy, dentistry, law, medicine and teaching.[97] Not surprisingly, perhaps, after ten years in England, Wharton applied to the Colonial Office for a post in the Gold

7. Arthur Wharton, goalkeeper for Sheffield United, c. 1894

Coast civil administration.[98] The British-based evidence suggests, there-fore, that Wharton's mother and uncle were prepared to defray the high costs of a British education, which included the expense of travel from the Gold Coast, and that he was expected to return to Cape Coast, when he left by sea for Liverpool in July, 1882.

Among the prominent Wesleyan Euro-African families of Cape Coast and Accra, there was a long and strong tradition of sending their sons to Queen's (formerly Wesley) College, Taunton, in Somerset. Wharton's older brothers and his Grant cousins were 'old boys' of Taunton. Why then did Wharton enter colleges in industrial Staffordshire and Durham rather than rural Somerset? Like Queen's, the Cannock and Darlington Colleges were ideologically sound. They both offered their students 'the comforts of a Christian home' and both principals, S. G. Gwynne and H. Brooks, were leading members of large and influential local Methodist communities. As lay preachers, elected representatives of the noncon-formist interest on the local School Boards, members of their local Liberal Party Association and acknowledged 'gentlemen' educational entrepreneurs, they fulfilled a series of confessional, commercial, humanitarian and political roles which, as a member of F.C. Grant's household, the young Wharton would have immediately recognized.[99] It is significant that the first recorded public performances by Wharton in the Cannock and Darlington press were, respectively, as a reader at meetings of the Wesleyan Sunday School and the Band of Hope and as a competitor in the 'athletic festival' of the Richmond Temperance Society.[100]

The choice of Shoal Hill and then Cleveland College may also be attributed to the influence of Samuel G. Gwynne, who was already well-known to the Whartons and the Grants. As an ex-mathematics teacher at the then Wesley College, Taunton, Gwynne had most probably taught Wharton's older brothers and cousins.[101] These 'old-boy' connections help to explain why F.C. Grant had already sent three of his younger sons to Shoal Hill by 1881 and why 62 advertisements for the Cannock college appeared regularly in Grant's weekly *Gold Coast Times* from 9 July 1881 to 2 June 1883. Upon his arrival in August 1882, therefore, Arthur Wharton increased the Cape Coast contingent in Cannock to four. It would be surprising if the cost of Gwynne's publicity in the *Times* was not reflected in a discount on their school fees![102]

Gwynne may also have been instrumental in securing Wharton's trans-fer to Darlington in August, 1884. Ill-health seems to have forced him to close Shoal Hill in July and, as a person entrusted with Wharton's education, it is probable that he recommended the young Gold Coaster to his old friend and colleague, Henry Brooks of Cleveland College.[103] Gwynne and Brooks were both born in the Somerset village of Nailsea in 1827.[104] Moreover, Brooks also had links with Cape Coast through one of Cleveland College's 'old boys', Timothy Laing, who was certainly well-acquainted with Arthur Wharton. The Rev. Wharton had been a close colleague of Laing's father, the Rev. Timothy Laing Senior, and before the latter's death in 1881, Arthur Wharton's uncle had appointed Laing Junior to the editorship of the *Gold Coast Times*. The fact that he reprinted extracts from recent editions of the *Darlington and Stockton Times* in the columns of the Grant press appears to confirm the continuation of his links with this northern town and perhaps with his *alma mater*.[105]

If Wharton's arrival in Britain may be ascribed to the existence of an imperial 'cultural bond', it was a confessional and educational rather than sporting one. The choice of the unfashionable colleges of the Midlands and the north, rather than the more favoured Queen's College in the south, may be attributed to the family's business acumen and the Wesleyan 'old-boy' network, which extended from Cape Coast to Darlington via Nailsea, Taunton and Cannock. It was as a student of these small colleges for young Wesleyan gentlemen, situated on the rural fringes of growing industrial towns, that Wharton's talents emerged in his college and then in local cricket and football clubs. The fact that Wharton chose to waste his family's substance and to deviate from the Euro-African code of patriotic conduct by becoming a sportsman helps to explain why his British success was ignored by his Gold Coast descendants and went unrecorded in the annals of Euro-African 'Men of Affairs'. It also explains why Wharton's application for an appointment in the Gold Coast colonial administration was rejected in 1893. The 'official' explanation, which was communicated to Wharton, listed the lack of vacancies and inadequate qualifications. The 'unofficial' reasons, which were recorded in the minutes and correspondence attached to the application in Colonial Office files, confidentially listed the inappropriateness of the status of '100 yards Amateur Champion of England' as a qualification for a Gold Coast civil servant. Moreover, it was felt that the association of Wharton's brother and sister with over-indulgence in 'indoor pursuits' in Accra made the employment of their young brother too great a risk for the Colonial Office to take.[106] These 'unofficial' explanations illustrate, perhaps, the wisdom of Euro-African 'anti-sporting' ideology and the weakness of the cultural 'bond' in the Gold Coast Empire – at least, where and when sport and 'native' Euro-Africans were concerned. The struggle for the salvation of Euro-Africans, in their unequal imperial contest with the British, required weapons of survival which were to be found in the classroom rather than on the playing fields. The case of Arthur Wharton reveals that only Blues, who were white but not black, could rule over Blacks in the Gold Coast Empire.

NOTES

This essay may be aptly described as a progress report upon recent attempts to reconstruct the biography of this little-known sportsman and to confront – as a West Africanist historian – three hitherto unknown and ostensibly unrelated domains of sport history and historiography: the British, the black British and the British Imperial. As a consequence, I remain indebted to the generous help or advice of many specialists in these fields. The names of some are recorded in the following footnotes; those who are not include the librarians of Cannock, Cheltenham, Darlington and Rotherham, Patrick Barclay and Derek Benning and Drs Owen Ashton, Duncan Scott, J.A. Mangan and Tony Mason.

1. E.g. *Manchester Guardian*, 5 July 1886; *The Times*, 5 July 1886.
2. *Cannock Advertiser*, 11 Sept. 1886; *Darlington and Stockton Times*, 18 Sept. 1886; *Newcastle Weekly Chronicle*, e.g. 21 Aug.–18 Sept. 1886; the *Sporting Chronicle*, e.g. 19 July–8 Sept. 1886; *Staffordshire Advertiser*, 18 Sept. 1886.
3. Details from club records were generously supplied by Mr E. Griffiths of Preston North End FC (16 Jan. 1985). These have been supplemented from match reports in the *Newcastle Weekly Chronicle*, e.g. 30 Oct.–18 Dec. 1886; the *Northern Echo*, 24 Sept. 1886, e.g. 31 Jan–12 March 1887.
4. *Cannock Advertiser*, 27 Aug. 1887. Wharton played for the Cannock Cricket Club and the Cannock and Cannock White Cross Football Clubs.
5. As a Darlington CFC player, Wharton was regularly chosen to play for Durham from November 1885. His selection, however, for Newcastle and Cleveland representative teams against Corinthians (twice) and Preston North End in January and April 1886, and the spate of rumours in the following September that he was to become a Bishop Auckland, a Newcastle East End or a Preston North End player all created lively controversies in the regional press. See e.g. *Darlington and Stockton Times*, 14 Nov. 1885, 12 Dec. 1885, 18–25 Sept. 1886; *Newcastle Weekly Chronicle*, 9 Jan. 1886, 24 April 1886, 1 May 1886, 18 Sept. 1886; *Northern Echo*,24 Sept. 1886.
6. *Darlington and Stockton Times*, 10 July 1886; *Cannock Advertiser*, 10 July 1886; *Newcastle Weekly Chronicle*, 22 May 1886–10 July 1886; *Sporting Chronicle*, 5–9 July 1886.
7. Editorial, *Darlington and Stockton Times*, 25 Dec. 1886.
8. In addition to evidence mined from contemporary press reports, this estimate of his versatility and athleticism is based upon two rare interviews in the *Athletic Journal* (26 June 1888) and the *Darlington and Stockton Times* (given in the summer of 1914 and reprinted with comment on 23 Dec. 1939) and upon residual oral tradition as reported by the club historians of Preston North End, Sheffield United and Rotherham United and by Darlingtonians. For clues to or details of these interviews and traditions, I am indebted to Peter Lovesey, Denis Clareborough, Peter Baxter, Alan Vokes, George Flynn and Herbert Burgin.
9. *Sporting Chronicle*, 28 July 1886; E. Illingworth, *A Short History of the Northern Counties Athletics Association, 1879–1979*, Leeds, n.d., pp.9–10 (hereafter *NCAA*); T. Keller, 'See why they ran', *The Guardian*, 9 March 1985; P. Lovesey, *The Official Centenary History of the AAA* (London, 1979), p.43.
10. From 1886 to 1888, Darlington CFC and Birchfield Harriers; Darlington CFC, Newcastle East End and Preston North End. From 1889 to 1896, Rotherham Town FC, Sheffield United FC and, most probably, Doncaster Rovers FC. Wharton's career from 1897 still remains obscure. While it seems likely that he moved to the Doncaster area, he played football for Stockport County FC after 1900 and in 1914, he was a professional cricket coach with a northern league club. *Darlington and Stockton Times*, 23 Dec. 1939; P. Baxter, *A Hundred Years of Football in Rotherham* (Rotherham, n.d.); personal communications: E. Illingworth, 20 Nov. 1985; D. Clareborough, 30 Nov. 1986; P. Baxter, 1 Feb. 1987; H. Jones (Stockport County FC), 20 Oct. 1987; Mrs E. Smith (Wharton's great-niece), 5 Aug. 1988.
11. *Post Office Directory of Rotherham*, 1895–96; M. Tyas, 'Rotherham United FC: an analysis of its origins and development, 1870–1914', unpublished BA dissertation, North Staffordshire Polytechnic, 1987, p.27.
12. *Athletic Journal*, 26 June 1888. Details of Wharton's displays of temperament are also to be found in the Minutes for 26 July 1887 and 22 Sept. 1887, *Minute Book of the Northern Counties Athletic Association* (transcripts generously supplied by Mr E.R.L. Powell of Chesterfield): Cf. E. Illingworth, *NCAA*, pp.9–10.
13. E.g. *Cannock Advertiser*, 29 Oct. 1887; *Darlington and Stockton Times*, 10 April 1886; *Northern Echo*, 5 April 1886.

14. *Athletic Journal*, 26 June 1888.
15. E.g. *Darlington and Stockton Times*, 10 July 1886, 17 July 1886 (reprints of reports from the 'national' press), 23 Dec. 1939; *Sporting Chronicle*, 5 July 1886, 20 July 1886.
16. In football club histories, the earlier association with 'Trinidad' seems to have become the accepted version; whereas in athletics historiography Wharton has been and continues to be described, variously, as a 'Negro', 'a West Indian' or a 'Jamaican'. See e.g. R. L. Quercetani, *A World History of Track and Field Athletics, 1864–1964* (Oxford, 1964), p. 2; M. Watman, *History of British Athletics* (London, 1968), pp. 19–20; P. Lovesey, loc. cit, 1979; E. Cashmore, *Black Sportsmen* (London, 1982), p. 15. Only Dr E. Illingworth, *ACAA*, has accurately recorded Wharton's West African origins and more recently R. Jenkins, 'Sportsman Extraordinaire', *West Africa*, 3 June 1985.
17. E.g. R. Hyam, *Britain's Imperial Century, 1815–1914* (London, 1976), pp. 151–2; J. Morris (ed.), *Pax Britannica. The Climax of Empire* (London, 1979), pp. 283–7; B. Porter, *The Lion's Share* (London, 1975), p. 346. For more circumspect treatments, see e.g. J. A. Mangan, *Athleticism in the Victorian and Edwardian Public School* (Cambridge, 1981); *The Games Ethic and Imperialism* (London, 1986); A. H. M. Kirk-Greene, *The Sudan Political Service. A Preliminary Profile* (Oxford, 1982), pp. 5–9; W. J. Baker and J. A. Mangan (eds.), *Sport in Africa:* New York, 1987, essays on 'Colonial Ways' by A. H. M. Kirk-Greene, A. Clayton, J. A. Mangan.
18. R. Jenkins, 'Wharton, Forgotten Hero', *South*, 86 (1987), 142–3 (hereafter *South*).
19. For a lively analysis of the difficulties inherent in the biographer's choice of present-oriented ideological 'contexts', see C. Ifeka, 'London in the Gold Coast. Problems with biography and some suggestions for a new approach', *Canberra Anthropology*, 4, 2 (1981), pp. 13–17 (c.f. Julian Barnes, *Flaubert's Parrot* (London, 1985), p. 38). The underdeveloped nature of West African sport history is noted in Baker and Mangan (eds.), op. cit., pp. vii–ix.
20. See note 17 above.
21. E.g. R. Cashman, 'The Phenomenon of Indian Cricket' in R. Cashman and M. McKernan (eds.), *Sport in History* (Queensland, 1979), pp. 180–203; B. Stoddart, 'Sport, Culture Imperialism and Colonial Response in the British Empire: a framework for analysis', *Proceedings of the 4th Annual Conference of the British Society for Sports History* (North Staffordshire Polytechnic, 1986), pp. 1–23; J. M. MacKenzie, 'Hunting in Eastern and Cental Africa in the late Nineteenth Century, with Special Reference to Zimbabwe' and T. O. Ranger, 'Pugilism and Pathology: African Boxing and the Black Urban Experience in Southern Rhodesia' in Baker and Mangan (eds.), op. cit., pp. 172–213.
22. For an extended discussion of the 'cultural' dimension to imperialism and of the methodological issues posed by the attempt of an outsider (in terms of time, space and race) to isolate and speculate upon 'insider' perspectives, see R. Jenkins, 'Gold Coast Historians and their pursuit of the Gold Coast Pasts, 1882–1917', pp. 92–100, unpublished Ph.D. thesis, University of Birmingham, 1985 (hereafter 'Historians') and T. C. McCaskie, 'Accumulation, Wealth and Belief in Asante History: I. To the Close of the Nineteenth Century', *Africa*, 1 (1983), pp. 3–43. McCaskie provides a singular examination of the place of 'moral and mental states' in the assessment of 'insider' perspective in the Ghanaian context.
23. See above, note 22.
24. For a guide to the geography, ethnography and the 'informal' commercial and confessional partition of the Gold Coast by 1866, the year of Wharton's birth, and until 1874, the year of Britain's 'formal' annexation of the littoral, see the map on p. 52.
25. W. Moister, *Henry Wharton, The Story of His Life and Missionary Labours in the West Indies, on the Gold Coast and in Ashanti* (London, 1875), pp. 119–20. 146–7, 150, 197 (hereafter *H. Wharton*); W. Hill, *An Alphabetic Arrangement of all the Wesleyan Ministers* (London, 1869), p. 147; *Certificate of Marriage*, Rotherham District, No 371: Arthur Wharton (aged 24) to Emma Lister, 21 Sept. 1890 (cf E. Illingworth, *ACAA*, includes date of birth as 1865).

26. B. Cruickshank, *Eighteen Years on the Gold Coast of Africa* (1853) (London, 1966), 2nd ed., I, p. 27
27. Moister, *H. Wharton*, pp. 160–2; Hill, op. cit., 1874 ed., p. 162
28. Victoria's 'little war' with Asante in 1873–74 generated an unprecedented degree of public interest in Britain in the Gold Coast. The pending General Election (with the new electorate of 1867), the first deployment of Cardwell's 'new model army' and the extension of the telegraph to the Gold Coast; all help to explain the presence of the large number of journalists in Cape Coast (e.g. F. Boyle, G. A. Henty, W. Reade, H. M. Stanley) and the consequent 'scramble' to publish books and articles on 'Gold Coast and Asante Studies'. Some 35 in number appeared within a year. For the historical background to the crisis, the desperate nature of the emergency in Cape Coast and the literary revolution in Gold Coast Africana, see W. D. McIntyre, *The Imperial Frontier in the Tropics, 1865–75* (London, 1967), pp. 121–51; R. Baesjou, *An Asante Embassy on the Gold Coast, 1869–72* (Leiden, 1979); A. B. Ellis, *West African Sketches* (London, 1881); Moister, *H. Wharton*, pp. 183–90; R. Jenkins, 'Confrontations with A. B. Ellis, a Participant in the Scramble for Gold Coast Africana, 1874–94', *Paideuma*, 33 (1987), 315–17 (hereafter *Confrontations*).
29. Moister, op. cit., pp. 180, 193; 'Obituary of Henry Wharton', *Methodist Magazine*, 97, II (1874), p. 920; H. Debrunner, *A History of Christianity in Ghana* (Accra, 1967), p. 157.
30. For details on Mrs Wharton's biography and Wharton–Grant genealogy, I am indebted to the generosity of Arthur Wharton's nephew, the Rev. F. C. F. Grant of Kaneshie, Accra, Ghana (16 Sept. 1985) and to the additional clues provided by the Rev. J. A. Stedman of Banjul, Gambia (7 June 1985).
31. *Gold Coast Times*, 13 Jan. 1883, 14 July 1883.
32. *The Colonial Office List*, London, 1883, 1884, 1886, pp. 92, 90, 478 respectively; *Gold Coast Times*, 2 Dec. 1882.
33. The following review of the career of Francis Chapman Grant (1823–94) relies heavily upon evidence from the *Gold Coast Times*, 1874–84, 'Obituary of F. C. Grant', *Gold Coast Chronicle*, 19 Nov. 1894; the testimony of the Rev. F. C. F. Grant (16 Sept. 1985) and the biographical study in Jenkins, 'Historians', pp. 577–8.
34. *Gold Coast Times*, 22 July 1882.
35. *Gold Coast Times*, 17 Sept. 1881, 1 Oct. 1881, 8 Oct. 1881, 24 Sept. 1881; A. B. Ellis, *The Land of Fetish* (1883) (Chicago, 1970), 2nd ed., Ch. 12.
36. E.g. E. A. Ayandele, *The Missionary Impact on Modern Nigeria, 1842–1914* (London, 1966), p. 8; C. Fyfe, 'Reform in West Africa: The Abolition of the Slave Trade', in J. F. A. Ajayi and M. Crowder (eds.), *History of West Africa*, II (London, 1974); O. Kalu (ed.), *The History of Christianity in West Africa* (London, 1980), Chs. 1,4.
37. D. S. Higgins, *Rider Haggard. The Great Storyteller* (London, 1981), pp. 52–89 (cf. P. B. Ellis, *H. Rider Haggard, A Voice from the Infinite* (London, 1978), Ch. 5). Between 1885 and 1887, Haggard wrote and published *King Solomon's Mines*, *Allan Quartermain* and *She*.
38. H. Rider Haggard, *Allan Quartermain* (written in 1885 and published on 1 July 1887), (London, n.d.), pp. 253–4. For a thorough examination of the debates on the nature and extent of the impact of Haggard and other imperial writers upon the British public, see J. M. Mackenzie, *Propaganda and Empire. The Manipulation of British Public Opinion, 1880–1960* (Manchester, 1984), pp. 1–10.
39. This and the preceding paragraph draw heavily upon Jenkins, 'Historians', Ch. 2; 'Gold Coasters Overseas, 1880–1919: With Specific Reference to Their Activities in Britain', *Immigrants and Minorities*, 4, 3 (1985), 5–10 (hereafter *Gold Coasters*); ' "West Indian" and "Brazilian" Influences in the Gold Coast-Ghana, c. 1780–1914. A Review and Reappraisal of Continuities in the post-Abolition links between West Africa and the Caribbean and Brazil'; paper presented to the 12th Annual Conference of the Society for Caribbean Studies, Hoddesdon, Herts, July, 1988, pp. 2–7 (hereafter 'Caribbean and Brazil').
40. Testimony of Rev. F. C. F. Grant, 16 Sept. 1985; R. Dumett, 'African Merchants of the Gold Coast, 1860–1905', *Comparative Studies in Society and History* (Oct. 1983), 680; Jenkins, 'Historians', pp. 577–8; Moister, *H. Wharton*, pp. 6–7. The Rev W.

Moister recruited Wharton into the service of the Wesleyan Missionary Society in Grenada in 1840. He knew Wharton's Grenadian family and conducted a lively correspondence with him until his death in 1873. The Wharton letters from the Gold Coast seem to have provided Moister with the principal source for his biographical memoir (e.g. p. 60).

41. For the history and historiography of this policy, see Jenkins, 'Caribbean and Brazil', pp. 1–2, 10–14; H.O. Russell, 'The Missionary Outreach of the West Indian Church to West Africa in the Nineteenth Century with particular reference to the Baptists', unpublished Ph.D. thesis, University of Oxford, 1972.

42. Henry Wharton, to Rev. J. Beecham, St. Vincent, 25 Sept. 1844, *Wesleyan Missionary Notices*, Dec (1844), pp. 682–3; W. Moister, *Missionary Anecdotes, Sketches, Facts and Incidents* (London, 1875), pp. 146–8.

43. Moister, *H. Wharton*, p. 148.

44. Ibid., pp. 146–7. William Moister Wharton (b. 1868?) was chronically ill during the years 1870–74. It is possible that he became a victim of the smallpox epidemic which accompanied the end of the Asante War in May, 1874. See *Gold Coast Times*, 28 May 1874.

45. Jenkins, *South*, pp. 142–3; 'Caribbean and Brazil', pp. 6, 7, 14, 20 (note 90).

46. Moister, *H. Wharton*, p. 27; R. Burton, 'Two Trips on the Gold Coast [in 1862]', *Ocean Highways, The Geographical Review*, I (1874), p. 451; K.A.B. Jones-Quartey, *History, Politics and Early Press in Ghana. The Fictions and the Facts* (Legon, Accra, 1975), pp. 69–71. For the 'developmental' politics of the Basel Mission and the Jamaica settlers of Akropong, see Debrunner, op. cit., pp. 108, 128–34; Jenkins 'Caribbean and Brazil', pp. 5, 9–12.

47. Moister, *H. Wharton*, p. 140.

48. See note 40 above.

49. This observation is based upon an examination of Sasines Records (1780–1830) at the Scottish Record Office, General Register House, Edinburgh and the Registrations of Births, Marriages and Deaths at the General Register Office, St. Catherine's House, London, for the years 1880–1920. A further insight into Wharton's genealogy was provided in the reported speech, which preceded the toast to his health at the Darlington dinner in Dec. 1886 (see note 7 above). The speaker, a Mr T. Watson, explained that, 'the famous athlete was of north country extraction, his ancestors having sprung from Stockton'. From the studies of concubinage and the emergence of 'free coloured' communities in the slave plantocracies of the Caribbean, it is possible that Wharton's grandmother's free status was granted by her white father, a Wharton from Stockton, whose name she retained and gave to her son Henry Wharton. Thus the latter's father, the Scottish sea captain-trader (who remains anonymous in the Moister biographical memoir) has still to be identified. See e.g. E.V. Goveia, *Slave Society in the British Leeward Islands at the End of the Eighteenth Century*, (New Haven, 1965), pp. 214–20; D.W. Cohen and J.P. Greene (eds.), *Neither Slave Nor Free. The Freedman of African Descent in the Slave Societies of the New World* (Baltimore, 1972), pp. 1–18; E.L. Cox, *Free Coloureds in the Slave Societies of St. Kitts and Grenada, 1763–1833* (Knoxville, 1984), pp. 10–32.

50. Moister, *H. Wharton*, pp. 23–4, 66.

51. Ibid., pp. 12–14, 119–20, 162; *Gold Coast Chronicle*, 19 Nov. 1894; I.S. Ephson, *Gallery of Gold Coast Celebrities*, (Accra, 1969), pp. 112–3; S. Tenkorang, 'John Mensah Sarbah, 1864–1910' *Transactions of the Historical Society of Ghana*, XIV, I (1973), 66–7.

52. Moister, *H. Wharton*, pp. 143–7, 160–1.

53. Inspired by the practice of the Basel Mission, the Rev. Wharton introduced the vernacular (Ga) as a medium of instruction in the James Town primary school in the 1860s: a unique attempt to Africanize Wesleyan Mission education before the late 1880s. Annual Reports on the 'Akrah Circuit', Feb. 1863–Feb. 1868, Boxes 266 and 267, *Archives of the Methodist Missionary Society*, London (hereafter *AMMS*).

54. Unless footnotes indicate otherwise, the following section draws upon Jenkins, *Gold Coasters*, pp. 10–12.

55. E.g. C. Bolt, *Victorian Attitudes to Race* (London, 1971); C. Fyfe, *Africanus Horton, West African Scientist and Patriot* (Oxford, 1972) (hereafter *Horton*); D.A. Lorimer, *Colour, Class and Victorians* (Leicester, 1978).

56. Captain H. Brackenbury, *The Ashanti War. A Narrative*, 1874, II, pp.321, 346, 352. Not untypical of the civilian journalist's view of the 'Cape Coast Fantee' was that expressed by the *Daily Telegraph's* correspondent in Cape Coast: 'Nothing but martial law, swift and strong, will make these natives take upon themselves the mere semblance of manly virtues. Fight they will not, though certain death were the penalty for refusal; work they may, perhaps, if a whip be behind them ... In the Prussian army they would have died there and then, but the dread of Exeter Hall ["the Evangelical groan"] is an abiding shadow over our officers'. See F. Boyle, *Through Fanteeland to Coomasie. A Diary of the Ashantee Expedition* (London, 1874), pp.108–9, 162–3.

57. From evidence in the *Gold Coast Times* after 1877, it is possible to reconstruct the growth of racial tensions in Cape Coast and in James Town and to gain 'insider' insights into the racist attitudes prevailing in Britain. The latter include the racial taunts experienced by an educated Fante-speaking Cape Coast woman (Wharton's sister, Clara?) in London streets and shops and on a train from the capital to Liverpool ('Darkie! Darkie!'; 'Blackymoor by the chapel-door') and the cynical editorial speculations on the dangers which faced the Zulu leader, Cetshawayo, while in London (from 'some designing showman who might see his way to a large profit by the exhibition of the captive King' or from 'a syndicate of fashionable ladies'), e.g. *Gold Coast Times*, 27 Dec. 1877, 25 Feb. 1882, 27 Jan. 1883.

58. Ibid., 9 July 1881. See also 30 July 1881, 1 July 1882, 16 Sept. 1882.

59. This early and, therefore, tentative outline of the diffusion of British forms of recreations in what became known in 1901 as the British Imperial Dependency of the Gold Coast (the southern Colony, Asante and the Northern Territories) is based upon the published accounts of expatriates, missionary (mainly archival) sources and the observations of the 'insider' contributions to the local Euro-African press. My proposed chronology for the spread of 'outdoor activities' does not conflict with A.H.M. Kirk-Greene's 'pioneering stage' as described by his 'Imperial Administration and the Athletic Imperative: The Case of the District Officer in Africa', in Baker and Mangan (eds.), op. cit., pp.86–9.

60. This attempt to define, describe and estimate the social and economic significance of 'indoor pursuits' is based upon a familiarity with a substantial number of expatriate eye-witness accounts from the reliable Willem Bosman (1688–1702) to the not always reliable Mary Kingsley (1893–5). For the Gold Coast years of Wharton Senior and Junior (1845–82), however, particular attention has been paid to entries from the diary for 1847–8 of C.A. Gordon, a Scottish naval surgeon, and to the cynical observations on the years 1873–83 of A.B. Ellis, an English officer in the First West India Regiment. See C.A. Gordon, *Life on the Gold Coast* (London, 1874) and above, notes 28, 35.

61. Before 1873–74, European expeditions into the interior, beyond the Accra plains and the Akuapem ridge, were notable for their infrequency. There is only one recorded visit by a European beyond the river Prah to Asante before the 1780s, when the Danes and then, after 1830, the Basel Missionaries began to establish bases in and beyond Akropong (Akuapem). The first British expedition to Asante was undertaken in 1817 and only two more were undertaken by white personnel before 1874. The Rev. Henry Wharton spent a year (1847) in Kumase, representing Wesleyan (and British?) interests in the Asante capital.

62. In 1866–68, the Sierra Leonean army doctor, Africanus B. Horton, published his influential studies of West African, including Gold Coast, diseases. For an examination of the 'insider' diagnoses, see Fyfe, *Horton*, pp.36–44, 84–9.

63. The English acquired a reputation for alcohol abuse among their fellow European expatriates in the Gold Coast townships. In his classic, but badly translated into English, account of his 14 years on the coast, the Dutch factor, Bosman, reported that excessive consumption of 'punch' contributed to the high death rate among the English rather than the rigours of climate and disease. W. Bosman, *New and Accurate*

Description of the Coast of Guinea (1704), reprint of the 1705 English edition (London, 1967), p.50.

64. Because of the close links between 'Christianity and commerce' and, perhaps, the influence of the Rev. T.B. Freeman, the black British 'father' of Ghanaian Methodism (who served on the coast 1837–90), expatriate Wesleyan missionaries did not always distance themselves from or denounce the 'unchristian' traders until the arrival of the 'new' muscular Christian missionaries in the 1880s. See Gordon, op. cit., pp.78–80; Debrunner, op. cit., pp.99, 131, 152, 205–6; A. Porter, 'Cambridge, Keswick, and the late Nineteenth-century Attitudes to Africa', *Journal of Imperial and Commonwealth History*, V, 1 (1976), 6–7; I Tufuoh, 'Relations between Christian Missions, European Administrations and Traders in the Gold Coast, 1828–74' in C.G. Baeta (ed.), *Christianity in Tropical Africa* (Oxford, 1968), pp.34–56.

65. Minutes and Reports: Gold Coast District, Box 266 (1842–66, e.g. 18 July 1848, Feb 1863), Box 267 (1867–79, e.g. Feb. 1874–76); Synod Minutes and Circuit Reports: West Africa, Gold Coast, Box 268 (1880–90, e.g. 31 Dec. 1880–83), *AMMS*; Annual and Quarterly Reports, Basel Mission, e.g. Akyem District, e.g. 1865, no. 32, 21 Jan. 1866; 1867, no. 8, 7 Jan. 1868; 1876, no. 222, 10 July 1876; 1880, no. 135, 10 Sept. 1880; 1885, no. 95, 6 Feb. 86 in P. Jenkins, *Abstracts of the Basel Mission Gold Coast Correspondence, 1854–99* (Basel, 1970); Log Book, 1887–95, Classwork Register, 1900–27: Christiansborg (Basel Mission and after 1919) Presbyterian Middle Boarding School Papers, *National Archives of Ghana, Accra*, EC7/17, 33; 'Educational Systems of the Chief Crown Colonies and Possessions of the British Empire, II', *Special Reports on Educational Subjects* (1905), 13, (London: HMSO, 1968 ed.), pp.13–4, 24–7.

66. It is possible that cricket was introduced in one of these schools, Richmond College or Mfantsipim (formerly, the Wesleyan High School, Cape Coast) in *c.* 1912, although 'hard' evidence has yet to be found to confirm this.

67. Skertchly had published a 'straight' account of his experiences in coastal Dahomey (*Dahomey as it is*) in 1874, the year in which his *Melinda* manuscript was completed. The latter draws liberally upon mainly recent (1873–74) published accounts of the Gold Coast and Asante and was clearly designed to exploit the new market for Gold Coast Africana as created by the Asante conflict. I am grateful to my colleague, Robert Fyson, for drawing my attention to and supplying a first edition of *Melinda*.

68. The novel has been ignored, hitherto, in British imperial literary studies and, given Haggard's apparent penchant for plagiarism, the similarities between *Melinda* and *Allan Quartermain* are not without interest. See Higgins, op. cit., pp.101, 117; R.I. Rotberg, *Joseph Thomson and the Exploration of Africa* (London, 1971), pp.170n, 187n.

69. Skertchly, *Melinda*, p.3.

70. Ibid., pp.82, 106.

71. M. Staniland, *The Lions of Dagbon. Political Change in Northern Ghana* (Cambridge, 1975), pp.48–50.

72. *Gold Coast Times*, 28 May 1874, 11 June 1874, 30 June 1874.

73. K.B. Dickson, *A Historical Geography of Ghana* (Cambridge, 1969), pp.258–9, Dickson's appraisal is based on the 'Memorandum on the Choice of the Seat of the Government of the Gold Coast', which was prepared for the Colonial Office by Capt. M.T. Sale of the First West India Regiment in 1875.

74. D. Kimble, *A Political History of Ghana, 1850–1928* (Oxford, 1963), p.94.

75. J.B. Anaman, *Gold Coast Guide for 1895–96* (London, 1894), pp.29–41. The Rev. Anaman, a Euro-African Wesleyan minister and pioneer Fante linguist from Anomabo, included 103 clerkships and 173 other posts (e.g. prison, postal and nursing services), which were held by Euro-Africans.

76. *Gold Coast Times*, 13 Aug. 1881; W. Brandford Griffiths [Junior], *The Far Horizon* (Ilfracombe, 1951), p.57. Griffiths Senior served in the Gold Coast as Lt. Governor and Governor from Dec. 1880 to April 1895. His son's 30-year association with the Gold Coast, 1881–1911, was interrupted by a seven-year 'break' in the West Indies, which coincided with his father's governorship!

77. W.H. Gillespie, *The Gold Coast Police Force, 1844–1938* (Accra, 1955), p. 23. Locally recruited soldiers were also expected to use simple apparatus and to practise 'free gymnastics' on a regular basis by *c* 1900. See C. Braithwaite Wallis, *West African Warfare* (London, 1906), p. 71.

78. G. MacDonald, *The Gold Coast, Past and Present. A Short Description of the Country and its People* (London, n.d) pp. 202–3. Macdonald served as the Gold Coast's first Director of Education, 1893–97. According to the Accra daily, the *Gold Coast Express*, 3 Aug. 1897, the Accra Club was opened by Governor Maxwell in August 1897 to celebrate Victoria's Diamond Jubilee. The occasion was also marked by a 'regatta' (surfboat and canoe races), a bicycle race and the Jubilee Handicap (in which six horses were entered by Euro-African owners).

79. This attempt to assess Euro-African perceptions of and responses to recreational pursuits is based upon local press evidence, my research into the complex web of ethnic, familial, generational and intra-confessional tensions which emerged in Cape Coast Euro-African communities after *c.* 1878, and Tom McCaskie's guidelines for the study of Akan ideas and attitudes from the 'inside out', See note 22, above.

80. The Gold Coast Education Ordinance of May, 1882, which introduced the payment of grant-in-aid upon results, confirmed Cape Coasters' suspicions that British officialdom preferred the Basel Mission's adapted 'vocational training' to the Wesleyan provision of an anglocentric liberal curriculum. See *Gold Coast Times*, 20 May 1882; Jenkins, 'Historians', p. 230, note 3.

81. E.g. between 20 May 1882 and 13 Jan 1883. *The Times* serialized, in 25 episodes, the first connected history of the Gold Coast in English, from an African perspective. These lessons from the past were designed to sensitize the younger generation to present dangers and future difficulties.

82. *Gold Coast Times*, 27 Aug. 1881.

83. Adverts which appeared (incongruously) in F.C. Grant's weekly *Times* illustrate this contradiction. On the 22 Oct. 1881, the Euro-African trader, J.M. Abadoo, announced the sale of moselles, hocks, champagnes, perfumes, toilet waters and soaps, cosmetics, hair lotions, billiard tables and bagatelle boards. Dumett's research indicates, however, that the leading Wesleyan merchants, like J. Sarbah and Grant (who was also the head of the Cape Coast Temperance Movement), avoided direct involvement in the liquor trade. On the 'temperance v liquor' controversy on the coast, see R. Dumett, 'John Sarbah the Elder and African Mercantile Entrepreneurship in the Gold Coast in the Late Nineteenth Century', *Journal of African History* (hereafter *JAH*), xiv, 4 (1979), 671–2; J.E. Flint, 'Mary Kingsley – A Reassessment', *JAH*, iv, 3 (1963), 98–9; S.T. McRory, 'The Competition for the Merchandise Trade in the Gold Coast, 1900–39', unpublished Ph.D thesis, Colombia University, 1980, pp. 31–3.

84. According to the *Gold Coast Times*, only five organized cricket matches were played on the Parade Ground of the First West India Regiment in Cape Coast in the 13 months between Dec. 1881 and Dec. 1882 and only the last one was reported in full, with individual batting, bowling and fielding details recorded. The reports do reveal that a number of the cricketers were Afro-Caribbean soldiers and the majority were Euro-Africans – a substantial core of whom had been educated in Sierra Leone and/or Britain. In addition to three Grants, they included T. Laing Junior (the new editor of the *Times*, see note 105 below) and Charles Wharton, Arthur's elder brother (see notes 32, 51). The *Gold Coast Times*, 10 Dec. 1881, 17 Dec. 1881, 13 May 1882, 20 May 1882, 30 Dec. 1882; Jenkins, *Gold Coasters*, pp. 43–51.

85. *Gold Coast Times*, e.g. 5 Dec. 1877, 9 July 1881, 30 July 1882, 1 July 1882, 16 Sept. 1882, 8 Oct. 1882, 14 Nov. 1882, 6 Jan. 1883; note 81 above. In a 'reformist' attempt to control or harness youthly interests in 'idle' pursuits, an afternoon of 'athletic sports' (leapfrog, blindman's buff, skipping, jumping, cricket and 'kicking a football') was introduced, alongside chapel services and a formal lecture on the evils of alcohol into the annual celebrations of the Order of Good Templars (two months after Wharton's departure for England) in September 1882 (23 Sept. 1882, 30 Sept. 1882).

86. Other 'reformist' moves included the Acme Billiard Club for 'gentlemen'. Ibid., 31 Aug. 1874, 26 Nov. 1881, 31 Dec. 1881; Anaman, op. cit., pp. 104–5.

87. *Gold Coast Times*, e.g. 10 Dec. 1881, 30 Dec. 1882; *Gold Coast Express*, e.g. 16 Sept. 1896, 21 Aug. 1897, 30 Aug. 1897, 6 Sept. 1897. In the late 1890s and early 1900s, the business and professional careers of a few young Euro-Africans seem to have been enhanced in ways already explored by T.O. Ranger and B. Stoddart in the Central-Southern African, Indian and Caribbean imperial contexts. See M. Sampson (ed.), *Gold Coast Men of Affairs* (1937), (London, 1968), p.181; A. MacMillan (ed.), *The Red Book of West Africa* (1920), (London, 1968), p.227; C.F. Hutchison, *The Pen-Pictures of Modern Africans and African Celebrities*, (London, n.d. (*c.* 1930?)), pp.187–8; T.O. Ranger, 'The Invention of Tradition in Colonial Africa', in E. Hobsbawm and T.O. Ranger (eds.), *The Invention of Tradition* (Cambridge, 1983), pp.237–9; note 21 above.

88. W. Brandford Griffiths, op. cit., p.185; note 58 above. On 8 July 1882, the editor of the *Gold Coast Times* declared that football was 'a pastime which owing to the heat of the country has only a few supporters here [i.e. in Cape Coast and Accra]'.

89. For biographical collections of Gold Coast Euro-Africans,. see M. Sampson and C.F. Hutchison, note 87 above; Jenkins, *Gold Coasters*, e.g. pp.13–15 (note 42), 43–4; 'In Pursuit of the African Past. John Mensah Sarbah of Ghana, 1864–1910', in R. Lotz and I. Pegg (eds.), *Under the Imperial Carpet. Essays in Black History* (London, 1986), pp.109–29.

90. Any attempt to identify and isolate a short list of prerequisites for the making of a 'model' late Victorian sportsman is likely to prove dangerous and controversial (see note 91). The aim here is to emphasize that before July 1882 there seems little in the history of the making of Arthur Wharton to prepare him for a sporting career.

91. Cashmore, op. cit., pp.4–10; cf. B. Carrington and E. Wood, 'Black Youth and Sport in the United Kingdom', in C. Brock (ed.), *The Caribbean in Europe* (London, n.d.), pp.225–8.

92. For inter-quarter town riots, burglary and larger-scale robbery in the Cape Coast and Accra localities, see *Gold Coast Times*, e.g. 13 Aug. 1881, 24 Sept. 1881, 18 Feb. 1882, 11 March 1882, 17 June 1882, 8 July 1882, 14 July 1883 (the latter reported a 'break-in' at Mrs Wharton's house-store-hotel); A.B. Ellis, *The Tshi-Speaking Peoples of the Gold Coast* (London, 1887), pp.279–80; T.J. Johnson, 'Protest: Tradition and Change. An Analysis of Southern Gold Coast Riots, 1890–1920', *Economy and Society*, i, i (1972) 167–73 (for increase in riots between 1850–89).

93. A campaign was also conducted against attempts to introduce 'lawn tennis' on the Sabbath. *Gold Coast Times*, 11 Feb. 1882, 16 Sept. 1882.

94. P.R.O., C.O. 96/238/2044. Confidential Despatch, Ag. Gov. Hodgson to Col. Sec. of State, Ripon, 2 Nov. 1893.

95. Wharton does seem to have acknowledged his Gold Coast origins in interviews with friendly local journalists in the Midlands and the North East of England. As late as 1955, he was still remembered in Darlington as 'a young man from the Gold Coast'. Thus, the references in the national sporting press to his Caribbean origins may be attributed to the British habit (which still persists) of describing blacks in Britain as 'West Indians' and to Wharton's unwillingness to refute them since the inhabitants of the Gold Coast were popularly identified in Britain with the Asante (real Africans) – Wharton's old enemies! See the *Cannock Advertiser*, 27 Aug. 1887; R. Scarr, 'Schools for Young Ladies and Gentlemen, Private Establishments in Bygone Darlington', *Darlington and Stockton Times*, 21 May 1955; Illingworth, *NCAA*, p.9.

96. Jenkins, *Gold Coasters*; for Wharton's proficiency in the use of English, see *Cannock Advertiser*, loc. cit.

97. E.g. *Gold Coast Times*, 11 Feb. 1881, 15 Aug. 1882; *Staffordshire Advertiser*, 21 Dec. 1872, 18 Jan 1873; *Cannock Advertiser*, 14 May 1881, 9 Feb. 1884, 26 June 1884; *Darlington and Stockton Times*, 11 Aug. 1883, 21 May, 1955; *The Northern Echo*, 1 April 1885.

98. P.R.O., C.O. 96/238/2044. Wharton seems to have planned, but failed, to return to his 'native land' in *c.* Sept. 1887. See *Cannock Advertiser*, 27 Aug. 1887.

99. Kelly's *Post Office Directories* (Staffordshire, 1880), p.78; Darlington and Stockton, 1885, p.265; Names and Residencies of Preachers: Wesleyan Methodist Circuit Plans for Darlington (e.g. Feb. – April, 1882) and for Cannock (e.g. Aug. – Nov., 1883),

Methodist Archives and Research Centre, J. Rylands Library, University of Manchester; *Cannock Advertiser*, e.g. 6 May 1882, 30 Sept. 1882, 12 April 1884; *Darlington and Stockton Times*, e.g. 19 July 1884, 9 Sept. 1884, 18 Oct. 1884, 28 Feb. 1885.

100. *Cannock Advertiser*, 28 Feb. 1884, 12 April 1884; *Darlington and Stockton Times*, 23 Aug. 1884.

101. *Staffordshire Advertiser*, 14 Jan. 1871; *Gold Coast Times*, e.g. 15 Aug. 1882.

102. *The Census Returns* for the District of Cannock in 1881 (R. G. 11/2783, p. 28) reveal that George P., Josiah M. and Justin (?) H. Grant of 'Cape Coast Castle Africa', aged 14, 12 and 11, respectively, were resident at Shoal Hill College. According to the testimony of the Rev. F.C.F. Grant, his father (George Peter) and his uncle (Josiah Mountford) were the sons of F.C. Grant and his second wife, Juliana (née Brown). Both returned from Cannock to Cape Coast in August, 1884, 'in good health' and 'successful in their exams'. *Gold Coast Times*, 22 Aug. 1884.

103. 'Obituary of S.G. Gwynne, F.R.G.S.', *Cannock Advertiser*, 22 Jan. 1887.

104. Ibid., *Census Returns* for the District of Cannock, 1881, and the Darlington District, 1871 and 1881.

105. *Gold Coast Times*, 27 Aug. 1881, 10 Sept. 1881, 11 Feb. 1882 (for the obituary of the Rev. T. Laing, 1824–81); *Census Returns* for the Darlington District, 1871; R. Jenkins, 'Historians', pp. 544–5. Laing Junior, whose career as editor, printer and proprietor of Cape Coast and Accra newspapers (including the first daily) spanned some 40 years, may be regarded as one of the most influential pioneers of Gold Coast/ Ghanaian 'nationalist' journalism.

106. See note 94 above.

CHAPTER FOUR

Emancipation, Exercise and Imperialism: Girls and the Games Ethic in Colonial Malaya

JANICE N. BROWNFOOT

Should you be interested in knowing something about the education of girls in Malaya, a visit to a local English-language school for girls would reveal all, suggested Miss Josephine Foss, headmistress of Pudu English School (PES or Pudu) in Kuala Lumpur (KL), in 1935. 'You will see there athletic, happy, healthy and normal girls, far better fitted to take their share in the struggle for existence in Malaya than their less fortunate uneducated sisters.'[1] She might also have added a comparison with their mostly 'less fortunate' mothers and grandmothers, few of whom had had any English or vernacular education, let alone played sport. Yet those of the older generations who had received such education and had experienced games or drill formed the foundation on which were built the inter-war developments that Miss Foss described. As Miss Mabel Marsh, headmistress of the Methodist Girls' School (MGS) in Kuala Lumpur, noted in 1930, 'a new attitude towards physical education is being engendered and a new spirit is pervading our schools to which the past generation was a stranger'.[2]

Both women agreed that by the 1930s changes in attitudes and approaches to the education of Asian girls, and in the health and happiness of many of the girls themselves, were obvious and fundamental. With their bodies physically liberated from restricting traditional clothes and customs, many of them were indeed better fitted for, and able to participate effectively in, 'the struggle for existence' because, through school, they had gained both physical emancipation and employable skills. In short, according to white women teachers, educated Asian females had been set free.[3] The new freedom was little short of revolutionary: and it had happened, or so it seemed, in the space of only a generation.

In this radical social change sport had apparently played a significant, if not fundamental role. The process began gradually with the introduction of gentle callisthenics and indoor exercises from about the 1890s. During the next twenty years physical exercise together with a limited number of outdoor sports became increasingly firmly established in a number of English-language girls' schools; by the inter-war period a quite astonishing transformation had occurred in the provision of sport for Asian girls and their participation in it. The time-frame was short and inter-linked with the three main periods in the development of girls' education. Of the first, from the earlier nineteenth century to the 1880s, little is known. The second from the 1880s to the 1910s was the period of 'take-off', while the years between the two world wars witnessed consolidation and expansion. The sporting transformation that took place and the effects associated with it happened at much the same time as games had similarly effected great changes in the lives of British – and American – girls and women.[4] Yet colonial society and gender relationships in the British Empire have usually been portrayed as exceedingly conservative and far slower to alter than in the metropolitan country.[5] Were Miss Foss and Miss Marsh correct then? If so, how and why had the emancipating changes they perceived come about, and what part had such an ostensibly simple curriculum development as introducing physical exercise played? What games did the girls play? What motivated white women educators to introduce physical education into curricula primarily for Asian girls from traditional, conservative societies, and were these physical activities symbols of female emancipation, or instruments for exercising control over, and achieving acculturation of, colonial subjects?[6] This essay attempts to answer some of these questions despite the severe paucity of available source materials.

Sport is defined here as any physical activities and events for improving physical, mental and/or moral health, whether recreational or competitive.[7] Serious studies of the relationship of sport to issues of gender and social change for females in colonial societies are virtually non-existent. Research has yet to be done on this subject for the British Empire.[8] Moreover, the difficulties are considerable. This essay itself presents research in progress, rather than definitive analysis and conclusions, because the source materials currently available are meagre, and the search for more continues. Few records from girls' schools for the period from the 1890s to the 1930s seem to have survived, partly as a result of the Japanese occupation, while missionary societies' materials are still being investigated.[9] Efforts to tap orally the memories of 'old girls' and former teachers are only now under way; published sources, such as colonial government annual reports, reveal[10] little about education in general for girls, and even less about sport and games. Newspaper articles give factual details but seldom address such issues as the women educators' aims or Asian girls' reactions to sport. Even printed and secondary sources that purport to describe education in colonial Malaya barely mention girls' education, if at all, and certainly do not consider girls and sport.[11] Indeed, in all the materials found so far the references to sport for Asian girls are perfunctory.

Accordingly this study describes the subject of physical exercise for Asian girls between the 1890s and the 1930s only in English-language education and through English-language sources. It considers what the white women educators' aims and opinions were, and what benefits and

changes they believed sport had contributed to for Asian girls. It does not
present any views from the girls themselves. Its findings, though revealing, are thus incomplete and obviously one-sided.

II

Although English-language schools for Asian girls in Malaya were
organized, primarily by white Christian missionary women, as early as
1817,[12] it was not until the 1880s that English-language education for
Asian girls really developed when the American Methodist Episcopal
Mission entered the Malayan field and the French and Irish Sisters of the
Holy Infant Jesus started to expand their convent network.[13] From the
last two decades of the nineteenth century these white missionary women
educators arrived in Malaya in increasing though never large numbers to
take up the cause of English education for Asian girls. Why did they go,
and what were their aims? In answer to the question 'For what purpose
are most missionary women in this land?', Ruth Harvey, a Methodist,
replied in sweeping, though only partial, explanation: 'To live with, and
work and play with the girls and women'.[14] Any work – and play –
especially educational, for and with Asian females had to be done by
women. But what work – and play – needed to be done and why? The
missionaries' answers to these questions incorporated attitudes concerning the roles and importance of women in society and the perceived needs
of the women themselves, and were linked to general missionary aims and
strategy. Women's missionary work – work for women, by women – also
inter-linked with nineteenth-century perceptions of the 'White Man's
Burden', and with the later nineteenth-century Women's Movement, the
fight for women's rights and the suffrage, and the changes occurring
slowly in the career opportunities available for women.[15]

The reasons why women missionary educators went to Malaya thus
reflected general societal and Christian aims and perceptions. These
included answering an appeal for help to mitigate the intolerable wrongs
and injustices reputedly suffered by their sex in non-Christian lands that
was linked to burgeoning beliefs in women's emancipation.[16] 'The very
social conditions that make women's lot in heathen lands an inferior one,
constitute the opportunity that calls for the missionary woman', affirmed
the Malayan Methodist Woman's Conference in 1911.[17] Missionary
women would help to 'free' Asian women and girls from centuries-old
traditions, customs and ceremonies which they believed were anathema to
the full personal development of the individual woman and her talents and
abilities, and prevented the re-structuring and modernizing corporate
development of Asian societies.[18] Thus their aim was to emancipate Asian
girls and women morally, physically, mentally, spiritually and professionally, using education and Christianity. Only women could get close enough
to Asian females, and gain the necessary entrée to Asian homes to achieve
these objectives for 'in her Western sister, the Eastern lady sees one whom

she does not fear, and whom she may learn to love and trust and confide in'.[19]

Indeed this sense of 'sisterhood' – 'woman's love for her sister woman of other hue and speech and faith'[20] – was a powerful motivating factor, along with the determination to transfer to Asian females the benefits and opportunities which Western women had won or were gaining. Having felt and responded to the 'Call', and fired by a profound sense of Christian altruism and idealism, the missionary women had a vocation to teach, and to bring the message of the 'good news', with all the benefits of a Christian education. As one Methodist missionary in Malaya summed up, they 'were stirred with a desire to give to other girls who had not had our opportunities, some of the good things that had come to us because we were living in Christian homes, and receiving the benefits of a Christian civilization'.[21]

Missionary teachers believed that education in English-language schools founded by Christian women would help raise Asian girls and women from inferiority and deprivation, and would develop females with better minds and physically improved bodies, whether they became converted or not. This was the missionary women's duty because 'the girls of this land to-day are to be the women of tomorrow . . . The responsibility as to what the women of the future in Malaya are, rests with us'.[22] One outstanding missionary educator, Mabel Marsh, was convinced from her arrival in Malaya in 1910 that Asians, especially women, needed 'our help' to free and uplift them from the circumstances and effects of dirt, disease, overcrowding, degradation and vice. In 1911, observing, for instance, that Asian women rubber-tappers, often born of child-mothers, had 'very little strength of body or mind', she had concluded that what all Asian women needed was physical and intellectual improvement.[23] The necessary changes were to be accomplished by providing an education for girls that incorporated in the curriculum lessons in Christian morals, modern hygiene and physical training.[24] This emphasis on the importance of both moral and physical instructions and of the philosophy that 'no people can possibly rise higher than its womanhood', was reiterated by the Methodist Bishop Lowe in 1927 when he dedicated the new buildings of the Suydam MGS in Malacca, in part 'for the purpose of aiding womanhood to attain the highest possible standard of physical well-being, of moral calibre and of spiritual understanding'.[25] 'We hoped', echoed Josephine Foss of the Anglican PES, 'that our foundation of Christian, moral and hygienic teaching would follow them [Asian girls] all the days of their lives.'[26]

The foundation was to be intensely practical too. The missionary teachers, some of whom, like Mabel Marsh, Thirza Bunce and Josephine Foss, were qualified professional educators, intended to fit each pupil to take her place in Malaya in a better and more effective way. Thus the aim of girls' education was, they agreed, many-sided: to prepare a girl for whatever course her future life might take, individually and as part of a wider society. This necessitated educating the whole person, body and mind. Accordingly, Asian girls were to be trained for a wide variety of vocations and worthwhile jobs and careers, partly to provide girls, who might or might not eventually marry, with employable skills, partly to train up women in occupations where they could help other women, notably teaching and medicine.[27] Even in 1935 the demand for suitable unmarried girls and women in commerce, the professions and schools exceeded the supply.[28] At the same time, however, women teachers wanted to educate 'their girls' to become better, more efficient wives, homemakers and mothers. Improved intellectual and domestic skills would fulfil various objectives:

> Educated lads will demand educated wives who will not only be companions to them but will bear them healthier children, and know how to bring them up, how to cook, and how to run a home in a healthier, more hygienic way than did their grandmothers.[29]

If they had been trained in the most efficient, advanced and hygienic techniques of domestic management, and were also Christian wives, then they would run Christian homes.[30] In short, as one MGS Report summed up, women educators wanted to make, with God's help and guidance, 'a better womanhood for Malaya'.[31] For this, physical improvement was mandatory.

In the decades under study missionary women educators in Malaya believed in the education of girls equally with that of boys. They regarded physical exercise as an integral and necessary part of that education. Consequently they introduced physical training and sport into the curriculum. How had they individually acquired their belief in the importance of exercise, and what prompted them as individuals to ensure that exercise was a constituent part of the syllabus? Regrettably, little is known about the personal views of each woman, and even less about how each came to endorse the importance of sport. They have left behind almost no evidence. But by interpreting the limited source materials and information available, including the backgrounds of some of the women, it is possible at least to suggest some answers.

In Malaya, there were three main groups of women missionary educators: American Methodists, French and Irish nuns, and to a lesser extent British Anglicans. Little is known about the Roman Catholics, although the 'muscular Christianity' of both American and British Protestants contrasted dramatically with the more demure Catholic nuns who presumably did not personally participate in sports.[32] But the backgrounds, upbringing and individual personalities of the women educators were no doubt fundamental to their perceptions about whether sport and exercise were important or not. Since the American women played such a significant role in Asian girls' education, it is worth looking at them in some detail. In America significant changes in education had occurred after the end of the Civil War in 1865. By the 1890s high school education was established, many Americans were going to some sort of college, often co-educational, and callisthenics and physical exercise were already part of the curriculum. By the turn of the century the role of physical education in nation-building was stressed, and from about 1905 a movement began to bring sports into the school and college curriculum to blend with callisthenics and gymnastics. For American women organized sport had become increasingly important from the 1860s, and the last quarter of the nineteenth century brought significant changes in attitudes towards games for females and to the female body, especially as the more emancipated 'New Woman' became common. By the early twentieth century Americans generally regarded sport and recreational activities as worthwhile and useful for both men and women.[33]

American Methodist missionaries like Mabel Marsh and Thirza Bunce, who were training as teachers in the late nineteenth century, must have been affected by the new attitudes towards exercise for women. Miss Marsh, who graduated from high school in 1897, trained as a teacher and taught in the USA before resigning in 1910 to answer the 'call' and become a missionary 'in a foreign field'.[34] Her own positive attitudes and those of her colleagues concerning both the importance of educating girls, and of incorporating exercise into the curriculum, must also have been stimulated and reinforced by the backgrounds and the particular American states from which they came. Limited information in published Methodist records shows that many of the Methodist women originated from mid-West states such as Minnesota, Ohio, Indiana, Kansas, Iowa and Illinois. Mabel Marsh was from Kansas, while Thirza Bunce hailed from Indiana.[35] Women born and bred in the American mid-West were, as Beran has shown, of fundamental importance to the introduction of organized games, notably basketball, to American girls' education in certain states, and to the formation of women's leagues for the advancement of sport for females. Beran shows too that women from such states frequently came from the kinds of pioneering backgrounds in which women had participated physically in the process of settlement, thus becoming role-models for their daughters and grand-daughters. They came also from immigrant ethnic origins whose traditions and education programmes had included physical activities as a major part.[36]

The more physically independent and less conservative background of the American women educators in Malaya benefited them in various ways for their teaching roles. Comparing them with Australian women who were similarly 'so friendly and approachable – much more like our American women than the female folk of England', Mabel Marsh thought the attributes of both came from growing up 'in a pioneer country [which] has produced a freedom from convention not possible in the older established countries'.[37] As a result of such freedom the American teachers were generally egalitarian in their attitudes to and treatment of other people, whatever their origins, and in their perceptions about the importance of play and sport for Asian girls. They participated alongside the girls and were friendly with, and close to, them.[38] In many ways their typical characteristics differed markedly from their English contemporaries. But in some respects they shared attitudes and philosophies, at least with individual English educators.

Miss Josephine Foss – the Anglican Englishwoman responsible for the development of Pudu English School (PES) from 1925 – came from a very different background. For her a Christian Anglican upbringing, coupled with individual force of personality, the influence of the Women's Movement, a Froebel teacher training, and her experiences as a missionary among the very poor in China, were far more important than egalitarian national and educational philosophies in determining her attitudes and beliefs. But in Malaya she became firm friends with her American Methodist contemporaries. Unfortunately evidence does not show whether she had participated in games as a girl, although she was a keen badminton player in the 1930s.[39] However, she had grown up in British society during a period when the British Empire was both expanding and consolidating, and she must have been at least aware of the emphasis on athletics and games in boys' and girls' public schools, and of the British belief that to maintain health in the tropics it was essential for white people to take regular exercise.[40]

For the American women it was not only being American that was important but also being Methodist. Methodist Episcopalian educational philosophy stressed the necessity for the development of a sound, well-ordered body for women as well as men, and thus gave physical exercise a significant place in the curriculum. Female Methodist educators like Mabel Marsh and her predecessors and contemporaries firmly believed that exercising the body must accompany the intellectual training of the mind for the rounded development of the individual. Sport, these women insisted, would improve Asian girls physically, and help develop physical and mental stamina. By contributing to girls' freedom physical exercise would, the teachers thought, help engender a love of life and the ability to enjoy it to the full without fear of hindrance or restriction. Changes in dress necessary for playing games would permit freer movement of the body and liberation from customary decorum. Spiritual growth and character development would also result as the individual learnt self-control, self-reliance and self-respect. In short, exercise would help girls gain freedom since a healthy body and a healthy mind, both part of a healthy upbringing, meant liberation. The Methodist women teachers were not alone in their conclusions about the advantages of exercise. Anglican teachers such as Miss Foss agreed.[41]

Participation in sports promised other benefits, too. Team games were particularly endorsed for providing a training ground for life. They taught discipline and imbued valuable moral and personal qualities. The methods of organization and structure necessary – rules, scoring systems, and standardized court and pitch dimensions – introduced each girl to new types of social relationships. Playing in a team thus developed co-operation together with understanding and experience of corporate action. Playing girls in other teams and other schools, women educators believed, also promoted healthy rivalry and competition, inculcated feelings of pride, loyalty and identity, and imbued approved ideals such as fair play.[42] Winning the game, and perhaps a prize or trophy too, were attractive incentives which then reinforced the individual's sense of self-worth and of corporate identity also. On a wider basis the qualities and values learnt through games-playing supplied a foundation for comprehending principles of community identity and civic service. Thus, through sport, inter-related with other school subjects, the girls were taught concepts of broader social organization and justice. Sport offered practical and theoretical lessons in democracy, both that of Christianity and of secular Western society, and so helped in preparing Asians for the eventual self-government promised by British colonial policy.[43]

Missionary women educators thought playing games contributed to the benefit of the local society and wider community in other positive ways. Malaya was a multi-racial society and each English-language girls' school became, very quickly in its history, a microcosm of this. By playing together the girls could learn about and better understand the various cultural and religious backgrounds of their team-mates and their teachers. Sport would assist inter-racial harmony. By playing games both teachers and students would come to realize, as Mabel Marsh believed, that humans and human nature were 'pretty much the same regardless of the color of the skin, the race, or creed'.[44]

Apart from cutting across ethnic community divisions, the women educators also believed that having their girls play games contributed to improving morals and combating the various vices perceived as prevalent in Asian societies – prostitution, concubinage, opium-smoking and gambling. Sport was wholesome. It helped train girls in wholesome ways of living so that not only would they refrain from vice, but would be positive examples for good in the battle against it. Games would keep young people away from temptation. After all, games had had many beneficial effects for Americans – and Britons. Surely what was good for them would be good for Asians too: thus by the 1930s it was noted with approval that the youth of Malaya, including girls, were as keen on games as young Americans.[45]

In discussing the provision of sport for Asian girls and the objectives underlying its introduction, it is fairly clear that in some respects, such as the types of exercise introduced and the justifications for it, the decisions and actions of white women teachers paralleled those of their metropolitan contemporaries. This is hardly surprising given the later nineteenth- and earlier twentieth-century movements to introduce and then expand sport for girls in the home countries.[46] But in some ways these women seem to have had a degree of freedom greater than many of their contemporaries in Britain and America, including being able to act fairly independently. This may seem surprising, yet it reflects the particular position and circumstances of Malaya during the colonial period. The Colonial Office in England had little direct interest in girls' education in Malaya, beyond endorsing schemes such as the grant-in-aid system for the financial support of the schools, staff and buildings. By comparison the Headquarters Boards of the Anglican and Methodist Missionary societies were both interested in the provision of girls' education in Malaya and were fundamentally important in recruiting teaching staff from 'home', the provision of whom caused constant headaches. However, their role in determining and controlling the precise sports or games played by the girls' schools appears to have been minimal. The Malayan Colonial Education Department, although it eventually laid down rules that games be compulsory, and although its inspectors of schools 'inspected' the games element of the curriculum, also seems to have followed rather than led. There seems no evidence to show that the preponderantly male colonial civil and educational services determined or instructed which sports girls' schools were to play.[47] As for the governing bodies of the Anglicans and Methodists in Malaya: the Anglican Bishop of Singapore may well have had the final say, but missionaries like Miss Foss (PES, KL), Miss Pring (St Mary's, KL) and Miss Lane (Church of England Zenana Mission Society, CEZMS School, Singapore) were independent-minded and strong-willed enough for their decisions to have succeeded. The Methodist women, in contrast, belonged to, and were agents of, the Women's Foreign Missionary Society [WFMS] (founded in 1869) which had always been a separate, independent part of the American Methodist Episcopal Church General Board. In Malaya the Methodist women had been invited by their Methodist male colleagues to join the First Annual Meeting in 1889, and by the early 1890s were holding their own Women's Conference as an integral though separate part of each annual meeting.[48] Thus it seems possible to conclude that white men did not exert dominant control over the nature, or speed, of the introduction and expansion of sport into English-language girls' schools in Malaya.

The most important factors determining what sports and games were introduced, when, and how quickly, were the attitudes and personalities of the women educators themselves, their perceptions of what would be helpful and appropriate for Asian girls and acceptable to their parents, and their knowledge of what was possible in relation to available space, finances and staff teaching skills. In many ways they were able to act quite independently and could be pioneering and innovative. Hence they could often keep pace with, and sometimes even be ahead of, metropolitan or other colonial situations. For example, in the United States and in the Philippines basketball was deliberately restricted as a sport for both American and Filipino girls from about the 1910s because it was considered unsuitably competitive and unladylike. Yet in Malaya it was introduced around the time of the First World War, and quickly grew in popularity so that even some inter-school matches and competitions were being played by the 1920s, with many more by the 1930s.[49]

III

Paucity of evidence does not enable a detailed chronological record to be given of the development and progress of sports for Asian girls from the 1890s to the 1930s. The available source materials are strangely and infuriatingly silent about the curricula of girls' schools in general, and sport in particular. That various types of physical education and games were initiated at certain times and then subsequently expanded can be inferred from the occasional scattered references. Although the information is fragmentary it suggests the trends. Much of it comes from the American Methodist women teachers, and it seems correct to conclude that where they led, others followed.

As already noted, from the late nineteenth century missionary women educators regarded the personal fitness and physical development of the individual Asian girl as integral parts of the educational process, even if they had to pursue these cautiously. However, it is unclear exactly when physical exercise in any form was introduced into Malayan girls' schools, although it was almost certainly during the 1890s, for a brief description of the Methodist Treacher Girls' School in Taiping in 1901 reveals that 'lively gymnastic exercises with piano accompaniment' were already an established part of the curriculum.[50] Indeed, the writer recommended that, in the apparently already competitive world of educational provision, 'the way to hold our own with other schools, especially the Catholics, is to take advantage of every help in the way of the best and newest educational methods, music, *calisthenics,* and trained teachers for the kindergarten'.[51] Physical education had become, she reported delightedly,

> one of the most profitable features of the school. It has not only benefitted the children mentally and physically but has elicited the interest of persons who have given financial and other aid to the school. We have held a monthly gymnastic competition for which prizes have been kindly presented by ladies of Taipeng.[52]

Regrettably, there is no evidence to indicate why the 'ladies' had decided to endow the school in this way, nor exactly what the gymnastics involved.

From the 1890s up to the First World War it seems that 'drill', gym and callisthenics, involving mechanical forms of exercise, were part of the regular educational programme in a number of the English-language girls' schools. In the Methodist Girls' Schools it can be assumed that these sorts of exercise were performed as a minimum, even if organized sport was not possible. Whether the then existing convents also required their students to take exercise is not known, although by the 1920s convent girls were certainly doing at least 'musical drill'.[53] Until the First World War the opportunity for physical education or athletics to be part of the girls' schools' curricula, other than as 'genteel exercises', was restricted. This was partly due to the limited interpretation of what 'physical education' meant at the time.[54] More importantly Asian girls then, even those at school, did not go out much, so any exercises they performed had to be 'intra-mural', and anyway their customary clothes severely restricted movement. Methodist Miss Bunce described the girls' typical dress around 1908: 'They wore long sleeves, long sarongs, long kabayas, long oily hair securely pinned in place with five long spikes'.[55] When they did venture out in public from school, perhaps to church, the missionary ladies escorted them, 'the older ones loaded into rickshaws and shielded from the gaze of men by a black oil cloth, covering them to the eyes'.[56]

Traditional Asian attitudes concerning acceptable and appropriate behaviour for young females also greatly restricted the girls' physical mobility and freedom. Mabel Marsh attributed the then limited development of all physical education in girls' schools in this period primarily to the attitudes of parents 'who considered a too free movement of the body as a sign of immodesty, and certainly would never have consented to outdoor sports in the open'.[57] Yet, as we shall see, by the 1920s a revolution had occurred. Meanwhile, traditional attitudes not only restricted participation in physical exercise, but mitigated against Asian girls being taught at home to use their leisure time in useful or enjoyable play. Missionaries believed that as a result any natural play instincts which survived childhood were often transposed into the 'gambling sort'. Mabel Marsh had a theory that the Chinese were inveterate gamblers because 'they have never had the play instinct developed and do not know a better way of spending their leisure time'.[58] One of the missionaries' objectives in teaching games was thus to impart beneficial use of leisure time. Given general Asian attitudes about physical exercise and play for females, it was therefore a significant achievement that even 'genteel exercises' were introduced to girls' school curricula, especially at such an early date. Although the exercises may have been performed behind closed school doors, away from the prying eyes of men, white and Asian, the remarkable point was that they were done at all.

Gymnastic exercise, limited as it might have been, laid the foundation on which later progress in sport was made. At the same time games-playing by Europeans generally, and by white women in particular, offered Asians practical examples of the importance their white rulers placed on exercise in the organization and peformance of colonial rule. Sport for European women in Malaya had become increasingly possible and popular from the 1880s and 1890s, with croquet, tennis and golf being generally available. Sometimes women initiated their own sports clubs or competitions independently of men; for instance the Ladies' Lawn Tennis Club (LLTC) of Singapore was founded in 1884 and the first Women's Golf Competition began in KL in 1897. By the 1890s swimming, too, had gained general acceptance, although at first women had to swim on separate 'Ladies' Days'.[59] Western women's enjoyment of games was openly observable and in addition, the missionary women themselves acted as role models for both their girl students and the girls' parents. When other Europeans commonly travelled in horse-drawn carriages, rickshaws and subsequently motor cars, missionary women typically rode bicycles, frequently in the face of opposition from their fellow whites who thought they were 'letting the side down' and probably exposing the whole community to ridicule. They ignored the criticism. Even in the mid-1920s Josephine Foss, as headmistress of PES, rode a bicycle until advised by her doctor to acquire a car because of the special demands of her work in the heat.[60] Missionary women also provided examples of 'rational' dress because, while conforming to the usual pattern of 'tropical kit' – long serge skirts, blouses and hats – for European females, they did not follow fashion but typically wore plain, practical, sensible clothes. When dress reform came after the First World War they changed with it.[61]

In the 1910s developments in the Methodist Girls' Schools in particular helped to pave the way further for the inter-war revolution in sports for Asian girls. Although 'drill' and mechanical forms of exercise with 'wands, dumb-bells and Indian clubs' continued to be common, the girls were by then also taking part in organized sports days, even with boys. Mabel Marsh records that the MGS KL Sports Day of 1913 was quite a success, the girls participating 'with fervour'.[62] The following year on Patrons' Day the girls 'all engaged in races, winning many prizes', and later that year the Government Boys' School invited the MGS to attend and participate in their own Sports Day. The MGS accepted 'and many of our girls carried off prizes', the Women's Conference minutes recorded.[63] Not only were these sports days held out in the open with spectators watching, but in some instances they were co-educational, an event that would have been unthinkable even a few years before.

From the First World War changes and developments in sports available for Asian girls, and in games-playing by them, seemed to occur rapidly if unevenly. Progress in the types of physical exercise and sports, and in acceptable forms of dress for white women were transferred in turn, sometimes quite speedily, to Asian females. Throughout the 1920s badminton, tennis, netball and basketball grew in popularity and availability. In 1921 Asian girls studying to be Bible Women at the Methodist Eveland Training Centre in Singapore played badminton on their own court. Physical culture was also part of the curriculum since their teachers believed in the principle that ' "all work and no play" makes girls dull just as it does Jack'.[64]

By the 1920s many Asian girls were also playing tennis, not only for exercise at school, but sometimes in competitions in public for prizes. The first recorded tennis tournament between young Asian ladies was played in 1924 in highly conservative Malacca, on the Methodist Epworth League courts, for prizes donated by local Chinese leaders. Many of those present could still remember the days when Chinese women were carried about in sacks 'for fear of being seen'. So it was hardly surprising that the tournament aroused both enthusiasm and opposition. Even so those who watched were apparently impressed, and overall gave approval for such tournaments provided they were 'conducted under proper supervision'.

Mr Tan Cheng Lock, Malacca's Chinese representative on the Malayan
Legislative Council, enthusiastically though somewhat inaccurately
'complimented the young ladies on their pioneer skills and [their] courage
in being roadmakers and pioneers in introducing wholesome games to the
womanhood of Malacca'.[65]

By the 1930s the progress made in sports in all girls' schools was
obvious. The 'mechanical' sorts of exercise which, even in the 1920s, had
remained fairly common, had largely given way to 'a happier, freer, more
satisfactory type of physical culture'.[66] Its hallmarks were team games,
with concomitant methods of organization, dress reform, and choice from
a wide variety of possible sports, including tennis, badminton, netball,
basketball, volleyball, quoits, ping pong, swimming and athletics, notably
relay games.[67] In the early days whether any physical instruction could be
given or not had partly depended on the room available in each school.
Most girls' schools had begun in Chinese shop houses, without adequate
space even for a playground, let alone for organized sport. Sometimes the
facilities of boys' schools or of organizations such as the Young Women's
Christian Association (YWCA) and Young Men's Christian Association
(YMCA) would be 'borrowed'.[68] By the 1930s adequate playground space
was considered 'a very necessary part of a school's needs these days when
girls are keen on all kind [sic] of sports, play good tennis, have inter-
school contests in netball and badminton and are coming to demand
hockey fields'.[69] Despite the need and the demand, not all girls' schools
had their own facilities, although most offered some choice of games.
Where possible, as finances allowed, larger premises with land had been
purchased – for example by Pudu and by some of the MGS. But neither of
the two 'flagship' MGS – MGS, KL and MGS Fairfield, Singapore – had
sufficient playing space to meet their girls' enthusiasm for extra-
curricular games.[70]

Despite insufficient facilities, the demand for, and popularity of, games
among Asian girls was reinforced by Education Department regulations
concerning both provision of physical exercise and of playing space for it.
By 1932 the FMS Education Annual Report stated baldly: 'In all English
girls' schools drill and games are now compulsory as in boys' schools'.[71]
Which games were available varied from school to school. Some had been
providing tennis and badminton in the 1920s, and by the early 1930s a
few offered basketball or netball too. These three team sports were the
main games played in girls' schools throughout the rest of the decade,[72]
their popularity confirmed by scattered evidence from individual schools.
At St Mary's, KL, in 1935 inter-school netball and badminton matches
were played, while at the CEZMS School in Singapore, where drill had
always been encouraged, progress in the 1930s was recorded in all three
games. Similarly at Pudu in KL by the mid-1930s the girls were enthusiastically playing all three and also volleyball: yet as late as 1929
many of the teaching staff had been apathetic about sport for their
students. In the same decade even swimming was fast gaining popularity.
Although schools like PES did not have their own pool facilities, they

made use of those of others such as the Victoria Institution, a major KL boys' school.[73]

Growth in the provision and popularity of games in the inter-war era was not confined to Asian girls in English-language schools. Although British colonial policy prevented missionary activity among rural Malays, even in those conservative Muslim Malay communities, games and physical education were allowed into the school curriculum. Thus by the early 1930s, perhaps amazingly, physical training was part of the weekly timetable in the Malay girls' vernacular schools, initially consisting of drill plus lessons in practical hygiene, but soon accompanied also by dancing and folk games. In 1935 when the Malay Women Teachers' Training College opened in Malacca it was recorded that among the teacher trainees 'Great keenness was exhibited at the start over badminton, netball and tennikoit [deck tennis] and there was soon marked improvement in skill, alertness and sense of play'. They were also taught class drill, country dancing and rhythm, and badminton tournaments were held too.[74]

Team games and the new style physical culture required methods of organization and other developments which reflected those of the metropolitan countries. The girls wore uniforms and were organized into groups or divisions similar to the house system, with captains, and teachers attached. Sports equipment was provided from central 'pools', shields and trophies were initiated. Sports days, inter-school 'friendly' matches, and occasional challenges and tournaments became common place, though the timing and pace of their introduction varied. As already noted, the MGS in KL had held annual sports days since at least 1913; by the late 1930s tournaments, notably in net/basketball and badminton, were also regular features.[75] By comparison it was not until 1935 that St Mary's, KL, tried 'for the first time, a real big sports day' on playing fields borrowed from the government boys' school. According to acting headmistress Miss Sprenger 'it was quite a success', much enjoyed by the girls, who competed for prizes bought from money donated by parents and friends.[76] One of Pudu's annual sports days, held on Empire Day in May 1935, is described in the first school magazine. With the girls in their purple and white uniforms, the school presented 'a wonderful spectacle', schoolgirl writer Lum Lai Ngor recorded. Watched by many spectators the programme included a children's crawling race, an obstacle race, a slow bicycle race, and an inter-school relay, which the MGS won, as well as a display of country dancing.[77]

IV

By the 1930s the effects of sports for Asian girls who had experienced an English-language education seemed both revolutionary and miraculous, particularly to the white women educators who had introduced games-playing. Summed up in two words – 'freedom' and 'independence' – they included dress reform, open participation in activities in public, physical emancipation, improved health, and enjoyment of life. But in assessing exactly what role sports and games had played, it was difficult to separate cause and effect. Mabel Marsh posed the problem:

> As one views this modern miracle, one wonders which came first – whether the sports made possible the freedom or whether the new freedom adopted the sports as its best means of expression.[78]

Whatever the case, a new freedom there certainly was, and sport was an integral part of it. Changes in dress were one of the most obvious manifestations. In sporting developments for Asian girls dress reform played a fundamental role. It was simply impossible to play energetic games like basketball and badminton, or to swim competitively, in traditional costumes and hair styles. Before 1930 skirts were already at knee level, sometimes even briefer, and hair was commonly short and un-oiled.[79]

Moreover the participation in sports which this dress reform enabled was increasingly carried out in public. So was the cycling which, by the 1930s, on cheap Japanese bicycles, was already immensely popular with Malayan youth, and which itself played a prime role in bringing Asian girls out into the public arena. Gertrude Owen, Young Women's Christian Association (YWCA) General Secretary for Malaya, emphasized the role of the bicycle as a means of female emancipation by the 1930s:

> This might be called 'the age of the bicycle' for it is bringing freedom to the young in an astonishing way. Who has not been amazed at the sight of the young Sikh, Malay, [and] Chinese school girls on their bicycles as they dash to school, or in boy and girl parties taking the air round the town's [Kuala Lumpur] beauty spots.[80]

Many girls were by now enjoying the same sorts of physical exercise and games as those enjoyed by Asian boys, notably badminton, basketball, volleyball, cycling and swimming.[81] Often the girls were playing them better. As the Straits Settlements Educational Annual Report for 1935 records:

> The standard of drill and games in the girls' schools was reported by the local Inspector of Schools to be markedly higher than that in the boys' schools, due to the large proportion of efficient women teachers and to the enthusiasm and interest they showed in the subject.[82]

The higher standards of girls' sport reflected the importance placed on physical education for girls, the new attitudes to it, and also the increasing demand for games in the inter-war period from the girls themselves.

Like the teachers, they too showed enthusiasm and interest, and they had fun playing. When they participated in some real sport the joy on their faces was obvious.[83] In fact what was more surprising was the girl who was uninterested:

> Show me a girl who does not enjoy such games and I will show you a girl whose home environment has inhibited all her desire for self-expression, or else one who is physically unfit to play[84]

asserted Mabel Marsh. Through the medium of sport the natural human instinct to play and to gamble had been turned to the benefit of the girls, and their physical and social emancipation.

As noted earlier, the women educators were also convinced that sport was contributing to the evolution of beneficial social and moral attitudes. As pride and loyalty were created in the individual school, the girls learnt self-control, the spirit of co-operation and fair play developed, and better understanding flowered between teachers and pupils. According to Miss Marsh, through games-playing: 'Racial discriminations are forgotten and self-interest sinks itself to the interest of the larger group – all spiritual by-products of the new Sports era'.[85] Eight years later the Methodist Report of 1938 echoed her sentiments. Apart from illustrating the freedom girls now had, outdoor games, it said, 'are breaking down racial antipathies and fostering friendliness between schools that a decade ago were bitter rivals'.[86] Methodist educators like Mabel Marsh also argued that morally sport resulted in a general decrease in vice as Asians who had once flaunted it openly, particularly opium-smoking and prostitution, instead took to playing badminton or tennis.[87]

Although the Chinese and Indian girls who formed the bulk of the Malayan English-language girls' schools population benefited more than Malay girls from sporting developments, nevertheless by the 1930s increasing numbers of Malay girls were attending schools such as MGS, and playing games.[88] They were said to be particularly gifted in 'rhythmics' 'with a special flair for all sorts of games.'[89] To Mabel Marsh the coming out of the Malay girls was one of the greatest satisfactions of all her work in Malaya. By the inter-war period the Chinese and Indian women were, she said, a generation ahead in learning, but Malay women were starting to take their place beside them, especially those with an English-language education.[90] It would be these Malay women who would direct the next generation 'toward better homes, a finer conception of life, better health and all the other blessings that follow in the train of an educated womanhood'.[91]

Taking physical exercise and playing games definitely contributed to improved health and healthier bodies for girls, which led in turn to other benefits. Commenting on Chinese women in particular, Mrs Ho Seng Ong, an MGS graduate and wife of one of Malaya's first Asian Methodist padres and headmasters, writing in 1927, noted that

> The woman of to-day is stronger and healthier. . . .. If she lives a

physical culture life, joins in all the outdoor sports that are offered to her, she cannot but develop a strong healthy body. When her body is healthy, her mind is healthy, her children will be healthy, and her home will be happy.[92]

Being healthier women meant not only having physically improved bodies from taking physical exercise, but also being able to obtain medical treatment when necessary, especially for specifically female needs. By bringing girls out in public, physical education and sport had, according to the Report of the 1938 Methodist Annual Conference, 'made it easier for girls to visit our hospitals and receive scientific treatment for ailments than when women were secluded behind brick walls'.[93]

The physically active and healthy girl also enjoyed life more, a feature which the missionaries as well as Mrs Ho had observed. Girls who, through games, gained physical emancipation, had much richer lives, they concluded. This new richness combined the girls' physical freedom with their enjoyment of various extra-mural activities, including sport, and the ability to choose their own lifestyle and perhaps a career too. Mabel Marsh commented with delight on MGS girls who once had been 'so stilted' but who, by the 1930s, were able to 'talk and laugh with a freedom born of a love of life with no fear of let or hindrance . . . and [with] a more sane and wholesome outlook on life in general'.[94] Their new-found emancipation and attitudes were typified by their physical freedom and their enjoyment of sport.

V

Although the material presented in this study raises more questions than currently available sources can answer, it is clear that what the white women missionary educators achieved by introducing sport along with English-language education for at least a proportion of Asian girls was quite revolutionary. Although constrained in the types of physical exercise they could initiate by both Asian and European attitudes, particularly in the decades before the First World War, these women nevertheless transferred to conservative Asian communities new beliefs about the importance of bodily health to, and thus new approaches towards physical exercise for, Asian girls. Moreover, this happened at almost the same time as, or not long after, similar developments were taking place in the West. Indeed, available sports for white females in Malaya seem to have been more circumscribed in some ways than those for Asian girls. Although sport for Asian females remained mostly separate from that of men, by the inter-war period mixing between the sexes on school sports days, while riding bicycles, and at leisure times, became increasingly common. The attitudes of white women educators, affected no doubt by the aims of the Victorian and early twentieth-century women's movement, led to the introduction of physical exercise for Asian girls who, as a result, were able virtually to 'jump' a generation in their progress towards equality and equal opportunities with men.

By the 1930s it was obvious that some astonishing changes had occurred. In less than four decades from the 1890s to the 1930s the lifestyles of many Asian girls and women had been transformed. From an almost purdah-like seclusion, at least for some, many had become almost as emancipated as their Western sisters. To many observers Asian girls who played sport or had regular physical training at school were noticeably happier, healthier and more independent. At school they were playing games once considered strictly for men only, and often they were playing in teams of mixed ethnic and social groups.[95]

The women educators had apparently achieved their aims. By locating physical exercise and sports within girls' schools and under women's control they were able to gain the benefits that sport offered physically, mentally and practically, and in the emancipation of women, without being accused of trying to 'masculinize' the Asian girls in their care. But to what extent did sport act as a powerful factor of moral, social and physical discipline for females as it was meant to for Asian males when introduced and developed by their colonial masters? By introducing sport for Asian males, white men apparently hoped to control social change for colonial subjects in ways that benefited the British Empire and colonial rule. The same objectives do not seem appropriate to white women educators. They were not aiming to exercise power over Asian girls or to acculturate them through sport into good colonial subjects. Their objectives and intentions were more humanist and international, and more subtle. They saw what they perceived as 'needs' and attempted to fill them. Asian girls and women were physically and psychologically restricted from fulfilling their potential by a variety of customs and attitudes which, in the world that was developing as a result of the industrial and technological revolutions, seemed increasingly anachronistic. The missionary educators wanted therefore to enable Asian girls to break free by passing to them the benefits they themselves had experienced through education, and especially physical exercise, since physical freedom was absolutely essential to female emancipation.[96] Thus they would fulfil their Christian calling and their sense of sisterhood, and at the same time liberate themselves also from many of the prevailing Victorian and Edwardian precepts of femininity.

McCrone has argued that sport has considerable potential for social disruption since it enables groups outside accepted institutions of power and of social norms to challenge existing political and social arrangements.[97] This study suggests that for some Asian girls in Malaya the sporting revolution, together with English-language education of which it was a part, helped challenge both Asian male views of the abilities and worth of Asian females, and Western colonial views of Asian subjects. Perceptions of women were revised, albeit sometimes with antagonism. One newspaper writer in 1933, claiming to speak on behalf of Western and Asian men, expressed horror at the modern, sport-playing, dancing, eman-

cipated Chinese girl in the Malaya of the 1930s whom he regarded as an
unacceptably 'ultra-modern development'.[98] Sport helped to transform
and liberate Asian females by helping to free them from both Eastern and
Western male perceptions of the appropriate roles, behaviour and social
relations for women generally. But just how important sport was as a
measure of social change, emancipation and greater equality for girls has
yet to be determined.

Currently not enough is known about the story of sport for Asian girls
in Malaya during the period between the 1890s and the 1930s for a full
understanding of the effects, implications and significance of sport within
the different Asian communities. It has been argued by various observers
and analysts of sport in the West that sport is 'a cultural artefact' both
determining and reflecting the dominant values of society.[99] It may well
have been doing just that for the white women educators who introduced
to Malaya Western sport for girls. But how could it be doing the same for
the Asian communities to whom it was introduced? What role, if any, did
games and sport play traditionally in their cultures? Much remains to be
done to identify and analyse the role of sport in the Malayan colonial
context generally, and for Asian females in particular.[100] What can be
concluded is that sport contributed to, and was a significant part of, the
social change that Asian females experienced over four decades. During
this period emancipation and liberation developed apace both for them
and for their Western educators. In the decades before the Second World
War Asian girls achieved various Malayan 'firsts' – the first female to pass
the Senior Cambridge certificate, the first woman doctor, the first woman
lawyer – together with gaining increasing freedom of, and control over, the
use of their own bodies, especially as dress reform progressed. In a mere 40
years they had advanced from being carried in 'sacks' or covered carriages
to riding bicycles and playing games in public.

The missionary women educators who had played such a fundamental
role in the changes that Asian girls had experienced, and from whom it
seemed the girls had benefited in various ways, could feel a degree of
pride in the successes they had achieved. Not only had a proportion of
Asian girls been able to develop at least healthy bodies, but at the same
time many were better prepared physiologically and psychologically to
take their place in the new Malaya that was emerging in the early
twentieth century. They formed an invaluable part of the foundation on
which an independent nation was later built. The values and advantages
they had gained would, many felt, serve them the rest of their days while
also reflecting commendably the efforts of the missionaries. As the Head
of the Standard Oil Company in Malaya remarked to Mabel Marsh in
March 1942, having watched the fall of Malaya to the Japanese:

> I have spent my life making money and working up a big business
> that is now all destroyed. You [missionaries] have spent your lives
> building character and personality. Nothing can destroy your
> work.[101]

In that work, it is suggested here, modern sport played a significant, perhaps revolutionary, part.

NOTES

1. J[osephine] Foss, MBE, 'The Education of Girls in Malaya', *St Andrews Outlook*, No. 83 (December 1935), 13. Note: the term Malaya is used in this essay to cover the Straits Settlements (SS), the Federated and Unfederated Malay States (FMS and UFMS), and the Borneo States.
2. Mabel Marsh, 'The New Freedom and Athletics in Girls' Schools', *Malaysia Message* 40, 11 (November 1930), 22.
3. Marsh, ibid., 7 and 22; E. [Thirza] Bunce, 'After Twenty-Five Years', *St Andrews Outlook*, No. 84 (April 1936), 41; Foss, 'Education of Girls', 11, 13.
4. On developments in Britain and America see J.A. Mangan and Roberta J. Park (eds.), *From 'Fair Sex' to Feminism: Sport and the Socialization of Women in the Industrial and Post-industrial Eras* (London, 1987) and Kathleen E. McCrone, *Sport and the Physical Emancipation of English Women 1870-1914* (London, 1988). There are also various articles scattered through the *International Journal of the History of Sport (IJHS)*.
5. This has been a commonly held view. For a discussion relevant to this article see Helen Callaway, *Gender, Culture and Empire: European Women in Colonial Nigeria* (London, 1987); Claudia Knapman, *White Women in Fiji 1835-1930: The Ruin of Empire?* (Sydney, 1986); and Margaret MacMillan, *Women of the Raj* (London, 1988).
6. The issue of sport and the socialization and control of women in Western societies and parts of the British Empire are discussed in, for example, Mangan and Park, op. cit., and J.A. Mangan, 'The Social Construction of Victorian Femininity: Emancipation, Education and Exercise', *IJHS* 6, 1 (May 1989), 1-9. On this subject for the Philippines see Janice A. Beran, 'Americans in the Philippines: Imperialism or Progress through Sport?', *IJHS* 6, 1 (May 1989), 62-87.
7. This is a paraphrase of the definition by Roberta J. Park in 'Sport, Gender and Society in a Transatlantic Victorian Perspective' in Mangan and Park, op. cit., p.58, and Mangan, op. cit., 1.
8. Some work has been done on sport and men in the British Empire, for example in India and the Sudan. But the issues of girls' education and the introduction of sport in the West are only now receiving serious study – see Mangan and Park, op. cit., and McCrone, op. cit.
9. Records which were lost include annual and teachers' reports, photographs, copies of registers, school magazines and so on. The writer has already researched most of the extant Anglican records. Some published Methodist records are available in Singapore but holdings at Methodist Board Head Quarters in New York have yet to be identified. For the Roman Catholic convents little is known about their records and any holdings at the mother house in France have yet to be explored.
10. These include the Educational *Annual Reports* of the Straits Settlements (SS) from the 1890s and the chapters on Education contained within the *Annual Reports* of the Federated Malay States (FMS) from the 1910s together with individual state reports in the 1890s and 1900s.
11. For example: *Education in Malaya*, Malayan Series, No XIV (Singapore, 1923), pp. 1-34, girls mentioned on pp. 20, 28-30 only; H.R. Cheeseman, 'Education in Malaya, 1900-1941', *Malayan Historical Journal 2*, 1 (July 1955), 30-47 – girls' education mentioned 32 and 41-2; Francis Wong, 'The Christian Missions and Education in Malaysia

and Singapore', *Teacher Education in New Countries* 12, 2 (1971), 143–53; and Philip Loh Fook-Seng, 'A Review of the Educational Developments in the Federated Malay States to 1939', *Journal of South East Asian Studies* 5, 2 (1974), 225–38, does not mention girls.

12. Hugh Bryson, 'The Education of Girls in the Nineteenth Century', *Malaysia* (November 1970), 11–14.

13. The first convent was opened in Singapore in the 1850s: S. Jenkins, *Where There is Darkness* (Kuala Lumpur, n.d.), p. 60.

14. Ruth M. Harvey, 'Girls', *Malaysia Message* 47, 2 (February 1937), 16.

15. Sources include Rev. H. P. Thompson, *Educational Missions at Work* (London, 1938), pp. 8–11; Helen B. Montgomery, *Western Women in Eastern Lands* (New York, 1910); James L. Barton, *Educational Missions* (New York, 1913), Ch. 5; and Ruth Rouse, 'The Ideal of Womanhood as a Factor in Missionary Work', *International Review of Missions* II (London, 1913), 148–64.

16. Montgomery, op. cit., *passim*; Rouse, op. cit.

17. W. T. C., 'Woman's Work in Malaysia', *Malaysia Message* 20, 9 (June 1911), 67.

18. Mabel Marsh, *A Wagon That Was Hitched to a Star* (privately published, Singapore, c. 1927), pp. 81, 90.

19. W. T. C., 'Woman's Work'.

20. Ibid., 66.

21. Harvey, 'Girls', 16.

22. Ibid.; Marsh, *A Wagon*, p. 53 and Mabel Marsh, *Service Suspended* (New York, 1968), *passim*.

23. Marsh, *A Wagon*, p. 53, and see also p. 34.

24. Ibid., p. 34 and *passim*, and Marsh, *Service Suspended, passim*.

25. 'Lady Guillemard Opens Malacca School-Buildings', *Malaysia Message* 36, 7 (April 1927), 12.

26. Josephine Foss, 'Not Worth A Bullet', *Autobiography*, p. 21, Mss, United Society for the Propagation of the Gospel (USPG) Files, held in Rhodes House, Oxford.

27. Foss, 'Education of Girls', 11; 'The Modern Girl in Malaya', *Malaysia Message* 34, 7 (April 1924), 46–7; John Skrine, Foreword, in John Gullick, *Josephine Foss and the Pudu English School* (Petaling Jaya, 1988), p. vii.

28. Foss, 'Education of Girls', 13.

29. Ibid., 11; see also 'Modern Girl', op. cit., 46; Resident Councillor's remarks in 'Lady Guillemard', 11–12.

30. 'Sidelights from the Malaysia Woman's Conference', *Malaysia Message* 30, 7 (April 1921), 52; Resident Councillor's remarks in 'Lady Guillemard', 11–12; 'Miss Olsen and a Chinese Girls' Boarding School', *Roda* 4, 11 (May 1935), 725, 727.

31. General Report of Girls' Schools – 1938, in *Minutes of the Malaya Annual Conference*, 46th Session, Methodist Episcopal Church, (Singapore, January 1938), p. 69.

32. No evidence on the nuns' views on, or participation in, sports has yet been located. But Beran makes the point for the Philippines, op. cit., 79.

33. Park, 'Sport, Gender and Society', pp. 65ff; Notes of a conversation between Professor Roberta Park and the writer at University of California, Berkeley, 2 November 1989; Beran, 'Americans in the Philippines', 72.

34. Marsh, *A Wagon*, pp. 1–2, and *Service Suspended*, p. 51. As yet no further biographical details, including her educational qualifications, have been found for Mabel Marsh.

35. Minutes of the Woman's Conference of Malaysia Mission, February 1915, in *Minutes of the Twenty Third Session of the Malaysia Conference*, Methodist Episcopal Church, Singapore 1915, pp. 90–1.

36. Janice A. Beran, 'Daughters of the Middle Border, Iowa Women in Sport and Physical Activity 1850–1910', *Iowa State Journal of Research* 62, 2 (November 1987), 161–81. In the copy which Professor Beran sent to the writer she has given additional information by hand on women from states other than Iowa: 165. See also Janice A. Beran, 'Playing to the Right Drummer: Girls' Basketball in Iowa, 1892–1927' in Roberta J. Park (ed.), *Centennial Issue of Research Quarterly for Exercise and Sport* (Reston, VA, 1985), 78–85.

37. Marsh, *Service Suspended*, p. 154.

38. Marsh, *A Wagon*, p. 22; Bunce, op. cit., 41–2 and Richard J.H. Sidney, *In British Malaya Today* (London, c. 1927), p. 178.
39. Foss, *Autobiography*, espec. Chs 1 and 2; Gullick, *Josephine Foss, passim*. Josephine Foss was a missionary in China between 1914 and 1919 where she saw the extreme poverty and difficult conditions of many of the people at close hand. She also observed the sufferings and problems of women with bound feet. See *Autobiography* Ch. 2. Pudu School was begun in 1915 by an elderly missionary from a comfortable middle-class English background, Miss Elinor Gage-Brown – see Gullick, *Josephine Foss*, pp. 28–50. Josephine Foss lodged with the American Methodist women in KL in their Women's Mission House on a bed-and-breakfast basis until her own house at Pudu was ready, *Autobiography*, p. 33.
40. On boys' athletics see J.A. Mangan, *Athleticism in the Victorian and Edwardian Public School – The Emergence and Consolidation of an Educational Ideology* (Cambridge, 1981). On girls and games in Britain see Mangan and Park, op. cit., and McCrone, op. cit., The British belief in exercise is discussed in John G. Butcher, *The British in Malaya 1880–1941* (Kuala Lumpur, 1979), *passim* and in my forthcoming thesis: Janice N. Brownfoot, 'White Female Society in Colonial Malaya 1890–1941'.
41. Methodist philosophy is outlined in 'The Aim of Methodism's Schools in Malaya', The Bishop's Page, *Malaysia Message* 36, 11/12, (August/September 1927), 10–11. See also Marsh, *Service Suspended*, pp. 46, 64–5 and Bunce, op. cit., 41. For Miss Foss's views see Foss, 'Education of Girls', 11 and 13, and *Autobiography, passim*. For the Philippines, cf. Beran, 'Americans in the Philippines', 76–7.
42. Marsh, 'The New Freedom', p. 22. Compare also Beran on the Philippines, 'Americans in the Philippines', 81–2.
43. Olsen, 'Miss Olsen', 725, 727, 729; and cf. Beran, 'Americans in the Philippines', 72, 81 – American teachers there thought sport and play one of the best ways of preparing Filipinos for democracy and self-government.
44. Marsh, *Service Suspended*, p. 48. By the inter-war period Methodist Girls' Schools had Chinese, Eurasian, Indian, Malay and a few European students. In MGS, KL by 1939/40 1 in 7 of the girls was a Malay, with a total of 113: Marsh, *Service Suspended*, p. 64.
45. Ibid., pp. 46, 48–9. American teachers in the Philippines thought likewise: Beran, 'Americans in the Philippines', 82. On vice in Asian societies: Marsh, *A Wagon*, pp. 29–30.
46. Mangan and Park, op. cit.; McCrone, op. cit.
47. Conclusions on the Colonial Education Department are made from the information contained in the Education *Annual Reports* for the SS and FMS. Government grants-in-aid and funding enabled girls from poor backgrounds to attend school.
48. Comments on Anglicans deduced from such sources as the *Annual Reports* written by the various women missionaries on their schools. On Methodist women see notes 30, 31 and 35, plus the Annual Woman's Conference Reports contained in the *Malaysia Message* each year.
49. Beran, 'Americans in the Philippines', 75 and Beran, 'Playing to the Right Drummer', 80, 81.
50. Mrs W. E. Curtis, 'Treacher Girls' School, Taipeng', *Malaysia Message* X, 7 (April 1901), 86.
51. Ibid., emphasis added.
52. Ibid.
53. Sidney, op. cit., p. 175.
54. In part a reflection of its nature in the metropolitan countries where in the late Victorian period physical exercise for girls frequently consisted of Swedish gymnastics: see Mangan and Park, op. cit., especially Chapters 5 and 6; and McCrone, op. cit., *passim*.
55. Buncce, op. cit. 41. A 'kabaya' is a long, fitted blouse.
56. Ibid. Miss Bunce is talking here about both day and boarding girls as the schools had both.
57. Marsh, 'The New Freedom', 7.

58. Marsh, *A Wagon*, p.91, and 'The New Freedom', 7.
59. Information on European women and their clubs is taken from Chapter 4 of my forthcoming thesis, 'White Female Society'.
60. Foss, *Autobiography*, p.32–3; Gullick, op. cit., p.55.
61. This is clear from photographs in the magazines of the period, e.g. the Methodist *Malaysia Message*, and the Anglican *Mission Field*.
62. Marsh, *A Wagon*, p.91.
63. Minutes of the Women's Conference, 1915, op. cit., p.100.
64. Miss C.E. Jackson, 'Eveland Training School', *Malaysia Message* 31, 1 (October 1921), 2.
65. 'Modern Girl', op. cit., p.47, and 'Two History Making Events', *Malaysia Message* 34, 7 (April 1924), 48–9.
66. Marsh, 'The New Freedom', 7.
67. Ibid.
68. The YWCA was a great initiator and supporter of sports for Asian women and girls, and provided various sporting facilities at most of its branches throughout Malaya. On the history of the YWCA in Malaya see Janice N. Brownfoot, ' "Sisters under the Skin" – Imperialism and the Emancipation of Women in Malaya c. 1891 to 1941', in J.A. Mangan (ed.), *Making Imperial Mentalities* (Manchester, 1990).
69. General Report of Girls' Schools, 1938, op. cit., p.67.
70. On the MGS see ibid. On Pudu see Foss, *Autobiography*, pp.31, 36, 43, and Gullick, op. cit., pp.53, 61.
71. M.B. Shelley, Acting Chief Secretary, FMS, *Annual Report for 1932* (Kuala Lumpur, 1933), Chapter IX, 'Education', p.52.
72. The Education Reports in the FMS and SS *Annual Reports/Records* for the 1930s make this clear.
73. For St Mary's see Miss O. Sprenger, Report [for St Mary's, KL] for 1935, Missionary Reports, Diocese of Singapore, USPG, E1935, [p.3]. For the CEZMS see K.J. Macfee and F.I. Codrington (compilers), *Eastern Schools and School Girls* (London, n.d.), p.68. On Pudu see Foss, *Autobiography*, p.43 and Gullick, op. cit., p.71.
74. Quote from FMS *Annual Report for 1935* (London, 1936), Chapter IX, Education, p.70. Malay Girls' schools are mentioned in most FMS *Annual Reports* on Education in the 1930s, especially 1933, 1935, and 1936, and in the SS *Educational Annual Report for 1935*.
75. Marsh, *Service Suspended*, pp.68, 78. In 1930 Mabel Marsh recommended that each child should pay $1 into a Central Sports Fund for each school to help pay for the purchase, use and upkeep of sporting equipment, and to help develop a sense of responsibility towards it: Marsh, 'The New Freedom', 22.
76. Sprenger, Report for St Mary's, 1935.
77. Lum Lai Ngor, 'Annual Sports', *Semper Fidelis, Pudu English School Magazine* (Kuala Lumpur, 1935), p.6, filed at Missionary Reports, Diocese of Singapore, USPG, E1935.
78. Marsh, 'The New Freedom', 7.
79. Ibid.; Bunce, op. cit., p.41; 'Emancipated Chinese Womanhood', article from the *Singapore Free Press*, reproduced in *British Malaya* 8, 6 (October 1933), 133.
80. Gertrude Owen, M.B.E., 'Aspirations of the Malayan Girls', *St. Andrews Outlook*, No. 84 (April, 1936), 36–7. The YWCA was itself of considerable importance in sponsoring and developing sport for women and girls in Malaya, see Brownfoot, 'Sisters under the Skin'.
81. However, the most popular team sports for boys were Association football, cricket and hockey. See FMS *Annual Reports* on Education for the 1930s.
82. SS *Educational Annual Report for 1935* (Singapore 1937), p.341.
83. General Report of Girls' Schools, 1938, op. cit., p.67.
84. Marsh, 'The New Freedom', 22.
85. Ibid.
86. General Report of Girls' Schools, 1938, op. cit., p.67.
87. Marsh, *Service Suspended*, p.48.

88. See figures in FN 44. But there were no Malays in Pudu because, according to Miss Foss, of 'feeding problems' regarding pork, Foss, *Autobiography*, p. 40.
89. General Report of Girls' Schools, 1938, op. cit., p. 68.
90. Marsh, *Service Suspended*, p.65.
91. General Report of Girls' Schools, 1938, op. cit., p. 68.
92. Mrs Ho Seng Ong, 'On the Women of China', *Malaysia Message* 36, 4 (January 1927), 8.
93. General Report of Girls' Schools, 1938, op. cit., p. 67.
94. Marsh, *Service Suspended*, p. 46.
95. Cf the time-scale in Britain – see McCrone, op. cit., especially Introduction and Conclusion.
96. Cf McCrone on Britain, op. cit., *passim*.
97. Ibid., p. 2.
98. 'Emancipated Chinese Womanhood', *British Malaya*, p. 133.
99. Mangan, 'Social Construction', p. 2; Park, 'Sport, Gender and Society', p. 70.
100. On sport and Europeans in Malaya see Butcher, *The British in Malaya, passim;* and Brownfoot, 'White Female Society', forthcoming, Ch. 4.
101. Quoted in Marsh, *Service Suspended*, p. 161.

CHAPTER FIVE

The Cambridge Connection: The English Origins of Australian Rules Football

G. M. HIBBINS

Australian Rules football was organized in the colony of Victoria in 1859, with Cup competitions in the 1860s, a premier competition in 1870, and the development of close community identification between club and suburb or town in the 1870s and 1880s, an identification which is only now dissipating. By the end of the century it was the major winter sport not only in Victoria, but in West Australia, South Australia and Tasmania. The eastern seaboard has taken less affectionately to the game but both Queensland and New South Wales have bought licences to enter teams (the Brisbane Bears and the Sydney Swans) in the recently expanded inter-state competition. This, run by the Australian (formerly Victorian) Football League from Melbourne, is acknowledged the best in standard of play and in attendance. Melbourne is Victoria's capital city and when over 100,000 fans surge into its enormous Cricket Ground for the Victorian Football League grand final each September, Australia's biggest annual sporting event is in full roar.

The code's spectator appeal has always attracted large crowds, but the 'National Game' has a particular place in the hearts of Australians for many reasons, not least because it is considered to have been born and bred in Australia. Its indigenous quality has recently been embellished by the notion that the game is sympathetic to the Aboriginal lifestyle. The game, it has been suggested, has a tribal appeal, implying kinship and the exaltation of reciprocal obligations and responsibilities which is the essence of Aboriginal law. An urban Aboriginal sportsman maintains Australian football has parallells with the *corroboree* (tribal dance) in its elements of flight and grace, and emphasis on ritual.[1]

Australian Rules Football is assumed to be the unique Australian contribution to world sport, unlike all the other sports played in Australia which have been imported. The letter to *Bell's Life in Victoria* in July 1858 which precipitated organized football in the colony of Victoria by suggesting that cricketers take up football in the winter to keep fit, has been described as 'the founding document, the Declaration of Independence, of a new national game'[2] and the game's continued success a possible 'example of colonial independence'[3] from English sporting imperialism.

Such a view is natural considering Victoria had made amazing progress during the 1850s following the discovery of gold. The population tripled between 1851 and 1854, and again more than doubled that increase between 1854 and 1861.[4] A contemporary observed: 'The superior energy of the Melbourne men is a necessary consequence of their having been the pick of the spirited youths of all the world, brought together by the rush of gold',[5] and it is tempting to visualize a dynamic, gold-euphoric society of enterprising and affluent young men prepared to flout tradition and to encourage innovation.

But it would seem that in reality the colony's essentially middle-class population wanted to imitate and improve, not to create. Rather than emphasize the independence of the Victorians in conceiving a national game, it should be conceded that the influence of English midwifery was substantial. Geoffrey Serle's authoritative study of the gold-rush decade in Victoria sets the background to a study of the origin of Australian Rules Football:

> Victoria provides an almost unique case of masses of migrants over a short period swamping a small existing society. This cross-section of the British Isles – with only the aristocracy, the paupers and the aged seriously under-represented – created, as it were, a new, large, self-governing county, automatically recreating British institutions and re-forming familiar clubs and societies. In a real sense they regarded themselves as part of Britain still . . . . They took an immense pride in their creation of 'another England', and assumed that it was the virtue of British institutions which made such success possible.[6]

The start of football in Victoria in 1859 is a fine example of this 'new county' syndrome, and the propriety of copying the English is suggested at the time by a local journalist who, in trying to explain the apparent eagerness to play football animating the colonials, referred to 'the natural anti-American tendencies of Victorians'.[7] Presumably he was suggesting that Victorians were happy to emulate the English, in contrast to the Americans whose anti-imperialist attitude had been evidenced by the War of Independence.

Two imperial views found an uncritical colonial compliance at the time, and both encouraged the introduction and growth of the football movement. At the beginning of 1860 the editor of *Bell's Life in Victoria and Sporting Chronicle* (itself an echo of an English counterpart) expressed the change: 'Within the last five years a different tone has pervaded society. The advocates of Muscular Christianity have become the majority. Such books as *Tom Brown's Schooldays* are among the most popular works of fiction ... That this gratifying change in public opinion has taken place in Australia to quite as great an extent as in Europe is evidenced by the events of the last year'.[8] The *Argus* was quick to associate Tom Brown with local football, suggesting 'that manly and healthy book' may well have 'produced a love for violent exercise' in the colony.[9] In April 1858 *Bell's Life in Victoria* reprinted an article on 'Muscular Christianity and Public Schools' from *The Times*, and another on 'Muscular Christianity' from the *English Weekly Despatch* in July 1859.[10] Thomas Hughes in his sequel *Tom Brown At Oxford* explained:

> The true muscular Christian has hold of the old chivalrous and
> Christian belief that a man's body is given to him to be trained and
> brought into subjection, and then used for the protection of the weak,
> the advancement of all righteous causes, and the subduing of the
> earth which God has given to the children of men.[11]

The colonials knew about 'subduing the earth': they had been busy cutting
down forests, mining gold, laying out railway lines, and building towns.
They took readily to the new quasi-religious concept and were just as
happy as their English contemporaries to concentrate on the demands of
physical vigour rather than on the spiritual stringencies.

Defence was a subject which exercised the minds of the colonials, again a
reflection of a concern gathering strength in England during the last half of
the 1850s. Victoria was not too far away from world events to feel immune;
indeed its minimal defence forces aggravated the vulnerability. In 1855 the
colonial elite dancing at Government House was reduced to ashen-faced
panic as firing in Port Phillip Bay set off fears that the Russians had landed.
Recently they had read in the colonial press of the carnage of Crimea, the
price of British unpreparedness being exacted in the Russian winter. As it
happened, the steamship *Great Britain* was celebrating its release from
quarantine by firing her guns, a response which was not entirely wasted, for
it shot home the lesson being painfully absorbed in England. Once again
the editor of *Bell's Life in Victoria* interpreted for the colonists the ethos of the
mother country, suggesting in 1860 that the Crimean war had awakened
the British to the need for manly sports as preparation for the nation's
defence[12] and his clear implication was that the colonists should follow suit.

Of the 'manly' qualities, 'bulldog pluck' was the one most often
associated with football. A mixture of physical courage, fortitude and a
dash of daring, 'pluck' was held in high esteem as one of the qualities
necessary for soldiering. It was a theme which was repeated *ad nauseam*
throughout the late nineteenth century.

> As a national pastime, football has an enhanced value, training youth
> in a vigorous, hardy sense, imbuing them with courage, tempering
> the self-control, and preparing them as they step into manhood to
> face many of the unlooked for difficulties which are encountered in
> the great battle of life. In forming their character who shall say it does
> not diffuse its usefulness, and in these days of 'war's alarms', when we
> look anxiously around for defenders, who are more calculated than
> those who valiantly meet breast to breast their adversaries in the
> mimic strife to protect our hearth and home?[13]

Not only did the English creed of muscular Christianity and the foot-
ball/soldier identification provide a sympathetic milieu for the introduction of football but the success of the Melbourne footballers in initiating
their code owed much to the status and organizational base already
established for that most English of sports – cricket. Victorians, in

particular, were considered to have a mania for the game: they 'live, move, and have their being in an atmosphere of cricket'.[14] Apart from horse-racing, cricket was undoubtedly the most prestigious game in the colony and the Melbourne Cricket Club was the oldest club in the colony. The influential young cricketers of Melbourne were 'mostly engaged in professional or mercantile pursuits'.[15]

Into this atmosphere Thomas Wentworth Wills (son of wealthy Victorian pastoralist and member of the Legislative Assembly, Horatio Spencer Wills) was welcomed on his return to Melbourne in December 1856. Tom already had a fine cricketing reputation made in England and Ireland, so his first practice match was anxiously watched and, although 'his peculiar style often caused much amusement', Wills had the last laugh, scoring 'upwards of fifty and carrying his bat'.[16] He was included in the match against the New South Welshmen in January 1857 in which the Victorians were defeated, and in September made Secretary of the Melbourne Cricket Club. In 1858 the Victorians were again defeated by the New South Welshmen and, in the winter of 1858, Wills wrote to *Bell's Life*:

> Sir, – Now that cricket has been put aside for some few months to come, and cricketers have assumed somewhat of the chrysalis nature (for a time only 'tis true), but at length will again burst forth in all their varied hues, rather than allow this state of torpor to creep over them, and stifle their now supple limbs, why can they not, I say, form a foot-ball club, and form a committee of three or more to draw up a code of laws? If a club of this sort were got up, it would be of vast benefit to any cricket-ground to be trampled upon, and would make the turf quite firm and durable; besides which, it would keep those who are inclined to become stout from having their joints encased in useless superabundant flesh.[17]

Three weeks later the first professional bowler the Melbourne Cricket Club had ever engaged, James Mark (Jerry) Bryant,[18] supported Wills. Maintaining 'an ounce of practice to be worth a pound of theory', Bryant would provide a ball for those who would like to play football in the Richmond Paddock, the area adjoining the cricket reserve at Jolimont and his own conveniently sited Parade Hotel!

Football! But what sort of football? In 1858 there was no national English football code to recreate in 'the new country'. The first – that of association football (soccer) – does not begin until 1863. So that in 1859 the colonists did the next best thing – they copied the process by which the English were themselves trying to develop a national code of football.

English football had been for centuries a rough-and-ready game with little regulation before the establishment of additional public schools to cater for the sons of the emerging middle class. The headmasters of such schools began to encourage team sports to keep their wayward pupils in some sort of order. The older established public schools, as well as these newer schools, devised their own football rules which only applied within each school and were not actually written down until the 1850s or early 1860s.[19] In the main the schools divided in favouring either a game in which the ball could be kicked and handled or a game in which the ball could only be kicked. The difference did not matter until ex-public school boys met at university and wanted to continue playing football, only to find that there was little concurrence, as 'the old Etonians howled at the Rugby men for handling the ball'.[20]

The great influx of Englishmen to the gold-rush colony brought with it this experience of playing football under school-prescribed rules and a belief in the English trend to gentrify and regulate football. So that when Bryant suggested that a ball would be available for those who would like to play football in the Richmond Paddock, the colonists found themselves in a similar position to the English undergraduates who wanted to play football together but were divided by the differences in school rules. 'A large and heterogeneous crowd put in an appearance', an early football player recalled, including a large percentage from England, but

> Each man played a lone hand or foot, according to his lights, some guided by their particular code of rules, others by no rules at all. Disputes, wrangling, and utter confusion were the inevitable outcome of such a state of affairs, but nevertheless we have to thank this football babel for many of the best points in the game ... Three or four Saturdays of this kind of play sufficed to show that something must be done to reconcile the different codes of rules.[21]

Three or four Saturdays brought the time to the end of winter and the beginning of the 1858–59 summer cricket season,[22] so it was not until the next autumn that something was done 'to reconcile the different codes of rules'. On 14 May 1859, the matches between pick-up sides resumed with the same problems: 'some of the players engaged following out the practice of catching and holding the ball, while others strenuously objected to it, contending that the ball should never be lifted from the ground otherwise than by foot'. On this occasion a meeting was held to form a football club, a number of members recruited and a committee selected.[23]

Three days later the rules were decided. The written document setting out the rules was accompanied by the names of the whole committee: T.W. Wills, T. Butterworth, W.J. Hammersley, [T.H.] Smith, J. Sewell, Alex Bruce and the Secretary J.B. Thompson.[24] But it would seem only four of the committee actually met to decide the rules, for only four names are most commonly mentioned in connection with this meeting: Thompson, Hammersley, Wills, and Smith.[25] The choice is significant because of the backgrounds of the four men, three of whom were very recent emigrants. Indeed, it seems likely that it was mainly because all four had recent experience of English football that they were elected to decide on the rules of an imitative colonial code.

In particular J.B. Thompson and W.J. Hammersley were vital inclusions because they had been at Cambridge University at a particularly significant time. They had both been accepted for Trinity College in October 1845.[26] Redit and exit registers for Trinity College show that Hammersley was there during 1846 and until June 1847; he played cricket for Cambridge in 1847. Similarly the register shows Thompson signing in and out of Trinity College during 1849 and until July 1850. It seems quite possible that he was there before that as his elder brother was tutoring at Trinity.[27]

Two important events for football occurred during this time at Cambridge University. In 1846 a short-lived Cambridge Football Club was formed. Even more importantly, a meeting in 1848, attended by representatives from Eton, Harrow, Shrewsbury, Rugby and Winchester schools, sought to frame a standard code of football amenable to all, and this meeting resulted in the Cambridge Rules, as they were called.[28] The meeting was held at Trinity College, the college of both Hammersley and Thompson. This discussion and amalgamation of rules at Cambridge University was the first attempted in England, and it was a notable precedent leading to a London conference in 1863 which set out to establish one set of rules for all English footballers. As Thompson emigrated to the Victorian goldrushes in the early 1850s and Hammersley to the colony in 1856, the Cambridge process of discussion and compromise was to prove no less influential for the colony of Victoria.

Thomas Henry Smith apparently played football before he came to Victoria and his military character would have endeared the game to him. It seems likely he had some exposure to Rugby School-style football, being educated at Trinity College, Dublin. Information on College football at the time of Smith's Bachelor of Arts is sparse but three years after he left in 1850, Trinity College began a Rugby School-type football club with nine players from Rugby School, 12 from Cheltenham College and 12 from Irish schools. Thus it seems likely that some form of uncodified football was played at the College at the time of Smith's education.[29]

Thomas Wills was native-born but educated between 1851 and 1855 at Rugby School, where he had captained both the cricket and football teams.[30] He had been back in Victoria for only two years at the beginning of 1859.

So it is natural that, in the absence of a national English code or codes of football to recreate, these four men followed the process taken at Cambridge University by considering the existing rules of the English public schools to find some acceptable amalgamation. It was also to be expected that the Rugby School Rules would figure prominently in this colonial consideration. It should be clearly reiterated that the colonists did not have either an Association (soccer) or Rugby organization to copy (or repudiate) for Association (soccer) did not come into existence until 1863, and Rugby football existed primarily as the game played at the school of the same name (just as Winchester football was played at Winchester, Harrow football at Harrow), although crudely imitative matches might be found wherever foot met ball. Indeed in 1859 only Rugby, Eton, Harrow, Winchester and Shrewsbury schools appear to have had written rules; an oral tradition governed the games elsewhere and, indeed, the Rugby rules presupposed an already existing knowledge of the game.

At this time Thompson wrote of combining the merits while excluding the vices of both Rugby School and Eton College rules[31] but writing to Wills some eleven years later he enlarged on that: 'You may remember when you, Mr. Hammersley, Mr. T. Smith and myself framed the first code of rules for Victorian use. The Rugby, Eton, Harrow and Winchester rules at that time (I think in 1859) came under our consideration ...'.[32] The result of this consideration was the formulation of ten rules, seven of which were fairly straightforward decisions, not differing significantly from their counterparts at Rugby School and Cambridge University.

The chief decision which was ultimately to give rise to a distinctive Australian football game was the Victorians' remarkable agreement to ban hacking, the name given to the practice of shin-kicking then prevalent in most English school games of football. Indeed Hammersley attributed the initiation of rules to the roughness of the free-for-alls which took place in 1858 when football in Victoria was first mooted: 'after a severe fight in the old Richmond Paddock when blood had been drawn freely and a leg broken, it occurred to some of us that if we had rules to play under it would be better'.[33]

According to Thompson, the rule-makers all believed that the sort of rules which adolescents or undergraduates would suffer 'would not be patiently tolerated by grown men',[34] the young professional and business adults who, pragmatically, were not prepared to risk being laid up with a time-consuming injury. Yet, again, this was not an independent colonial view; it would seem that English attitudes were significant. Opposition to violence in football had been building slowly during the 1850s in England and, emigrating with the new colonists, just happened to be put into practice earlier in Melbourne than it was in London.

In both places the argument was identical: hacking might be acceptable for schoolboys but it was not advisable for men.[35] In 1860 Melbourne footballers were being reassured that:

> Though still manly, [football] has become a decorous and, to a certain extent, tame pastime. Under the humane legislation of the Melbourne Football Club ... 'hacking' renders a member liable to excommunication. These rare old 'bullies' so famous at one time at least, at Winchester, Eton, and Harrow, have no place in Victoria and in vain do we in these degenerate days anticipate the spectacle of a dozen players rolling on the ground together. But if sore shins and aching shoulders are less common and the excitement less intense, we make up in some measure by increased good humour and the absence of severe accidents. So that perhaps after all, football under the rules of the 'Humane Society' is preferable to the horseplay we so much glorified in as schoolboys, when our hebdomadal bruises were deemed trophies of pluck, and a good limp or black eye a thing to talk about and be proud of. Besides, fully a moiety of the football players

THE ENGLISH ORIGINS OF AUSTRALIAN RULES FOOTBALL

here are grown men, and don't take a kick as they would a dozen years ago. Black eyes don't look so well in Collins Street [Melbourne's financial centre].[36]

In London three years later it was asserted: 'men of business ... to whom it is of importance to take care of themselves', would be unwilling to play football which allowed hacking.[37]

The significance of the anti-hacking decision made in Victoria lay in the *unanimity* of the decision rather than in the actual decision itself. This point is made clear when it is appreciated that it was on the issue of whether to allow hacking in football or not that the English footballers disagreed, and *that it was this disagreement in 1863 which led to a split and the two codes of soccer and rugby*. In England, so firmly did some football players of the handling/running persuasion feel that football was emasculated by the abolition of hacking that they withdrew their support from the new Football Association which was trying to form one set of laws for all players of football. Considering hacking and running an integral part of 'the true football game', the hackers went their own way and took with them the handling/running style of game (the style which, of course, was formalized as Rugby Union in 1871), leaving the advocates of a game which emphasized kicking to form the Association, or soccer as it was later called.[38]

In Melbourne there was little vested interest in retaining hacking or, at least no articulate opposition to its abolition, and consequently no split occurred between the proponents of the two types of game. At this point the colonists supported the English anti-hacking progressives against the English pro-hacking traditionalists. Why?

Some Australian historians have suggested that the concern about violent play was stronger in the colonies where making one's way was more urgent for the participants than for the aristocrats of England who could afford an enforced break. Certainly the football beginning in Melbourne involved mainly young men earning a living, whereas in England regulated football had begun in the schools. Indeed anti-hackers in England in 1863 were attacked with the gibe that they objected to hacking because 'too many of the members of the clubs began late in life and were too old for that spirit of the game that was so fully entered into at the public schools and by public school men in after life'.[39]

In Melbourne there was likely to be a greater age-range playing together. With the initial shortage of players, the colonists appreciated the danger to the boys who sometimes played with adult sides, and in school teams when masters or ex-pupils helped to make up the numbers. The injury rate may have been aggravated by the dryness of the Australian grounds, lacking the soft mud of English winters. Or perhaps it was simply recognized that there were numerically not enough football followers to afford two camps and that agreement was indispensable if football was to be favourably advanced. Whatever the reason or reasons, the important result was that the colonial rule-makers had the opportunity to consider the rules of the various forms to *both* the handling/running game and the kicking-only game in formulating their own code, rather than just copying one model.

Not that dissension did not exist but some compromises were quickly made. From the English handling/running type of game, catching from a team-mate's kick (marking) followed by a free kick, and picking up the ball after one bounce were features included in the 1859 Melbourne game but the kicking-only (incipient soccer) proponents in 1860 ruled out running while holding the ball. The problem for the 'kickers-only' was that, although they had the numbers at meetings such as the 1860 one at which more than just the Melbourne Football Club was represented, the silent majority it would seem were already playing, and inclined towards Rugby School-style football.

Most of the colonials would lean to Rugby School-style football because they identified with its adherents. According to one English commentator on the origin of the two English codes, 'the data available at present suggest that most leading proponents of the embryo soccer game [kicking-only] were Old Etonians, Old Harrovians and old boys of other established public schools, whilst most protagonists of Rugby were Old Rugbeians and former pupils of the newer schools formed to accommodate the educational aspirations of the expanding middle class'.[40] In England this resulted in a delicately balanced tussle between the two class factions. Not so in Melbourne where the more aristocratic were outnumbered. In 1861 two out of three people in Victoria were migrants, the bulk being from the same class which had supported the newer schools in England[41] and therefore much more likely to support Rugby School football in the colonial environment. Early references to the sort of football played in Victoria refer constantly to Rugby, meaning the game played at the school of that name. An early football player claimed (some 40 years later) that games 'under Rugby [School] rules were played by the miners on many of the and during these exciting times a small coterie of Rugbyites [sic] kept the ball rolling in Melbourne'.[42] Better evidence is provided by the contemporary Melbourne daily papers, the *Herald* and the *Argus*, which refer to a modification of Rugby School rules being used in the games preceding the advent of the Melbourne Club Football rules.[43]

Rugby footballs were quickly in favour. Melbourne's sporting goods entrepreneur attractively advertised the 'famous Rugby Footballs which took the Prize Medal at the Exhibition ... [and] will fly many yards further than the old-fashioned sort'. Old Rugbeian Tom Wills was soon insisting on their use in the matches which he captained and the oval ball was being used by Melbourne and Geelong, certainly by 1862.[44]

It bounced less predictably than the round ball and in reality the impracticality of deciding when a ball had been picked up on the first bounce caused constant dispute and eventually meant that this rule was soon disregarded, the players being allowed to pick up the ball on any bounce. This in turn encouraged the already prevalent Rugby School habit of running with the ball, as presumably it was difficult to stop on the spot having chased a bouncing ball, just as running was necessary in the movements preliminary to kicking a ball or in dodging an opponent. After a dispute broke out in a Geelong-Melbourne match, running with the ball and then deliberately bouncing it at intervals evolved, although 'some players bounced the ball every 10 or 12 yards while others would run 40 or 50 yards and even further without bouncing it'.[45] In 1864 the football writer of Melbourne's sporting weekly, *Bell's Life in Victoria*, complained: 'The rule as to taking up and carrying the ball was very much infringed, and frequently a player would run 20 yards with ball in hand. This may be in accordance with Rugby [School] rules but certainly is not with those of Melbourne ... The best players, it was noticed, were very often those to set the worst example in this particular'.[46] This was probably a reference to the play of H.C.A. Harrison, the cousin of Tom Wills and the sprint champion of the colony, and it may be surmised that the bouncing rule may well have been introduced to bring the fastest players, and Harrison in particular, back to the field.

The 1865 meeting of the Melbourne Football Club did not discuss the problem,[47] but this year saw the resolution of the conflict. In a match between the MFC and Royal Park, a goal was 'run' – clearly a breach of the Melbourne rules but allowed by the umpire. Theodore Marshall later explained how the situation arose:

> I was captain of the Royal Park [side] and in the team was J.E. Clarke, second only in fleetness on the football field at that time to Harrison ... it was arranged that if Clarke got the ball, he was to tuck it under his arm and run as far as possible without bouncing it. Clarke, seizing a favourable opportunity, bolted with the ball along the wing, dodging several Melbourne players on the way and, without once bouncing it, flew towards the goal and kicked it. When Clarke had overrun the orthodox 40 or 50 yards, the Melbourne men stood wondering at his audacity, and ceased to interfere with him. Harrison who was nearly a 40 yard man himself, asked me what it meant! I answered that I simply wanted to settle once and for all how far a man should be allowed to run with the ball without bouncing it. After consultation it was agreed that the ball should be bounced at least once in every ten yards, and so this important point in our game was brought about.[48]

A year later bouncing the ball every five or six yards was written into the rules. If empiricism entered into the development of Australian Rules, this was the entry. The advent of the bouncing rule was the important modification sought to conciliate both views of football: it mollified those opposed to running with the ball, for bouncing the ball at frequent intervals, particularly with the unevenness of bounce occasioned by balls containing animal bladders, must have discouraged running. The basis of the game had been reached. That the unanimity of the decision to ban hacking was of considerable consequence is emphasized by the consideration that if the English had not been unable to agree on whether to allow

hacking or not, it seems likely that they too could have had one code of
football and, by a similar process of compromise, one resembling Aussie
Rules.

The battle against rough play and running without bouncing the ball
continued throughout the 1860s and was severely tested by the advent of
the British regiments returning from the Maori wars in New Zealand and
based in Melbourne during 1867. Their game involved running with the
ball, but also tackling so fierce that the matches became legendary for their
violence and Harrison (who had a fair reputation for courage) declared
wryly after one game that he thought the soldiers had [mis] 'taken his
Melbourne side for the enemy'.[49] By that time the opposition to violent
football in England had increased and the colonial stand against it was
affirmed in reprints of English sporting articles, such as John D.
Cartwright's survey of the new (1863) Cambridge University Rules and of
the football rules of each of the main English public schools.[50] The English
magazines themselves were also available: 'We would recommend all
[colonial] players ... to read up the improved game, described and
discussed in the latest numbers of the English *Bell's Life* and *Field*, as
thereby they may discover what those journals are so strenuously striving
for – how to make football as scientific and as popular for winter exercise as
cricket is for summer.'[51]

The other crucial decision for the future of the game was to omit any
offside rule. According to Hammersley 'we decided to draw up as simple a
code of rules, and as few as possible, so that anyone could quickly
understand' [them]. It would seem that this feeling was partly responsible
for the decision not to take up Rugby School rules in their entirety for, as
Hammersley also recalled: 'Tom Wills suggested the Rugby rules but
nobody understood them except himself'.[52] It was difficult to appreciate
when a player was 'off his side', which in the Rugby School code of 1846/47
needed six rules to clarify.[53] Although the Victorian game began originally
with the two opposing sides ranged on opposite sides of a centre line, no
offside rules meant that, as free-ranging 'goal sneaks' become successful,
captains learnt to deploy their men and create the pattern of paired
forwards and defenders recognized today.

The Football Club Rules sub-committee elected in May 1859 were not
only men with English football experience or knowledge.[54] Importantly for
the steady advance in spreading those rules, Wills, Hammersley and
Thompson who comprised the Rules sub-committee (with Smith), also
had some reputation for playing cricket in England. They were among the
'laurelled warriors' of the Victorian team which had finally succeeded in
defeating the New South Wales eleven in Sydney only four months
previously. The match had brought business and Parliament to a stand-
still, and excitement in Melbourne knew few bounds when Victoria won by
two wickets. Wills, in particular, was hailed as a hero, for not only had he
captained the match but endured a broken finger while batting.[55] 'Everyone belongs to a cricket club at Melbourne, everybody talks learnedly and
eruditely about the game, and what is more everybody identifies himself

with the fame which its champions of the bat and ball have achieved either at home or in friendly contest with their neighbours,' wrote the *Sydney Morning Herald* editor, trying to explain the defeat to its New South Wales readers.[56]

The emerging football club, to the committee of which these cricket heroes had been elected, could only have been helped by the Victorians' identification with such cricketing glory. It is little wonder that the Melbourne Football Club soon established the legitimacy of its claim to construct binding rules. The early dominance of the Melbourne Football Club players, quickly known as the 'invincible whites' from their constant victories and the colour of their long (cricket?) trousers, helped impose the Melbourne Football Club rules on the clubs springing up around Melbourne and in the country, and which initially could not challenge this strength.

The fourth member of the Rules Committee, Thomas H. Smith, was also a cricketer but possibly his place on the committee was an acknowledgement of his position with that other English institution of prestige – the public school. Smith was the classics master at Scotch College, the oldest public school in Melbourne. Scotch College had been followed by the establishment of St. Patrick's College in 1854, the Geelong and Melbourne Church of England Grammar Schools in 1858 and Geelong College in 1861. Soon it was being written:

> Of late years the mentors of youth have more than ever practically recognized the fact, that the cultivation of the physical powers is absolutely necessary to the full development of the intellectual faculties, and the objects of their solicitude have not been slow to show their appreciation of this truth. Thus cricket and other outdoor sports have become almost a portion of the curricula of the public schools in England, and this attention to muscular development has extended to society at large, producing a very noticeable revival in favour of manly pastimes. *The colony of Victoria in this, as in other respects, has not been slow in following the example of the parent stem* ...[57]

The Melbourne public schools varied not one whit from the English public schools in the growing passion for games.

At the same time that the cricketers had advertised to entice football enthusiasts of all persuasions to kick a ball around the Richmond Paddock, the Scotch College began a three-day match against Melbourne Grammar School. Forty a side, the public-school match was an epic struggle with distinct Rugby School aspirations. Thomas Wills acted as one umpire and Robert Hervey, Thomas Smith's assistant classics master at Scotch, who played in the match (as did Smith), is reputed to have imported six Rugby balls from England and taught the boys to kick them.[58]

The colonial public schools, lacking the individual traditional games of their English counterparts, adopted Melbourne Football Club rules, and so did Melbourne University which began a Club in 1860. The schools formed a recruiting pool which provided continuing support in the nineteenth century, a practice which still has a role today. The school involvement also augmented the gentlemanly status which football had assumed in its association with the Melbourne Cricket Club. Skill at football arguably suggested that the owner had enjoyed a public-school or university education.

Australians have generally given the credit for the advent of Australian Rules football to the native-born Tom Wills and his cousin Colden Harrison. Both were as near as possible Victorian, having come as infants when Port Phillip (Victoria) was being first settled. Yet of the four men primarily involved in founding Australian Rules, three of them were immigrants of the 1850s. While borrowing considerably from England in the development of Australian Rules Football, did a burgeoning nationalist movement later demand that Australians be credited with its success?

Tom Wills, as has already been described, wrote 'the founding document', the seminal letter to *Bell's Life in Victoria* which suggested football as a winter recreation for cricketers, and he also brought to bear the Rugby School influence on the original rules. His initiative fortunately met with considerable support, for without the propitious English-inspired climate of opinion, football in Victoria may well have eventuated later as either Association/soccer or Rugby. Wills' alternative suggestion in the same letter that cricketers form a rifle club, for example, did not have the same impact despite the defence fears of the time, and a later letter suggesting athletics had no immediate result.[59]

Wills had the best of both worlds, being native-born and benefiting from his English schooling at Rugby and his status as an English cricketer. Researchers have also been intrigued by the rest of his life. Both his cricket and football careers were interrupted in 1861 when his family set out to establish a sheep station in Queensland. Soon after the end of the nine months' pioneering trek north, Wills' father and 18 family servants were murdered by Aboriginals in allegedly the biggest massacre of white men to take place in Australia. Tom was absent from the homestead on that particular day. He struggled to establish the station until early in 1864 when, returning to what he loved most, he played cricket against the touring English team. Almost certainly the best Australian cricketer of the 1860s, he coached the Melbourne Cricket Club and (oddly, considering the death of his father), an Aboriginal cricket team which subsequently toured England. He also returned to football but his main input into Victorian football had taken place in those first three years before he left for Queensland. In 1869 he was replaced as captain of the Victorian eleven and it was not long before his drinking problem was the subject of explicit public comment.[60] He was a gifted but undisciplined sportsman, afflicted by guilt at his own lack of material success, yet jealous of his honour. A confirmed alcoholic, he had alienated most of his family and friends by the time he committed suicide at the age of 44. Nevertheless Wills' cricket brilliance, family tragedy and melancholy end have attracted chroniclers ever since, few of whom have resisted the opportunity to tell his romantic tale in connection with the establishment of Australian Rules Football.

In contrast his cousin, Colden Harrison, tended to show more reverence for things 'at Home' (England) and little pride in his mother's fine but convict-stained colonial ancestry of intellectuals and entrepreneurs.[61] Very much the muscular Christian, Colden Harrison became well known between 1859 and 1862 as the champion amateur runner of the colony and as an excellent football player. He was an able administrator, which his experience as a public servant in the Victorian Customs Department no doubt assisted. His work was quiet, but effective enough not to go unnoticed by his contemporaries who praised his efforts and who consistently nominated him to positions of responsibility as the organization developed. Thus it was in 1866, when Wills, Hammersley, Smith and Thompson were all either not in Melbourne or involved with other sport, that Harrison represented the Melbourne Football Club at a club conference and that he was asked to draft the latest set of rules.

The new game after its initial spurt needed a period of consolidation and consistent supervision to succeed and 'there never was a harder worker than H.C.A.; a little vicious in his play, perhaps, but still an undeniable good 'us'.[62] He was involved in football administration at least until 1905 when he was elected chairman of the first Australian Football Conference, and then continuously famed for his loyal support of the Melbourne Football Club and love of the game until he died, aged 93, in 1929. He had outlived the members of the first rules committee by some 40-odd years[63] and this fact in itself may well have been significant; it meant that publicists seeking home-grown heroes to celebrate in a time of growing nationalism found Harrison the answer, as numerous newspaper articles testify. Harrison's stamina – his ability to outlast everybody on and off the field – was held in high regard, particularly as it laid to rest some disquiet that Australia's convict origins had led to a 'tendency to decay among the descendants of the early colonists'.[64]

At the inaugural meeting of the Australasian Football Council in 1906 Harrison was officially designated 'father of the game' and honoured as such at the Jubilee of Australian Football in 1908.[65] The history of this epithet is illuminating. Some 16 years after the founding of the Melbourne Football Club, a writer under the *nom de plume* of 'Tom Jones' wrote the first history of the game in an article called '*Football in Australia*'. It began: 'Football in Victoria was practically ushered into existence in the year of grace 1858 [*sic*] when, through the agency of Messrs. H.C.A. Harrison, W. Hammersley, J.B. Thompson and T.W. Wills, the Melbourne Club was called into being, as autumn nodding o'er the yellow plain came jovial on'.[66] Now, as has been indicated, Hammersley, Thompson and Wills were certainly involved but it seems unlikely that Harrison was actually at the meeting of Melbourne cricketers which formed the Melbourne Club in the autumn of 1859, as he played cricket for the suburb of Richmond. Certainly Harrison is not included in the committee which that meeting elected.

Nevertheless this naming of Harrison as a founder of the Melbourne Club has since been repeated by most writers on the subject, despite the challenge to its accuracy early in 1876 when Thomas Smith wrote to

complain about his own omission, stating: 'Mr. Harrison had nothing to
do, directly or indirectly, with its formation. The Melbourne [Club]
originated with Mr. Wills, Mr. Hammersley and myself, as we walked from
the cricket ground. Mr. Thompson was not then present, but joined us
afterwards ...'.[67] This description apparently refers to the Rules meeting of
the committee rather than the meeting of Melbourne cricketers which had
formed the Club three days earlier. It is supported by later accounts of the
Rules meeting written by Wills and Hammersley, neither of whom refer to
Harrison being present. In his reply 'Tom Jones' ungraciously acknowledged Smith's right to be included as a founder of the Club, and, by
omitting to defend the inclusion of Harrison, tacitly conceded his mistake.[68]
In the next issue of *The Footballer* an 'Old 'Un' reminiscing in print had a dig
at Smith and also asserted that H.C.A Harrison 'may justly be called the
Father of Victorian Football', thus apparently first bestowing on Harrison
this accolade.[69] *The Footballer* did not last beyond 1881 but when a new
paper called *Football* briefly appeared in 1885, its first issue featured a
drawing of Harrison with the caption 'The Father of Victorian Football'
and the writer quoted 'Tom Jones' extensively from the first inaccurate
article often years earlier. The same error appears in T.S. Marshall's paper
on the history of the game read to the Football Association in 1896[70] and so
this factoid passes on into the twentieth century.

Harrison would have claimed in his autobiography to have helped found
the club or write the 1859 rules, if he could have done so legitimately, for he
was not a man to shun the limelight. In a chapter entitled 'Football. Father.
of the Australian Game', he does claim to have drafted the 1866 rules which
he lists in detail[71] and these have frequently been dubbed the first written
rules until the original document setting out the 1859 rules was found in the
Melbourne Cricket Club archives. Harrison's name is not on the latter.

Given that Wills' claim to football fame rests mainly on the letter he
wrote suggesting the game to keep cricketers fit, and that Harrison's should
rest solely on his long and conscientious record of football administration
and not on any role in actually founding the game, is that sufficient to select
them for the honour of beginning Australian Rules Football? Indeed why
have the other three – Hammersley, Smith and Thompson – been ignored
almost completely? The only detailed academic work to appear so far on
Australian Rules Football[72] follows this erroneous tradition by including
Harrison in a committee of five. It names and details the lives only of the
Australians, Wills and Harrison. Popular accounts skate over the beginning of Australian Rules with a fine disregard for the holes abounding in
their accounts and rest on the wealth of information which exists about
these two men, partly owing to Harrison's own autobiography, *The Story of
an Athlete*.[73]

Occasionally recognized is William Josiah Hammersley, who played as
a Victorian cricketer after a career in England, and was also well known as
the sporting editor of the *Australasian*. It is obvious, from his sporting
reminiscences published in a Sydney paper[74] not long before he died, that
his interest lay mainly with cricket and racing. He was a good shot and also

involved in the administration of athletics until disillusioned by its growing professionalism. He admitted that his interest in football waned after he actually gave up playing (probably in 1865), and his main contribution can be said to be helping to decide on the first rules in 1859 possibly from the benefit of his Cambridge experience, and publicizing the matches in *Bell's Life in Victoria* for which he worked before it was incorporated in the *Australasian* in 1867. He died in 1886 at the age of 59 of 'softening of the brain'.[75]

Smith is the sort of name one uses to indicate anonymity and certainly this Smith has suffered from just that. Even on the 1859 Rules document his initials have been omitted from his name, presumably because the writer did not know them at the time, and until recently it was not known that the 'H' in Thomas H. Smith stood for Henry. Thomas Smith came to Victoria in the 1850s, appears first as the classics master at the Scotch College in 1858, became the headmaster between 1860 and 1863 of the National Model School which was a prestigious government-funded school, and then the Inspector for Schools in the Sandhurst Region from which he was dismissed late in 1864 for 'official negligence and improper conduct' (details unknown), thus effectively ending his teaching career in Victoria; it seems he left for South Australia. Not surprisingly his contemporaries were not effusive about him after this. The impression one gets from reading his reports and the odd comment made in passing about him is that he was a rather stiff, military-minded man and not much liked: Hammersley referred to 'Football Smith' as having a 'very peppery temper', (a likely cause of his downfall).[76] He was obviously a good footballer and is reluctantly conceded to have 'contributed materially towards the advancement of football in its early day'.[77] Certainly he helped to frame the 1859 and 1860 rules and possibly his contribution was also a role in liaising between the public schools and the Melbourne Football Club.

Similarly the identity of J.B. Thompson has been masked by the fact that he is only given his initials in contemporary reports. He was, in fact, James Bogne Thompson. An important role in transmitting to Melbourne the Cambridge process of considering and amalgamating different English public school rules to find an agreeable consensus game has already been suggested for him.

Thompson did not favour Rugby School football or its 'abnormal' ball but his continual efforts to publicize football as a game of importance have not been acknowledged at all. As the sports reporter from at least 1859 (and probably earlier) until 1861 for the *Argus*, a Melbourne daily, it seems a reasonable assumption that Thompson wrote the *Argus* paragraphs on football. Describing football as 'a most manly and amusing game', Thompson hoped that it might 'continue to grow in favour until it becomes as popular as cricket'. He tried to attract spectators, maintaining that 'a well-contested football match is as interesting a sight as can be conceived; the chances, changes, and ludicrous contretemps, are so frequent, and the whole affair so animated and inspiring'.[78] The *Argus* column promoted 'this excellent game' with practical details about the whereabouts of matches and formation of new clubs followed by fulsome praise of the games and recruitment of members.

Thompson should be credited with successfully promulgating the new code, for to have any set of rules accepted by a great mass of players was no easy task. At first 'during the infancy of the game it was kept alive by scratch matches played between the members of the Melbourne Club or any spectators willing to take part. As these matches were played by sides varying from 15 to 30, a large number of young men soon became conversant with the rules'.[79] However, this in itself would not have been sufficient to publicize the new game, and diffusion of the Melbourne Football Club rules was, in fact, facilitated by publication. After the first meeting in May 1859, the *Argus* said: 'This complete code will be printed and distributed amongst the members of the [Melbourne Football] club, of whom there are now about 70 on the list' and, by June, the paper was referring to 'the lately published rules which appear to give general satisfaction'.[80] Indeed some swift work meant they were published in the 1859 edition of *The Australian Cricketers' Guide*, with its summary of the just past cricket season, as 'The Laws of the Melbourne Football Club as played in the Richmond Paddock 1859' along with 'The Rules of Football as played in the Rugby School' and 'The Rules of Football as played at Eton School' [*sic*]. The following year Thompson edited the first edition of *The Victorian Cricketers' Guide* in which only the Melbourne Football Club Rules were given space for, as he pointed out, 'we seem to have agreed on a code of our own', those 'of the Melbourne Club by whose rules ... the game in Victoria is now universally played'.[81]

In the *Argus* Thompson embraced and advertised each rule change and reassured the bellicose that the game had not become less manly by becoming less dangerous.[82] He also continually worked to ensure that the Melbourne Football Club Rules were the only ones recognized, no doubt aware that a plethora of different football games with different rules was not a practical precondition for organized football, as South Australian footballers were discovering.

Thompson's influence extended beyond Melbourne as the metropolitan and country papers customarily reprinted each other's material. For example, the goldfields' *Ballarat Times* of the 23 May 1859 quoted his assertion that the 'rules determined upon at a meeting of the [M.F.C.] Committee ... will be be strictly adhered to'. That was only six days after the Rules had been settled upon! Thompson's enthusiasm for football and his constant publicity make it noticeable that when Thompson departed for the country gold-mining centre of Bendigo to work on the *Bendigo Advertiser* in 1861 that the interest of the *Argus* declines, and it may not be coincidental that his departure was followed by an apparent loss of support for football in Melbourne during 1862–64.[83] Nothing succeeds like success, Thompson evidently believed, and he propagated the fiction that the game was spreading like 'an epidemic', so much so that the wary historian must be aware of Thompson's orchestration and, in the interests of truth, make allowance for some exaggeration by the *Argus*.

8. The Colony of Victoria's Intercolonial Cricket XI, 1859. This picture – a collage of photographed figures superimposed on a painted background supposed to represent Sydney Harbour – shows three of the four men who framed the first football rules: T. Wills and J. B. Thompson (seated left) with W. J. Hammersley standing between them. It emphasizes the role that cricket had to play in the colonial sport of football

9. Football being played in the Richmond paddock, Melbourne, a lithograph taken from the *Australasian Sketcher*, 1875

All four members of the rules committee therefore had a short association with Melbourne football, yet all had something to contribute. Thompson deserves considerably more credit than he has received when one compares his contribution with that of Wills. Hammersley and Smith could at least be rescued from obscurity. The roles of Wills and Harrison in the development of Australian Rules Football seem to have been singled out for recognition perhaps because there is much accessible biographical knowledge of the two. Wills, particularly, is a fascinating character and his alcoholic end could be excused as a result of his family tragedy. However, Thompson's death from broncho-pneumonia and alcoholism when he was 47 and Smith's ignominious removal from the Victorian education system may well have been embarrassing defects for 'founding fathers.' In contrast Colden Harrison's rectitude and administrative involvement made him a desirable choice for such a position. His longevity rubberstamped this elevation and made him a legend in his own lifetime. That Wills and Harrison were Australian, rather than English, no doubt was a powerful part of their attraction, particularly in the 1880s and 1890s when Australian nationalism was making itself felt.

Certainly today Australian Rules football is a unique game. Yet it originated with a number of cricketers participating in the English trend to gentrify football and copying the Cambridge University precedent to put together a consensus code by consulting the rules of English public-school games, and in this case those mainly of the dominant Rugby School. It was nourished by the English creed of muscular Christianity, and sustained substantially by the unacknowledged work of two English journalists and one Irish schoolmaster. Australians may now feel sufficiently secure in their national identity to reject any notion of football fawn in recognizing more fully this colonial response to the imperial bond.[84]

NOTES

1. M. Flanagan, 'Aboriginal Olympics', *Age*, 5 September 1987.
2. L. Sandercock and I. Turner, *Up Where, Cazaly? The Great Australian Game* (Sydney, 1981), p. 19.
3. W.F. Mandle, 'Games People Played: Cricket and Football in England and Victoria in the Late Nineteenth Century', *Historical Studies*, 15, (1973), 521.
4. Census figures: 1851: 77,345, 1861: 540,322.
5. G. Blainey (ed.), *Greater Britain, Charles Dilke visits her new lands, 1866 & 1867* (North Ryde 1985), pp. 95–6.
6. G. Serie, *The Golden Age: A History of the Colony of Victoria, 1851–1861* (Melbourne, 1963), pp. 380–81. For a colony which 'made a fetish of copying everything English', Serie (p.365) was surprised to find a later (1923) description of the early development of Australian Rules Football as an empiric 'rather go-as-you-please affair at first, [with] a set of rules ... gradually evolved, which experience taught us to be the best', A. Mancini and G.M. Hibbins (eds.), *Running with the Ball: Football's Foster Father* (Melbourne, 1987), p. 119.
7. *Argus*, 18 April 1859.
8. *Bell's Life in Victoria* (hereafter *BLV*), 7 Jan. 1860.

9. *Argus*, 16 August 1858, 18 April 1859.
10. *BLV*, 3 April 1858, 30 July 1859.
11. T. Hughes, *Tom Brown At Oxford* (London, 1880), pp.112–23.
12. *BLV*, 17 Jan. 1860.
13. *The Footballer*, 1877, 120.
14. Editorial, *Sydney Morning Herald*, reprinted *Argus*, 25 Jan. 1859.
15. *BLV*, 26 Sept. 1857.
16. *Australian Cricketers' Guide* (Melbourne 1857), p. 55.
17. *BLV*, 10 July 1858.
18. *BLV*, 31 July 1858. Profile, *BLV*, 2 July 1864. Obit., *Australasian*, 17 Dec. 1881, 779. Surrey cricketer, came to goldfields, played against the English, went to Sale about 1865 and ran a hotel.
19. Rugby 1845–46, Eton 1849, Harrow 1850s, Winchester 1850s, Shrewsbury *c.* 1855, Westminister *c.* 1860, Charterhouse 1862. E. Dunning and K. Sheard, *Barbarians, Gentlemen and Players: A Sociological Study of the Development of Rugby Football* (Canberra, 1979), p. 98.
20. Ibid, p. 104.
21. T.S. Marshall, 'The Rise and Progress of the Australian Game of Football', 1896, manuscript.
22. The summer in Australia is from December to February.
23. *Herald*, 16 May 1859; *Argus*, 16 May 1859.
24. Document held by the Melbourne Cricket Club (hereafter MCC) museum.
25. Accounts by the first three all mention just these four: only Smith recalls Bruce as being added to this number later. Mancini and Hibbins, op. cit., p.165, fn.42.
26. W.W. Rouse Ball and J.A. Venn, *Admissions, 1801–1850, Trinity College, Cambridge*, Vol. IV, pp. 579–80.
27. Exit and redit registers for Trinity College, 1843–49, 1849–53, Wren Library, Trinity College. These registers do not prescribe the limits of residence but do prove that Hammersley and Thompson were in Trinity College between these times.
28. J.R. Whitty, 'Early Codes' in A.H. Fabian and G. Green, *Association Football*, 1 (London, 1960), pp. 141–2.
29. Letters to author from MSS department, Trinity College, University of Dublin, 10 Oct. and 14 Nov. 1986. He played football in 1858 in the Richmond Paddock.
30. Mancini and Hibbins, op. cit., pp. 6–8.
31. J.B. Thompson (ed.), *Victorian Cricketers' Guide, 1859–60* (Melbourne), preface.
32. J.B. Thompson in T.W. Wills (ed.), *Australian Cricketers' Guide, 1870–1871* (Melbourne), pp. 114–15.
33. *Sydney Mail*, 25 August 1883, 363.
34. Thompson in Wills, op. cit.
35. Dunning and Sheard, op. cit., Ch. 5.
36. *Argus*, 14 May 1860.
37. G. Green, 'The Football Association' in Fabian and Green (eds.), op. cit., p.52. Also 'If we have hacking, no one who has arrived at the years of discretion will play football, and it will be entirely relinquished to schoolboys.'
38. Ibid., pp. 50–54.
39. Ibid., p. 52.
40. Dunning and Sheard, op. cit., p. 101.
41. G. Serle, *The Rush to Be Rich* (Melbourne 1971), p. 6.
42. Marshall, op. cit.
43. *Herald*, 23 Aug. 1858; *Argus*, 16 May 1859
44. Advertisement by George Marshall in *BLV*, 28 April, 1860; *Argus*, 14 May 1860; *BLV*, 6 Sept. 1862. The balls were made across the road from Rugby School.
45. Marshall, op. cit.
46. *BLV*, 28 May 1864.
47. The meeting agreed only that the losing side should kick off from the centre after a goal and refused Tom Wills' motion to have a bar across the goal posts eight feet from the ground, *BLV*, 13 May 1865.

48. Marshall, op. cit., claims this occurred in 1863 but see also *BLV*, 22 July 1865, for probable account of the same match.
49. *Argus*, 27 Sept. 1869.
50. Republished from *Field 1863* by *BLV*, 21 May–2 July 1864.
51. A Geelong paper, 1 April 1862, cutting in H.C.A. Harrison's Scrapbook, private collection.
52. *Sydney Mail*, 25 Aug. 1883, 363.
53. Dunning and Sheard, op. cit., p. 91.
54. Mancini and Hibbins (eds.), op. cit, preface.
55. *Argus*, 25 Jan. 1859.
56. As reprinted in the *Argus*, 25 Jan. 1859. The delights of Sydney harbour encouraged water sports, the editor asserted.
57. *Yeoman*, 17 Sept. 1864. Italics not in original.
58. Robert Hervey, listed in Scotch College Speech Night Programme for 1858; Scotch College Diamond Jubilee (booklet), Oct. 1911, p. 68. Scotch College archives. Nothing is known of Hervey's further involvement with football and the interest in football attributed to him may have arisen from some later confusion of Hervey with T.H. Smith.
59. *B.L.V*, 23 April 1859.
60. *Australasian*, 13 March 1869; 25 Jan. 1873; MCC minutes 27 Sept. 1869. MCC Annual Reports 1869–1870, 1870–1871.
61. Mancini and Hibbins, op. cit., pp. 2–5.
62. T.P. Power (ed.), *The Footballer*, 1876, 17.
63. Thompson died in 1877, Wills in 1880, Hammersley in 1886. Smith's death date unknown.
64. Mandle, op. cit., p. 526.
65. As the Vice President of the Melbourne Cricket Club from 1892, Harrison had a stand named after him at the Melbourne Cricket Ground, and the new administrative headquarters of the Victoria Football League was named Harrison House in his honour.
66. T.P. Power (ed.), *The Footballer* (1875), 7. Autumn in Australia is from March to May, so this no doubt refers to the May meeting of 1859 and therefore 1858 is not correct.
67. *Australasian*, 26 Feb. 1876, 269. Letter dated 17 Feb. 1876, South Australia.
68. *Australasian*, 11 March 1876, 333.
69. T.P. Power (ed.), *The Footballer* (1876), 17. It seems possible that the editor, Tom Power, was both 'Tom Jones' and the 'Old 'Un' and in the latter case hiding behind the folksy style so often affected by writers in lieu of a white beard and prodigious memories. If this was Power writing, he was not an 'old 'un' at all, being 14 in 1859 when the club began and ten years younger than Harrison.
70. Marshall, op. cit.
71. Mancini and Hibbins (eds.), op. cit., Ch. 7.
72. Sandercock and Turner, op. cit., pp. 19–20, 23–4.
73. Mancini and Hibbins (eds.), op. cit.
74. *Sydney Mail*, 18 Aug.-15 Dec. 1883.
75. Death certificate.
76. Mancini and Hibbins (eds.), op. cit., pp. 24, 46.
77. By 'Tom Jones' who is a hostile witness. *Australasian*, 11 March 1876, 333.
78. *Argus*, 16 August 1858.
79. Marshall, op. cit., p. 3.
80. *Argus*, 23 May 1859, 6 June 1859; *BLV*, 14 May 1864.
81. J.B. Thompson (ed.), *The Victorian Cricketers' Guide for 1859–1860* (Melbourne), p. 110.
82. See, for example, the quotation attached to footnote 36; also *Argus* 18 June 1860.
83. *BLV*, 7 June 1862, 7 May 1864; *Argus*, 13 June 1862
84. Verbal and written responses to Mancini and Hibbins, *Running with the Ball*, op. cit., in which an early version of this research was published, suggest that this is not so. Wills seems to have been elevated at the expense of Harrison but Thompson, Smith and Hammersley continue to be ignored.

CHAPTER SIX

Symbols of Imperial Unity: Anglo-Australian Cricketers, 1877–1900

RICHARD CASHMAN

I

Australia was one of the parts of the Empire most susceptible to ideas and practices symbolizing the bond of empire. At the beginning of the twentieth century virtually the entire population (98 per cent) was Anglo-Celtic: they were either born in, or were descendants of migrants from, England, Scotland, Wales and Ireland.

Pro-imperial sentiment was particularly strong in the colonial middle class which drew its greater proportion from England and Scotland. When an indigenous nationalism began to emerge from the 1860s, it was not in any sense anti-British; rather, it was decidedly Anglicist and expressed in terms of Anglo-Australian ideals. This concept suggested that middle-class Australians viewed themselves as dual citizens, as much British as Australian; they were citizens both of a particular nation and a wider empire. In the minds of middle-class Australia, there was no clear distinction between an Englishman or a Scot and an Australian. The essential difference was between a metropolitan and a colonial citizen. The common reference to Britain as 'home'[1] underlines the strength of the British attachment. A successful return to England or Scotland was a desirable form of progression for middle-class Australians. Most regarded 'home' as culturally superior.

The first stirrings of nationalism in Australia were hesitant and tentative. One of the central aims of Australian middle-class thinkers was to establish that the colonial British were not inferior to the metropolitan variety. One recurring colonial theme up till the 1880s, reflecting the Social Darwinism of the era, was that British culture and citizens could flourish in the southern hemisphere and that the hot sun did not weaken 'British blood'. The *Sydney Morning Herald* of 24 January 1874 stated that colonial victories against the English tourists proved that British blood 'has not yet been thinned by the heat of Australian summers'.

Not everyone in Australia subscribed to Anglo-Australian ideals. The working class, with much greater Irish proportions, were far less sympathetic to ideals which were Anglicist and pro-imperial. They contributed to the development of a more indigenous nationalism which found greater expression by the 1890s and challenged some of the pro-British tenets of the older nationalism.

As the most English of English games, cricket was thought to express imperial ideas and the concept of cultural bond better than any other sport. There developed from the late nineteenth century, note Sissons and Stoddart, an 'unshakeable belief in cricket as a code of cultural behaviour throughout the British Empire'. The same authors quote a comment in *The Times* on the deaths in 1933 of the Indian prince Ranjitsinhji and the cricketing Viceroy, Lord Chelmsford, that although 'a whole world of race and custom separated them . . . the greatest of English games brings men together in the most satisfying of associations'.[2] Preference for the game was, in the opinion of Major Philip Trevor, linked with English character: 'when you find a man completely out of sympathy with cricket, you will generally find some other rather un-English trait in his character'.[3]

Influential cricket apologists in the late nineteenth and early twentieth century had no doubts that cricket was one of the most important links of empire. Lord Harris claimed in 1921 that 'cricket has done more to consolidate the Empire than any other influence' while the Indian prince and imperial cricket symbol, K. S. Ranjitsinhji (1872–1933), stated that 'cricket is certainly amongst the most powerful links which keep our Empire together. It is one of the greatest contributions which the British people have made to the cause of humanity'. Ranjitsinhji, according to Derek Birley, viewed the Empire as 'the world's greatest cricket team'.[4]

Cricket had an added advantage for imperial thinkers in that it was believed to be beyond the comprehension of non-English nations. 'The game is', as the Rev. James Pycroft put it, 'essentially Anglo-Saxon' and 'foreigners have rarely, very rarely, imitated us'.[5] Europeans, such as the French and Germans, were considered unable to fathom, let alone play, cricket. There was even the fanciful suggestion, aired from time to time, that had the Germans played cricket they would have been far less inclined to have indulged in warfare with Britain. Some rather crude comparisons between British and German culture appeared during the First World War, as for instance in E. W. Hornung's poem 'Lord's Leave 1915':

> Cricket? 'Tis Sanskrit to the super-Hun . . .
> Playing a game's beyond him and his hordes
> Theirs but to play the snake or wolf or vulture:
> Better one sporting lesson learnt at Lord's than all their Kultur.[6]

With its clear English and imperial associations cricket was the favoured middle-class team sport in Australia for much of the nineteenth century and became a significant element in the development of Australian nationalism, as W. F. Mandle pointed out in his seminal article 'Cricket and Australian Nationalism'. Success at cricket, matching and even defeating the English masters of the game, was proof positive that British society, culture and institutions were flourishing in the Antipodes. Since Australian middle-class nationalism was initially so hesitant and defensive – colonial culture was accepted as an inferior to the metropolitan product – 'thrashing the motherland' at cricket, as Mandle has shown, was an important colonial priority.

Success at cricket enhanced claims of the 'white' Empire that they were superior in the pecking order to the 'black' and 'brown' Empire. The influential English cricket administrator, Lord Harris, thought that 'Asiatics' (Indians) were far too 'excitable' to play cricket well in that they lacked the necessary 'phlegmatic' qualities of 'Anglo-Saxons'.[7] Defeating the Englishmen proved that Australians had their share of desirable Anglo-Saxon qualities such as pluck, courage and stoicism.

II

The ideology of cricket proved a powerful construct cementing the cultural bond of Empire because it was more than a theoretical construct: it had a number of practical dimensions in which the ideals were given tangible form.

Regular English tours to Australia from 1861–62 did much to enhance interest in the game and to improve the skills of colonial sides. Although the aims of English tourists, mostly professionals, were to make money and to have a good time, the tours performed important educative roles. Some of the English tourists of the 1860s, notably William Caffyn and Charles Lawrence, remained in Australia after the tours to coach local sides. As the first international sporting team to visit Australia the English tourists enhanced interest in a game which was already popular and at the same time reinforced a British frame of reference. The appearance of star players, such as the bowler George Tarrant and the batsmen brothers, E. M. and later W. G. Grace, provided attractive symbols which proved appealing to colonial society. The tours also underscored the superiority of British culture, as matches were played against the odds. During the first two tours an English XI was usually pitted against a colonial XXII. Even though it played every match against a colonial XXII, George Parr's 1864 touring side was undefeated with seven wins and five draws. Colonial sides had the incentive to reduce this disparity between the two sides; local teams were reduced to XVIII, then to XV, and eventually, in 1877, played the tourists on even terms.

Australian tours to England, organized on a regular basis (every two to three years), from 1878 assumed even larger proportions in the colonial mind. Such tours represented a form of cultural pilgrimage to established shrines of England, such as Lord's, which were and still are highly regarded. Great store was placed on winning in England, and at Lord's in particular, since it was regarded as the ultimate achievement to triumph on the hallowed proving ground, at the cathedral of cricket, as it were. It is ironic that Australians have set and continue to set such store on success at Lord's – much more store than English sides. This is probably the principal reason why they have outplayed England in all but one Test there in the twentieth century and have a record vastly superior to their performance on any other English ground.[8]

The creation of imperial heroes, and their endorsement by the English media, was another practical way in which the cultural bond was furthered. Cricket heroes such as W. G. Grace were initially English domestic heroes. But the colonial interest in all things British determined that this dynamic symbol of the game was soon exported and embraced as an imperial hero as well.

But from the late 1870s, with the arrival of the Australian Fred Spofforth (1853–1926) as a world-class bowler, the English media accepted colonial cricketers as heroes and in fact contributed to Spofforth's elevation as an imperial symbol. The rise of Spofforth is an interesting case-study, to be explored below, because although he was as popular in England as Australia, his media image was rather different in the two societies.

The most famous imperial hero was K. S. Ranjitsinhji. From the time he attended the Indian elite Rajkumar College to the completion of his education at Cambridge University, Ranji, as he was popularly known, imbibed British cultural traditions, including the practice and ideology of cricket. Although English cricket authorities were rather slow to embrace this brilliant but unorthodox cricketer, he became in time England's 'pre-eminent example of cricket's imperial value'.[9]

Ranji was a powerful cultural symbol because he succeeded at the highest level of the game, scoring 64 and 154 not out in his first Test in 1896, playing for England against Australia. He was the first of a number of Indian-born princes who represented England, partly because India itself did not become a Test-playing nation until 1932. Ranji became an enthusiastic and effective apologist for cricket as an important bond of Empire. His English tutors did such a good job inculcating the games ethic that Ranji became an active supporter of recruiting campaigns during the First World War and helped raise money for patriotic funds.[10]

The opportunity for some players to represent both England and Australia was a further telling illustration that they were cricketers of the Empire. They were all really brothers, who were part of a great imperial team. This was achieved by a deliberate slackness in the qualification rules for national sides before 1900. It was easier in some instances for an Australian to represent England than to qualify for an English county. English tours to South Africa, which included Australian players along with English, also demonstrated common imperial ties. English teams right up to the 1930s, in addition, had a distinctly imperial character with Duleepsinhji and Pataudi Senior following the earlier tradition established by Ranjitsinhji.

During the period 1877–1900 five Australian players represented both Australia and England, and a sixth was keen to do so but did not get the opportunity. By exploring the circumstances in which the five changed their allegiances, we will gain further understanding of some of the practices which furthered the ideology of imperial union through cricket. But first, consideration of the career of the sixth Australian player, Fred Spofforth, throws light on another important cultural practice, the creation of imperial heroes.

III

The day before the Australian cricket hero, the 'Demon' Fred Spofforth, left Australia for good to take up residence in England he made some revealing comments about his identity. The occasion was a farewell dinner at the Oriental Hotel, Melbourne, on 7 June 1888, and Spofforth's remarks were in response to what was said by his former captain and cricketing colleague, William Murdoch (1854–1911). In his speech Murdoch suggested that Spofforth would arrive in England (in late July) to be of some possible assistance to the 1888 Australian tourists who had left Australia some two months before. Murdoch added that he hoped 'whatever his [Spofforth's] success in England, [he] would never be found opposing an Australian eleven'.

Spofforth responded that he believed that he was in fine form and far from a spent force as a Test bowler. He added that 'Australian associations would ever remain very dear to him' and he hoped that when he arrived in England he might be of 'some service to the Australians'. However, he disagreed with Murdoch at one point: 'If England paid him the compliment of picking him' and 'if as a member of an England team he was instrumental in beating an Australian eleven, he would feel all the more proud of it for the sake of Australia'. His audience, made up of many who believed fervently in Anglo-Australian ideals, cheered this comment.[11]

Spofforth did not play again for Australia or England. Five other cricketers of this era, 1877–1912, played Tests for both countries: J.J. Ferris (eight for Australia, one for England), William Midwinter (eight for Australia, four for England), William Murdoch (18 for Australia, one for England), Albert Trott (three for Australia, two for England) and Sammy Woods (three for Australia, three for England). While there were different reasons why each represented two countries – working-class players were rather more concerned with professional advancement and financial rewards than those from the middle class – this unique double was a reflection of the strength of Anglo-Australian ideals in this era. There were two sides to this practice. Australian players were quite amenable to the idea of playing for the English side. English officials for their part accepted colonial players who had already appeared against the mother country.

Frederick Spofforth (1853–1926), who was born in the Sydney suburb of Balmain, was proud of his colonial upbringing and clearly relished uprooting the stumps of Englishmen.[12] He always saved his best for his arch rival and one of the best-known symbols of Victorian England, W.G. Grace. Although Spofforth came from a comfortable middle-class family and was a banker by profession, he had a love of the Australian bush and spent much time as a stockman on the large country property of his brother-in-law. Long periods spent in the saddle on the estate enhanced his stamina as a bowler.

However, Spofforth was also very conscious of English antecedents as were most middle-class Australians of this era. An autobiographical essay, published in 1903, began with the following comments:

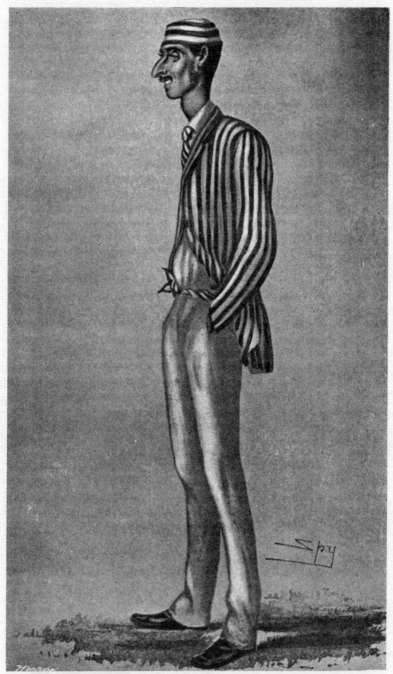

10. The English approximation of an Australian hero. The famous cartoon by 'Spy' of Spofforth, the Demon Bowler, from *Vanity Fair*, 13 July 1878

11. Tours generated enormous public interest and enhanced the cultural bond. This illustration from the *Sydney Mail*, 30 November 1878, shows the 20,000-strong crowd at Circular Quay, Sydney, on the return of the 1878 team

My father came from a very old Yorkshire family, who fought for
their country in 1066, and suffered defeat at the hands of William the
Conqueror, and in consequence lost all their property, it being given
to one William de Perci, to whom, I believe, one of the present dukes
owes his inheritance.[13]

Being an Australian, to Spofforth, was synonymous with being a colonial
Englishman or Scot. He was not at all unique in this perspective. During
the 1882 tour Spofforth's team-mate George Bonnor (1855–1912) was
involved in controversy at Nottingham when he tangled with the fiery and
patronizing Secretary, Captain Holden. The Australians were not
impressed with Holden's failure to provide them with lunch which was
akin to treating them as professionals, and there was a heated debate
between Holden, Bonnor and Australian Manager Beal. After Bonnor
became so angry that he had to be restrained, Holden took out a cigar and
enquired pointedly: 'Will some *Englishman* give me a light?' This unsubtle
aside was too much for Bonner who retorted instantly; 'I can tell you, sir, I
am as much an *Englishman* as you or any gentleman present: I can trace my
family back for six generations, and perhaps you cannot do more'.[14]
Spofforth's espousal of Anglo-Australian ideals made him a very acceptable symbol for the English cricket public. Although he cut down and even
humiliated many English teams, the English cricketing public never
demonstrated any hostility to the 'Demon'; in fact he became England's
favourite Australian sportsman. Undoubtedly there were also sound cricketing reasons for this popularity. Spofforth probably performed better on
English wickets than Australian, and some of his most memorable performances were in England. He was also a perfect foil for the champion
batsman of this era, W.G. Grace, and the rivalry between the two great
players did much to put international cricket on the map.
But other factors made Spofforth acceptable to the English cricketing
public. From very early in his career the English press seized on the fact
that Spofforth was really one of them and claimed that his success proved
how Anglo-Saxon culture could flourish even in remote and less civilized
parts of the world. Within months of Spofforth's first great English success
– the demolition of the MCC on 27 May 1878[15] – the English media were
acclaiming him as a great symbol of English imperial greatness. Spofforth
was only the second cricketer (W.G. Grace being the first) to appear in a
'Spy' cartoon in the *Vanity Fair* series which was published on 13 July 1878.
Alongside the cartoon 'Jehu Junior' wrote that 'Mr Spofforth is Australian
by origin and breeding, yet like the better kind of Australians, he is not
distinguishable from an English gentleman. He comes, indeed, of a good
English family . . . He is withal of excellent manners, modest and diffident,
and has become a favourite with all who have known him in England'.
Similar views appeared in other sources: *Home News* pointed out to its
readers on 27 May 1878 that 'Spofforth is a Yorkshireman by extraction'
whose 'father rode as straight as the best with the Yorkshire and Ainsty [*sic*:
Ainstey] and other hounds'. *Home News* added that it welcomed the

prowess of Spofforth and his colleagues because it was proof that 'our flesh and blood' was 'not degenerating in those far-off lands'.

The above comments suggest that Spofforth was not only revered and respected, as were Trumper and Bradman and some other twentieth-century Australian heroes, he was acclaimed and adopted as a British or an imperial hero. This was more possible in the late nineteenth century because there were so many overlapping areas between British and middle-class Australian culture. Heroes reflected symbols which were appreciated equally in both societies.

There were, however, slightly different reasons why he was lionized in each country. To the British he was an imperial symbol whose success established the vitality of their culture in exotic climes. To the Australians he was a symbol that colonial culture, which it was feared was inferior, was worthwhile. Spofforth was also a symbol of an emerging but hesitant Australian nationalism.

Spofforth was a member of five Australian tours to England, 1878–1886, and at the end of the last tour he married Phillis Cadman, the daughter of a wealthy Derbyshire tea merchant. The Spofforths decided initially to live in Australia, settling in Melbourne in 1886. It was the country where Spofforth had spent virtually all his life, his immediate family (his mother and three sisters were still living there) and Spofforth had a job as a banker in Melbourne.

But two years later the Spofforths decided to leave Australia for good and return to England. His wife, Phillis, was unhappy with her life in Australia. Then there was the prospect of moving into a senior position, and eventually managing, the business of his father-in-law, the Star Tea Company. But it is likely that Spofforth was also amenable to the idea of reclaiming his English heritage and of acting out Anglo-Australian ideals, which placed high status on making it in England.

After returning to England Spofforth concentrated mostly on building up the Star Tea Company though he was interested in playing some games for Derbyshire. Spofforth became embroiled in controversy when there was considerable debate about whether he had to abide by a residential rule which required a two-year qualification period. Spofforth himself, supported by the Derbyshire Cricket Club, provided some interesting grounds as to why this rule should be waived. He believed he had a 'moral right' to play for Derbyshire, then a weak county club, because he had come to Derby for business and private reasons and not as a cricket professional. He then added a revealing comment reflecting his Anglo-Australian ideals: 'Personally, I regard myself as an Englishman, but other people seem to take a contrary view'.[16]

The Spofforth case appeared to be based on two grounds. As an amateur and a gentleman he was not intent in making profit from any waiving of the rules to accommodate himself in the Derbyshire side. His intention was simply to provide 'a lift' for a struggling county side. Spofforth also raised the issue as to whether the framers of the rule had ever considered the question of an Australian player who by virtue of his birth outside England was not qualified to play for any county.

Spofforth played only nine games for Derbyshire between 1889 and 1891 before he moved to London where he played club cricket for Hampstead until the age of 51. He became a successful London businessman with a fine house and garden south of London. He visited Australia briefly in 1902 and 1925.

Spofforth was not the only Australian who was equally at home in England. William Murdoch, who was Spofforth's captain during tours of 1880–84, was Australia's premier bat in the early 1880s and generally regarded as a very astute and able captain. After captaining the 1890 Australian side Murdoch remained in England and, like Spofforth, reclaimed his English heritage and became an Englishman.

In Murdoch's case there was no pressure from an English wife hankering to return to relatives and friends in England. Murdoch married an heiress, Winsome Jemima Waton, daughter of a Bendigo mining magnate. His immediate reason for settling in England was to join the Sussex Club. Murdoch, it seems, had become disillusioned with Australian cricket and his prospects of leading his country again and set out to discover new cricket pastures.

But cricket was only one of the reasons why Murdoch moved permanently to England. As a solicitor, he too, like Spofforth, clearly placed much emphasis on making it in England. The ease with which middle-class Murdoch settled into English life was reflected in an interview published in *Cricket Field* on 16 July 1892 when he stated that 'English country life suits me very well'. He added that 'some day or other I hope to go back to Australia' but 'not to live there, for I have settled in England now . . . but to see the old country again'.

It was ironic that while Murdoch had still a year before he was eligible to play for Sussex he was deemed eligible to play for England. In the 1890s it was easier to transfer from one Test country to another than to qualify for a county. Admittedly Murdoch was a member of W. W. Read's mostly amateur side to South Africa; this was largely a second-string touring team playing against an opposition that had yet to establish itself as formidable. Murdoch played for England in the only Test match of the tour at Cape Town in March 1892 just 19 months after he had captained Australia against England at the Oval.

Murdoch died on 18 February 1911 while watching a Test at the Melbourne Cricket Ground against South Africa after he had returned to Australia for a short visit. Given that Murdoch was born and bred in Australia, married an Australian and achieved his greatest cricket as an Australian, it is surprising that Murdoch was not buried an Australian. This was not to be. His body was embalmed and shipped back to England where he was buried at Kensal Green, London, on 18 May 1911. The Murdochs, like Spofforth, had reasserted their English identity. They believed, like other Anglo-Australians, that England was ultimately home.

In a sense the English team to South Africa in 1891–92 was an imperial team as it included another Australian, J.J Ferris (1867–1900), who played alongside Murdoch in the 1892 Test at Cape Town. Ferris, too, had been a member of the 1890 Australian team. However, the circumstances of his transfer were rather more controversial. Unlike Murdoch and Spofforth, who were both in the twilight of their careers, Ferris was only 23 and was an integral member of the Australian bowling attack. During the 1888 and 1890 tours the Australian team depended heavily on their opening duo of C. T. B. Turner ('The Terror') and Ferris ('The Fiend'), for after that the bowling was decidedly thin.

W. G. Grace appears to have played an important role in recruiting Ferris to Gloucestershire which was strong in batting but weak in bowling. In order to reduce the qualification period Ferris signed an agreement for a tenancy of a small house near the Bristol County Ground on 24 June 1890 while he was on tour with the 1890 Australians. It was an unorthodox and presumably secret agreement made before the two Test matches of 1890 were even played. The poaching of Ferris strengthened Gloucester and weakened Australia.

After the tour Ferris returned to Australia to settle business matters and played some domestic cricket, representing New South Wales in several matches, before returning to England in March 1891. Because of the fiddle with the residential rules, Ferris was able to play for Gloucestershire from the beginning of 1892 rather than 1893. Ferris, a bank clerk in New South Wales, joined a Gloucester stockbroking firm.

There were many in the cricket world who looked upon the move to Gloucester as a mistake because the Gloucester attack was weak and Ferris had to shoulder a very heavy load. The critics were proved right. After three seasons Ferris became worn out and was never the same bowler again. Ferris could have played for Gloucestershire again in 1894, but by then he was disappointed with his form and returned to Australia. He played twice for New South Wales and once for South Australia but was unable to reproduce his form. He was one of the first colonials to enlist in the Boer War, enlisting with the Imperial Light Horse, but died on 21 November 1900 of enteric fever at the age of 33 and was buried at Durban.

Ferris differed from Spofforth and Murdoch in that he did not settle in England permanently and his move to England appears to have been inspired more by cricket reasons than by Anglo-Australian ideals. However, his experience throws light on the priorities of cricket officials who made it much easier to move from one national side to another than to qualify for an English county.

The careers of S. M. J. 'Sammy' Woods (1867–1931) and Spofforth were intertwined at one point as they were both touted as candidates to prop up the ailing 1888 bowling side. By the time of the First Test it had become clear that the side had real bowling problems as all-rounder S. P. Jones was seriously ill and the support bowling, to back up Turner and Ferris, was proving inadequate.

Although Spofforth, who arrived in England a day before the First Test, was keen to play for Australia and was supported by some prominent pundits, he was not picked to play in any of the three Tests. The Australian team co-opted Sammy Woods instead. It was a very unusual and largely unsuccessful move. Woods played in the three Tests but in no other games on the tour. The more intriguing aspect was that Woods was not an Australian cricketer in the strict sense of the term. He had played no first-class cricket in Australia whatsoever. Born at Glenfield, New South Wales, he had completed part of his secondary education at Sydney Grammar School and Royston College but had 'made England my home' from 1883, his sixteenth year.[17] He completed his secondary schooling at Brighton College before continuing on to Cambridge University.

When he was co-opted to the Australian side Woods was already playing for Somerset and represented the county for 25 years. He was a member of Lord Hawke's team to South Africa in 1895–96 and represented England in all three Tests.

Two working-class cricketers, Albert Trott (1873–1914) and William Midwinter (1851–90) had different reasons for representing two countries. Financial gain and professional advancement were the more immediate concerns. However, both players benefited by playing in an era when Anglo-Australian ideals were prominent among the organizers of cricket enabling Trott and Midwinter to advance their professional interests by playing for more than one country.

Albert Trott, born in Abbotsford, Victoria, was employed as a ground bowler at East Melbourne. He made a highly successful Test debut with both bat and ball against Stoddart's 1894–95 team, playing in the last three Tests of this series. His form deteriorated in subsequent seasons and he was not selected for the 1896 tour, which was captained by his brother, George Henry Trott. Disappointed at not making the Australian side, Albert Trott migrated to England where he secured a position on the Lord's ground staff. He qualified to play for Middlesex in 1898 and became a very valuable player for this county side for the next twelve years. Selected for Lord Hawke's 1898–99 tour of South Africa, Trott played two Tests for England.

Albert Trott, who was lost to Australian domestic and international cricket after 1896, died in London by his own hand in 1914, leaving his wardrobe and £4 to his landlady.

William Midwinter, professional cricketer and publican, was the most interesting of the six cricketers considered in this study, being the only one to represent Australia against England and England against Australia. His changing allegiance from one national side to another even attracted criticism from commentators committed to Anglo-Australian ideals.

Midwinter was born at St Briavels, Forest of Dean, Gloucestershire and spent his boyhood years there until his family migrated to Sandhurst on the Victorian goldfields in 1862. After gaining selection for Victoria in 1874–75 he represented Australia in the first two tests in March 1877, playing an important role in Australia's historic First Test victory. During the English

summer of 1877 Midwinter travelled to England and played for
Gloucestershire. Over the next five years he became cricket's first international mercenary, following the cricket sun and commuting regularly
between Australia and England.

Midwinter was selected in the 1878 tour of England and joined the
tourists when the side arrived in England. He had only played eight
games for the tourists before he was virtually 'kidnapped' by W.G.
Grace, when Midwinter was padded up about to open the Australian
innings against Middlesex at Lord's. Grace persuaded Midwinter that
he should really be playing for Gloucestershire against Surrey at the
Oval.

Midwinter was a member of the English 1881–82 tour to Australia
and played for England in all four Tests. Despite his ever-shifting
loyalties Midwinter was keen to play for Australia for the 1882 tour of
England. The nationalist journal, *The Bulletin*, made a wry comment on
7 January 1882 about Midwinter: 'Midwinter is very anxious to go with
the next Australian team. In Australia he plays as an Englishman; in
England, as an Australian and he is always a credit to himself and his
country, whichever that may be'.

Midwinter made a strenuous effort to return to the Australian Test
side against the 1882–83 English tourists captained by the Hon. Ivo
Bligh. He proclaimed that he had now 'left England to return no more'
and that he considered himself 'an Australian to the heart's core'. He
objected to being dubbed an 'Anglo-Australian' by the colonial press,
which he regarded as a pejorative term, because 'he felt as much an
Australian at heart when playing for Gloucestershire county as he does
now, or as he did when learning how to play the game in Sandhurst,
which he looks upon virtually the land of his birth'.[18] This was yet
another use of the term 'Anglo-Australian' which represented the nega-
tive side of the ideal. An all too frequent shift of allegiance from Englishman to Anglo-Australian made a mockery of the ideal.

The colonial press was sceptical of Midwinter's rediscovery of his
Australian identity. He was castigated in the *Sydney Mail* on 16 December 1882:

> *A propos* of Midwinter, I would ask seriously, are the cricketers of
> the colony, and especially those of Victoria, going to submit to
> another season of vagaries from this very slippery character? One
> day he is an Australian, and next day an English player. Last
> season he played with England against Australia, and wanted
> badly to go to England immediately after as a full-blown
> Australian cricketer in Murdoch's team. Failing to induce the
> Australians to take the giant to their arms, he journeyed back to
> the old country with Shaw's team, and played for his county
> Gloucestershire during the whole of their last cricketing campaign.
> In order to ingratiate himself with the colonial cricketers, who will
> not forget his base desertion of the first Australian Eleven at

Lord's, he returned to Australia with Murdoch and his companions, announcing his intention of 'never never' returning to the old country.

Despite such misgivings Midwinter was selected for Australia in the Fourth Test in the 1882–83 series against the Hon. Ivo Bligh's team and was a member of the 1884 Australian side to England, representing Australia in two Tests. His selection for the 1884 tour drew less criticism because from 1882 until his death in 1890 he resided in Australia.

In retrospect it seems that Midwinter was criticized because he denied Anglo-Australian idealism and exploited the slackness in international qualification rules. The actions of Spofforth and Murdoch were more acceptable in the eyes of middle-class Australians because they did not flout, but rather enhanced, a prevailing nationalism, which was pro-imperialist.

However, during the 1880s there were stirrings of a more indigenous nationalism. While a middle-class Melbourne audience cheered Spofforth's suggestion that he would regard it as an honour to play for England against Australia, the more radical paper, *The Bulletin*, was not all that impressed by this effusion of patriotism. It made some sarcastic comments in the issue of 9 June 1888 about Spofforth's departure:

> Spofforth, the erstwhile demon bowler, having come in for money, leaves next month to take up residence in England.

> If Turner keeps up his present form with bat and ball the Britishers will forget about Spofforth who at his best was only a one-part demon.

In the following issue of 16 June *The Bulletin* ridiculed the remarks made by Spofforth in his valedictory oration. Spofforth, it argued, would not be of much use to the Australians who were short of batsmen rather than bowlers; nor would the British need any extra bowling resources. *The Bulletin* then proceeded to denigrate the performance of Spofforth:

> The long'un, in his day funked the Britishers, who (Grace always excepted) had lapsed into a mechanical style of batting unfitted to master a new method of attack. But they have come to modify their former opinion of Spof.'s powers very considerably.

The strength of the Anglo-Australian ideal has been diluted in the twentieth century. Since 1900 no player has represented both countries. By 1900 Australia was producing more indigenous heroes in keeping with emerging nationalism, and the thought of playing both for Australia and England became quite foreign to working-class heroes such as Victor Trumper. With the rise of a more confident local nationalism, which drew less on British traditions, Australians like Trumper were less inclined to regard England as home. Residential qualifications, imposed much later, have restricted the movement of players from one international side to another.

IV

Anglo-Australian ideals played an important role in many sports in colonial Australia in the era up to the First World War. There was no absolute distinction between Australian and British competitors at the initial (1896) Olympic Games. Stan Rowley won three individual gold medals as an Australian in athletics and then won a fourth when he competed for Great Britain in the 5,000 metre Cross Country event at the 1900 Paris Olympics. Australia's first Olympic champion, Edwin Flack, was nominated for the 1896 Games by the London Athletics Club and his two gold medals were claimed as British, as well as Australian, victories even as late as 1936.[19] Sport then helped to dramatize that special bond which was meant to exist between the countries which made up the British Empire.

From 1877–1900 a number of Australian Test cricketers had the opportunity of representing both Australia and England. In the absence of international qualification rules some Australian cricketers were able to act out and make a reality of Anglo-Australian ideals. Because Australians and Englishmen shared so much common cultural territory, some of the first Test heroes, notably Spofforth, were as much English as they were Australian heroes.

Anglo-Australian idealism diminished in importance after 1900 as a more indigenous nationalism emerged. Tighter legislation, to restrict entrance to the English side, was not required after 1900, because Australian cricketers no longer believed it was an honour to play for both England and Australia.

Anglo-Australian cricketers played a significant role in the rise of international cricket as an important institution. Spofforth, who was an acceptable English as well as an Australian hero, helped to make Test cricket the pinnacle of cricket competition. He and the others discussed in this chapter symbolized a belief that Britain and Australia were an integrated, indivisible 'Anglo-Saxon' community bound by ties of common cultural activities, not least of which, of course, was cricket.

NOTES

The author is indebted to Dr J. A. Mangan for his constructive comments on an early draft of this study.

1. An Australian cricket annual, for instance, published in 1878, referred to the 1878 tour as 'the trip home'. P.E. Reynolds, *The Australian Cricketers' Tour Australia, New Zealand and Great Britain in 1878* (J.W. McKenzie reprint, Cambridge, 1980), p. 13.
2. Ric Sissons and Brian Stoddart, *Cricket and Empire: The 1932–33 Bodyline Tour of Australia* (Sydney, 1984), pp. 29, 33.

3. Quoted in W.F. Mandle, 'Cricket and Australian Nationalism in the Nineteenth Century', *Journal of the Royal Australian Historical Society*, LIX (Dec. 1973), 226.
4. Derek Birley, *The Willow Wand: Some Cricket Myths Explored* (London, 1979), p.13.
5. Quoted in ibid., p.11.
6. Quoted in Mandle, 'Cricket and Australian Nationalism', 227.
7. See Richard Cashman, *Patrons, Players and the Crowd: The Phenomenon of Indian Cricket* (New Delhi, 1980), p.37.
8. Since 1900 Australia has won 9, lost 1 and drawn 12 Tests played at Lord's. This is vastly superior to Australia's overall Test record (since 1880) in England: 34 wins, 37 losses and 58 draws.
9. Sissons and Stoddart, *Cricket and Empire*, p.29.
10. For a discussion of the influential tutor Chester Macnaghten see J.A. Mangan, *The Games Ethic and Imperialism* (London, 1987), pp.133–5.
11. *Australasian*, 9 June 1888; *Leader*, 9 June 1888.
12. Richard Cashman, *The 'Demon' Spofforth* (Kensington, 1990).
13. F.R. Spofforth, 'In the Days of My Youth: Chapters of Autobiography', *M.A.P.*, 28 November 1903, 672–4.
14. Quoted in *The Bulletin*, 12 Aug. 1882.
15. Australia 41 and 12 for 1 defeated a strong MCC side 33 and 19 in less than a day in only the second match of the 1878 tour. This shock result, in which Spofforth took 10 wickets for 20 runs, played an important role in the rise of international cricket.
16. *Birmingham Daily Mail*, 10 June 1889.
17. S.M.J. Woods, *My Reminiscences* (London, 1925), p.9.
18. Quoted in *Cricket*, 16 February 1883.
19. W.W. Dent, 'Australia's Participation in the Olympic and British Empire Games, 1896–1938', unpublished MA thesis, University of New England, 1987, pp.11–16.

CHAPTER SEVEN

Football on the Maidan: Cultural Imperialism in Calcutta

TONY MASON

Brian Stoddart has recently reminded us that the unity of the British Empire was not only a product of economic, political and military ties. It was also maintained by sinews of cultural power of which the English language was the most notable and sport by no means the least.[1] Sport was a means of transmitting a set of British beliefs and standards about fairness, honesty and straightforwardness in a context of respect for traditional authority which may have been summed up in the idea of 'playing the game' but which went far beyond it. Sport was also something that rulers and ruled could not only share but, in certain circumstances, do together. Sport could provide a cultural common ground among otherwise disparate groups.

Team games in particular were thought valuable for teaching conformity and solidarity and football, cricket, hockey and rugby were rapidly being established as central parts of the curriculum in schools all over the Empire from the 1880s. The role of organized sport in the public and grammar schools of Britain was repeated in schools as far apart as Wellington and Port of Spain, Melbourne and Calcutta. This study concentrates on the impact of one sport, football, at one particular moment, in 1911, in a location not always thought of as being synonymous with the generation of footballing passion: Calcutta. It attempts to analyse and describe the cultural importance of the first victory of a native team over a European one in the Bengali equivalent of the FA Cup Final: the final for the Indian Football Association Shield. Even the London *Times* drew the attention of its readers to this startling happening.[2]

But first we must sketch in the most important landmarks in the development of football in Calcutta up to that exciting pinnacle of 1911 and note, in particular, the role in that development of another important British institution, the Army.

There were about 75,000 British troops in India at the beginning of the twentieth century and it cannot be said that it was a very attractive posting, especially for the other ranks. Poorly paid and generally underprivileged, life was boring, brutish and hot. There was a limit to the amount of training and military manoeuvres which could be undertaken and sport in general and football in particular came to be not only a boon to physical fitness and an outlet for the physical needs of young men, but a crucial boost to morale. As one old soldier told Charles Allen, 'We had one great weapon against boredom. The answer was sport, sport, sport'.[3] Sport was something officers and men could share, and inter-unit, inter-battalion, inter-regimental competition did much to cement army solidarities. A place in a battalion or regimental eleven provided opportunities for travel, improved personal status and must have relieved the tedium of ordinary soldiering. Moreover, casual games often provided a link between British and Indian other ranks, as one private in the Royal Scots described:

> In the evening we used to go along to have a chat with the Gurkha boys. We would invariably find them playing football and they would immediately split up and demand that we should join them. From then on it was everyone for himself, with about forty Gurkhas on each side, each having two or three British ranks playing with them and with the ball being passed to the British ranks by every Gurkha on their side. ...[4]

The first regular, organized football competition in India was probably the Durand Trophy competed for by Army teams in Simla from 1888. The Army's influence on the footballing life of Calcutta was bound to be considerable because the garrison there was so large. Calcutta had been the headquarters of the East India Company and remained the formal capital of British India until 1912. It was one of the great commercial cities of the world with a population of 1,222,313 by the beginning of the twentieth century. 'Street after street of grave business houses like huge neo-classical factories to process the trade of the interior' dominated its modern core.[5] This role, together with its administrative, educational and military importance is clearly reflected in the rise of organized football there.

Scratch football games were probably no more uncommon in India, and particularly in Calcutta than elsewhere in the Empire. The evidence so far is thin but it is clear that the mandarins of the Indian Civil Service occasionally indulged themselves in a vigorous kickabout such as the one in 1868 in which Etonians beat the Rest by 3–0 and Lord Vansittart scored twice.[6] Formal clubs appeared a little later. Dalhousie may have been the first: some of the young British males engaged in business and commerce formed a Trades Club in 1878 but the unprepossessing name was soon altered to the Dalhousie Athletic Club, from the Dalhousie Institute which had once been the headquarters of the Trades Association of India.[7] This important organizational impetus not only set up the Trades Cup, which from its inception in 1889 appears to have been open to both European and native teams, but was also crucial in the establishment of the Indian Football Association in 1893.

The Calcutta Football Club itself was an elite European foundation in 1872. Its historical notoriety rests on the fact that the members actually played rugby until 1876 when the attempt to establish that game was given up as a bad job and the club disbanded. The club silver was melted down and reshaped as a cup to be played for annually by the rugby teams of England and Scotland: the trophy has been known as the Calcutta Cup ever since. The club itself was reformed in 1884 and, though still flirting with rugby, took part in the Trades Cup and appears to have concentrated on football from about 1894. Its status and resources meant that it would inevitably become a power in the local football world. Other European clubs had joined Calcutta by the mid 1880s including Calcutta Rangers and Howrah United.

By that time, young Bengalis were also beginning to play football and form clubs for regular play. The colleges may have been first, with the Presidency College FC begun in 1884 and a rash of followers soon after: Sibpur Engineering College, Bishops College, Medical College, St. Xavier's College and La Martiniere. By the middle of the 1880s, at the moment when professionalism was being introduced in England, other Indian clubs began to appear in Calcutta, Sorabazar (1885), Mohan Bagan (1889) and Mohammedan Sporting (1891) who had been dissatisfied with three previous incarnations as Jubilee, Crescent and Hamidia. Many others must have been quickly formed and as quickly faded. We do not know much about the social origins of the players, but it seems likely that they came from the educated lower-middle and middle classes, an expanding group without whose existence and positive support such a structure as the British Empire in India could not have been sustained.

Clubs usually lead to the organization of regular competitive matches and, with the example of sporting events at home as the model, that soon happened in Calcutta. We noticed earlier the Trades Cup, first played for in 1889. It was in one of the early rounds of that competition, in 1892, that a Bengali team, Sorbazar, first defeated a British regiment. The following year saw the foundation of the Indian Football Association (IFA) in Calcutta but very much on London lines. It immediately announced its own knock-out Shield to be played for by European clubs only and this limitation of the premier competitions to the dominant group was continued in 1898 when the Calcutta Football League was formed.[8] Mohan Bagan won the Trades Cup three years in succession between 1906 and 1908 and it may have been this success which prompted the British-dominated IFA to allow them to enter the Shield in 1909.[9]

By 1911 the popularity of football in Calcutta had expanded dramatically, reflected in a plethora of cups and leagues and with numerous Bengali and British clubs. There was, however, a clear hierarchy among these competitions. The IFA Shield attracted competing teams, civil as well as military, from far afield in the sub-continent and brought the season to an exciting climax. The Shield was taken very seriously indeed. The 2nd Battalion East Yorkshire Regiment team from Fyzabad, for example, began preparing for it in June, although they were also en route for Simla and the Durand Trophy in September and the Delhi Durbar Tournament in November.[10] Matches in the Shield were given extensive coverage in the city's newspapers who characterized it as the hot season's major attraction.

The football season in Calcutta lasted from mid-May until early August. This was not only the hot weather but was often wet too and always humid. The games were usually played in the relative cool of the early evenings between about 5.30 and 7.00pm, before the sacred dinner hour of the dominant Europeans. In that weather thirty minutes each way was enough for the most enthusiastic. Spectators were attracted, partly because it provided some variety and excitement in an otherwise dull season and partly because entrance to most grounds was free. Some clubs were private, run by the members, and had enclosed grounds; others had been allotted part of the Maidan. This was a large open space in front of Fort William in the centre of Calcutta originally designed to provide a clear field of fire in the event of attack. By 1900 it had become a huge pleasure garden with tennis courts, golf links, bicycle tracks, riding roads and cricket and football pitches. When charges for admission were made for football matches the receipts usually went to local charities. It was here that Indian footballing history was made in 1911.

The British played in boots, of course, but the Indians tended to play in bare feet. When the Mohan Bagan played Aryans, for example, in the Bengal Gymkhana tournament in 1911 only one player on each side wore boots. There was some suggestion that bootless players were at a disadvantage when the pitch was wet and the leather-cased balls heavy. One can imagine that that was not the least of the drawbacks.[11] But boots or not, Mohan Bagan had already defeated the Calcutta club in 1911 and this can hardly have failed to have whetted the appetite of a football public whose attention, by early July, was daily being drawn to the excitements to come.

The competition began on July 10 and Mohan Bagan had an easy passage to the next round against the young boys of St. Xavier's College. The *Englishman*, a touch sourly perhaps, offered the opinion that if Mohan Bagan were the best native team then it did not say much for the rest and 'great as the rejoicing was in the Indian camp after last evening's victory, the lamentations on Friday may be much greater'.[12] Friday was the day scheduled for the next round when Mohan Bagan would come up against Calcutta Rangers. The paper also drew attention to 'the supporters of the native team mustered in full force around the field ... in spite of the excellent arrangements (of the Rangers' Secretary) it was at times difficult to keep the hordes of Bengalis off the ground of play'.

Friday evening was wet, conditions not always thought to favour the barefoot Bengalis, but a 2–1 victory for the Mohan Bagan side had the *Englishman* overturning conventional interpretations. The Rangers found it difficult to keep their feet on the wet ground whereas the 'nippy Bengalese were quite at home'. Nor could the British draw much satisfaction from the way 'their' team reacted to defeat. They 'indulged in excessive rough play' and one player was sent off. On the other hand, the Bengali eleven appeared to have learned the lesson of British sportsmanship well, because the player against whom the foul had been committed intervened with the referee on his opponent's behalf and he was allowed to resume play.[13] This chivalrous gesture provided an interesting contrast to the scene a few days later when the East Yorkshire Regiment beat the Royal Scots in a replay by 3–2. The East Yorks had been awarded two penalties, one of which had provoked vociferous Scottish protests. In the last few minutes of the game, the East Yorks repeatedly kicked the ball out of play to waste time. 'After the match, the East Yorks called for cheers for the Royal Scots, but the Scots, who took their defeat sulkily, did not respond with cheers for the winners.' What they did respond with was a protest and the match was again replayed: but the Scots lost once more.[14]

In the third round Mohan Bagan came up against their first military opponents, the Rifle Brigade, and won with a somewhat fortuitous goal two minutes from the end. According to the report in the *Englishman*, the snipers' goalkeeper kicked the ball against an opposing forward from whom it rebounded to another who tapped it in. The soldiers wasted many chances and should have won. Criticism was directed at Mohan Bagan for being a 'picked team, several of them being men from up country and from the sister province of Eastern Bengal'.[15] But the *Statesman* said there was no fluke about the result. Mohan Bagan won because of their 'superior excellence in almost every department of the game.'[16] By this stage, the crowds were beginning to attract as much attention as the football. The *Statesman* thought the crowd which had come to the Dalhousie club ground to see the match between Mohan Bagan and the Rifle Brigade had produced a scene unparalleled even for a football match in Calcutta.

> As early as 4 o'clock excited Indian youths and men – some of whom had travelled twenty to thirty miles from small suburban stations – came and took their places and before half past five there was scarcely standing room left. A vast sea of eager, excited faces thronged the galleries, tables and boxes and about 16 or 18 deep fringed the ground. From it there arose a continuous crackle of chatter – mostly in the vernacular – and the crowd was an entirely different one from the crowds that generally witness other football matches, full of fire and enthusiasm with only one thought – the thought of victory.[17]

There were now only four teams left in the Shield. The East Yorkshire Regiment would meet the Calcutta club in one semi-final while Mohan Bagan took on the Middlesex Regiment in the other. This latter game was also played on the Dalhousie club ground. It was clear that the public's interest in the game surpassed everything that had gone before. By three o'clock in the afternoon on the day of the match several thousand had already taken up the best positions. Even the correspondent of the *Englishman* was swept up by the excitement:

> At 4 o'clock the field was lined by several rows of spectators and every minute saw the crowd growing denser and denser ... from all sides the crowds poured in and the wonder was that at that early hour, so many of Calcutta's citizens were available. However, if the truth were known, many an ardent Bengali football enthusiast absented himself from work in order to see the game and the Clerks in almost every office in the city went so far out of their ordinary course as to clamour for early dismissal to witness the game. Indeed Bengali Calcutta has gone football mad and the result is not relished so far as those

European lovers of football is concerned, who, unable to leave their
daily avocations before the usual hour, arrive on the ground to find
the crowd of such gigantic dimensions that a clear view of the game is
utterly impossible. Last evening the box wallahs and stool wallahs
who ply their trade in furnishing stands and miscellaneous bric-à-
brac from which late comers view the game did a roaring trade, but
even their resources were taxed to the utmost and many thousands
had to leave the field disappointed at not being able to obtain a
glimpse. ... The trees around the field swarmed with spectators who
climbed up to the very tops. Many a man came down and had a nasty
fall and an immense branch of one of the trees behind the Dalhousie
tent, unable to bear the strain, crashed to the ground with its load of
human freight. Several persons were injured ... .

All existing arrangements to keep the crowds under control were
swept away and from as far behind as was possible, right up to the
very touch lines, the spectators swarmed and actually fought for
places. Once it looked as if a vast riot was in progress at the S.W.
corner. ... The multitudes in front being pushed by those behind into
the football field, rose in a mass to contest their ground. A free fight
ensued in which sticks and umbrellas were freely used, and only the
arrival of the military picket helped to restore order. ...[18]

After all this the match itself ended in a draw and was replayed two days
later. This time, the Bengali team won 3–0 but not without a smear of
controversy. All their goals came in the last twelve minutes after the
regimental goalkeeper had been injured. The *Englishman*, true to form, said
he would have saved all the goals if he had not been hurt.[19] The East
Yorkshire Regiment had won the other semi-final and the final tie was to be
between the pride of the Bengalis and the best of the English soldiers.

The interest was so great that the press demanded that the game should
be played on the Calcutta cricket ground and that it should be declared a
charity match in order that admission could be charged. The *Englishman*
claimed that charges would be supported by both English and Indian
football enthusiasts in spite of the fact that it would obviously reduce the
number of spectators. It was too tempting to resist. The IFA declared a
charity match with admission charges of two rupees and one rupee.
Soldiers would be admitted free to the southern enclosure of the Calcutta
club's ground and there were some seats which could be booked in
advance.[20]

It cannot be accurately ascertained exactly how many people turned up
for the Shield final on 19 July 1911. The *Statesman* claimed 50–60,000,
characterized the crowd as 'magnificent' and asserted that 'it was managed
by that happy aptitude which our police have for handling big crowds'.[21]
The writer who communicated the event to the monthly journal of the East
Yorkshire Regiment underlined the phenomenal interest in the match and
claimed that two rupee seats were being sold for 15.[22] The majority of the

crowd in the enclosure supported the soldiers but those outside were for the Bengali team. The East Yorkshires scored first, early in the second half, but two late goals provided Mohan Bagan with the victory. The *Statesman* claimed that the better side had won and there was no use minimizing the victory to soothe East Yorkshire feelings. 'It is part of the game to take defeat and it is just as much part of the game to take unbiased criticism afterwards in the columns of the Press.'[23]

There were equally exciting scenes after the match. The Mohan Bagan team went to their tent on the Maidan where they were acclaimed by 'thousands of Bengali youths'. Some of the players were carried shoulder-high. When they then drove to the residence of the secretary of the club, Mr S. Bose, the carriage was followed by a large band of cheering young men. There were 'unique' scenes on the Shambazar and Chitpore tramcars with each carrying 'at least ten times more men than the Company byelaws allowed ...'. It was clearly a moment to be savoured. Did it have anything other than a sporting significance? The press reaction gives us some idea.

The London *Times* reported the result of the match with a touch of astonishment and an anxiety to reassure those readers who shared it that the victory had been won in an absence of all racial feeling. The European spectators were good-humoured and the Bengalis cheered the losers.[24] The *Statesman* suggested that both communities had something to celebrate; victory for the Indians, and dignified acceptance of it by the English. 'One great lesson that the English devotion to sports teaches is that defeat should be accepted with a good grace and the English people must have been bad pupils in the national school of good temper and chivalry if they did not welcome the triumph of the Mohan Bagan team and cherish a strong desire to defeat them at the earliest opportunity.'[25] It seems that both sides were trying hard to live up to the image they wanted the other to have of them. So, although it was proper to mark the victory, demonstrations should be avoided which might turn the heads of the victors. The refusal of the Mohan Bagan club to participate in an entertainment in their honour – their secretary was quoted as saying that success, as the club in general and the players in particular looked upon it, was the result of practice and study of the science of the game under the guidance and with the help of their numerous friends, both European and Indian – left the *Englishman* feeling that that was maturity; that demonstrated that English values were more than skin-deep.[26]

A *Statesman* editorial suggested that the triumph ought to be marked by encouraging other Bengalis to play. In particular students should be provided with facilities for both cricket and football because outdoor activities were better than office employment for young men and the community they served. Agriculture demanded trained minds in healthy bodies and the writer thought it would be strange if young men who had been disciplined and stimulated by sport did not feel attracted by farming or other work which demanded strength and endurance.[27]

What did the native language papers say? It would not be surprising for a major sporting event to be given a political interpretation in the context of

early twentieth-century Calcutta. The Hindu elite's relations with the
British were always ambivalent. But the educated Hindu was well aware of
the British sneer that they were a low-lying people in a low-lying land with
the intellect of a Greek and the grit of a rabbit.[28] Moreover, there were
recent political differences between British and Bengalis. In 1905, the
British had partitioned Bengal and created a new province, East Bengal. It
was not at all a popular change and the anti-partition movement injected
new vigour into the politics of Bengal in particular and India in general.
Japan's defeat of Russia in the war of 1904–05 also encouraged Asians
everywhere.[29]

Even without the benefit of being able to read the local language press we
are able to look in a little more detail at Indian opinion about the
significance of the outcome of the 1911 Shield final because the Bengali
language press was being monitored and translated by the British administration in Calcutta, and some of those translations have survived. The
Indian Mirror was a Calcutta daily paper with an estimated circulation of
about 1,000. It was edited by the head of the Maha-Bodlin Society and,
perhaps with a touch of extravagance, claimed that the recent Japanese
victory over Russia 'did not stir the East half as much as did that of Mohan
Bagan over the East Yorks'. But the paper also emphasized the 'large
mindedness of the European community in admitting a Bengali team to
take part with them in sport' which 'ought to arouse a deep sense of
gratitude'.[30]

Another weekly, *Basumati*, thought the victory of the Bengali foot-ballers
offered more complex lessons.

> We have seen Bengalis assembled on various occasions of danger,
> distress and sorrow, such as that of the Partition. ... But never before
> did we witness such a vast concourse, such a demonstration of joy.
>
> Mohan Bagan has infused a new life into the lifeless and cheerless
> Bengali ... (who) will never be able to repay the debt they owe you for
> infusing the revivifying nectar into their lifeless body.
>
> They are greatly mistaken who seem to find race-antagonism in
> this national victory. Race-antagonism has nothing to do with it.
> There is nothing of meanness in the tide of patriotism that has rushed
> into the silted up life stream of the Bengali.
>
> By your victory sport has been turned into a unifying force, an
> occasion of common rejoicing. ... [Mohan Bagan have] held up
> before the Bengali an ideal of striving in concert.
>
> The Bengali must ever remain indebted to those who have, in these
> dark days of disunion, found the secret of union. ...
>
> There are no players today in the play-room of the Indian Associa-
> tion. The Congress play-room has been blown off by one blast like a
> house of cards. Revered leaders ... have not been able to unite their
> adherents by the tie of unity. In a country where union takes place
> only to dissolve, where repulsion is more powerful than attraction,
> you have been able to knit together so many hearts. You silently

worked to bring about union, and your effort has now been crowned with victory.[31]

Another paper made a sharper and more cynical appraisal of these events. *Hitavadi* was a weekly with an estimated circulation of 30,000. It told the story of the semi-final day meeting between an Englishman and a native Christian travelling together in the same railway compartment. The Indian asked, in all innocence, who had won the match between Mohan Bagan and the Middlesex Regiment, but the only reply he received was a slap on the cheek! '... The day this note of resentment is absent from the Englishman's report of a defeat sustained by him, you may be sure that he is become quite as spiritless as ourselves.'[32]

But the idea that both Indian and Englishman emerged with credit was never far away. A small-circulation Calcutta daily, *Nayak*, was very excited that Indians, who had shown themselves capable of holding their own with the English in almost every walk of life, had now crowned all by beating them

> in that peculiarly English sport, the football ... It fills every Indian with joy and pride to know that rice-eating, malaria-ridden, bare-footed Bengalis have got the better of beef-eating, Herculean, booted John Bull in that peculiarly English sport. Never before was there witnessed such universal demonstration of joy, men and women alike sharing it and demonstrating it by showering of flowers, embraces, shouts, whoops, screams and even dances. ... The rice-eating Bengali is capable of learning everything to perfection and beating even his teachers. Teach him warfare and he will prove as clever as the Japanese. ...

But the paper also underlined the

> magnanimous equanimity of the Englishman. Amid the taunts and jeers of exultant Bengali youths Englishmen, even at the bitter hour of defeat, never lost for a moment their equanimity, nay, had the generosity to express their admiration for their conquerors, to take them up on their shoulders and dance with glee, so that everyone could see why the English are the rulers of India! May the English be victorious! Would that they showed the same equanimity in the work of administration that they have shown in sport![33]

This was a sporting event which both British and Indians interpreted as having nationalist, racialist and therefore political significance. The newspaper evidence shows, however, that both sides were treading cautiously. It also reflects, perhaps, a less hostile attitude, despite the partition of Bengal – soon to be reversed – than might have been shown once Indian demands for self-rule really got under way and Congress became a mass movement. Mohan Bagan's victory did not produce a bombardment of Fort William by Bengali athletes, nor did it provoke a military revolt against peace and order. It clearly injected some confidence into some of the native peoples of Calcutta and convinced them that they were as good as their masters. But it also seems to have reinforced admiration for those masters. Perhaps that is the essence of the mystery of hegemony.

As for football in Calcutta, it went from strength to strength. By 1929 the IFA had affiliated to it 140 Indian clubs and 14 European or Anglo-Indian ones. The IFA Shield had record entries in 1936, with 12 military teams, 12 civilian visitors and 21 local teams taking part. From Razmak and Chakrata, Dacca and Kohat, Agmere and Bombay, Favidpur and Lucknow, they came. Local radio provided running commentaries on some of the matches. In an annual representative match between a team selected from the Indian clubs and one chosen from the Europeans, the Indians won for the first time in 1929 before the Governor of Bengal, his lady and at least 25,000 others with many locked outside.[34] The popularity of the game had produced the importation of players from other parts of India and probably the first signs of professionalism. By 1939, the Indian Tea Market Expansion Board were using Jumma Khan, a full-back for Mohammedan Sporting, in press advertising for their product.[35] Of course Indian football continued to mirror the main features of the society of which it was part. Equal representation between Indians and Europeans on the Council of the IFA was only obtained in 1930 after threats of secession by the Indian clubs and the setting up of a reconciling commission chaired by the Bengali Advocate General. Bad refereeing sometimes led to allegations that it had been racially inspired. There were few clubs which were racially mixed. Nor were the differences simply those of rulers and ruled: when India played China in an international match in 1936 some commentators noted wistfully how all the crowd were unified in their desire for an Indian victory and lamented that such unity between Indians could not be sustained off the football field.[36]

Mohan Bagan flourished too, and 80 years later was still the premier Hindu club in Calcutta, though competing for the position with East Bengal. It was, perhaps, a pity that the English Football Association did not route one of their Empire tours to Calcutta nor that the North Calcuttan Hindu elite were able to fund a tour by Mohan Bagan to England to match the visits of Parsee cricketers. For although it was a real achievement to lower the colours of the representatives of the occupying power on 28 July 1911, the three bandsmen and eight privates who made up the East Yorks side could hardly be said to represent the best of the English game. Indeed, the 1st Battalion of the East Yorks themselves were probably more formidable and in 1911–12 had won the Faber Cup, East Riding Cup, Yorkshire Charity Cup and York and District League. What would Mohan Bagan have made of Everton or Liverpool, Newcastle or Manchester United or of top-class amateur teams?[37] Yet it *was* a famous victory and was recalled with pride 50 years later when the club honoured the memory of the four surviving players and said Hindu prayers for the peace of the departed souls. The victory of Mohan Bagan in 1911, a club official declared, had launched football in Bengal towards the status of national institution which it had become today. The Indian government should honour the surviving players not only for their services to sport but for their services to the nation. The twenty-eighth of July ought to be declared National Football Day.[38]

NOTES

1. Brian Stoddart, 'Sport, Cultural Imperialism, and Colonial Response in the British Empire', *Comparative Studies in Society and History*, 30, 4 (1988).
2. *The Times*, 31 July 1911.
3. Charles Allen (ed.), *Plain Tales from the Raj* (London, 1976), p. 156.
4. E. S. Humphries in Allen (ed.), op. cit., pp. 109–10. For more on the importance of organized and unorganized football in India see Frank Richards, *Old Soldier Sahib* (London, 1936), pp. 227–8, 295–7. Sport also provided opportunities for the largely European officers to mix informally with the native other ranks in the Indian Army and the Police.
5. James Morris, *Pax Britannica. The Climax of an Empire* (London, 1979 ed.), p. 104.
6. Some of what follows is based on Anthony de Mello, *Portrait of Indian Sport* (London, 1960), Ch. X.
7. The Earl of Dalhousie had been Governor-General in the 1850s.
8. It is interesting that the Europeans were able to sustain a league even though, according to the 1911 census, the number of males in the 15–30 age-group was only just over 3,000. No Indian team was admitted to the Calcutta League until 1914. After that, the League rules only allowed two Indian teams to play in the first division at any one time, a stipulation not removed until 1925.
9. *The Illustrated Weekly of India*, 1 July 1984.
10. On the East Yorkshire's preparations see their regimental magazine, *The Snapper* VI, 9 September 1911, 158.
11. *The Englishman*, 5 July 1911. Mohan Bagan appear to have fielded their first entirely booted team as late as 1936, the same year in which Mohammedan Sporting still played barefoot but had boots ready for all the players if required. Booted play was not made compulsory until 1953. *Calcutta Statesman*, 26 May, 14, 16 June 1936.
12. *The Englishman*, 11 July 1911.
13. Ibid., July 15, 1911.
14. Ibid., 18, 21 July 1911.
15. Ibid., 20 July 1911.
16. *Calcutta Statesman*, 20 July 1911.
17. Ibid. Apart from the weather it might have been Manchester or Middlesbrough.
18. *The Englishman*, 25 July 1911.
19. Ibid., 27 July 1911. How the goalkeeper was hurt may be one of those sporting tales which has gathered baroque accoutrement down the years. According to a recent article a thundering drive by a Bagan forward brought down the cross-bar and injured the head of the regimental goalkeeper. But the *Statesman* at the time reported that he received a cut over the eye from the *boot* of a Bagan player, lost consciousness and resumed with his eye bandaged. *The Illustrated Weekly of India*, 1 July 1984. *Calcutta Statesman*, 27 July 1911.
20. *The Englishman*, 25, 26 July 1911. *Statesman*, 27 July 1911.
21. *Statesman*, 3 August 1911.
22. *The Snapper*, VI, 9 September 1911, 158.
23. *Statesman*, 3 August 1911.
24. *The Times*, 31 July 1911.
25. *Statesman*, 3 Aug. 1911.
26. Ibid., 10 Aug. 1911. *The Englishman*, 3 Aug. 1911.
27. *Statesman*, 3 Aug. 1911.
28. Quoted by John Rosselli, 'Physical Education and Nationalism in nineteenth century Bengal', *Past and Present*, 86 (1980), 121–48.

29. Ronald Hyam, *Britain's Imperial Century 1815-1914: A Study of Empire and Expansionism* (London, 1976), p.237.
30. *Indian Mirror*, 30 July 1911, Indian Office Library L/R/5/38.
31. *Basumati*, 5 Aug. 1911.
32. *Hitavadi*, 4 Aug. 1911.
33. *Nayak*, 30 July 1911.
34. *Statesman*, 17 May, 6, 7 July, 1929, 21 June 1936. The Indians won 3–0.
35. 'A hot cup of tea is an excellent pick me up for an athlete. In all outdoor games there is nothing like a cup of tea as a drink.' *Statesman*, 31 July 1939.
36. On the IFA dispute see *Statesman*, 17–31 May 1929. On the India v China match, which ended in a 1–1 draw, see *Statesman*, 8 July 1936.
37. They lost 1–0 in November 1937 to the touring English amateurs Islington Corinthians.
38. *Statesman*, 30 July 1961.

CHAPTER EIGHT

Viceregal Patronage:
The Governors-General of Canada and Sport in the Dominion, 1867–1909

GERALD REDMOND

Modern imperialism and the Victorian era are synonymous, representing an age of expansion and the concomitant extension of British customs and rules. One dictionary definition of 'imperialism' states:

> ... extension of British Empire where trade required protection given by imperial rule; (Hist.) union of different parts of British Empire for purposes of warlike defence, internal commerce, etc.; ... acquiring colonies and dependencies; ...[1]

During this period several former colonies acquired self-governing status through political action and subsequent legislation, but retained membership of the Empire cementing the 'union' referred to above. As the title and contents of this volume make clear (as well as other recent research),[2] sport was one of those customs which became a significant 'cultural bond' within this unique family of nations. A love of *sport*, for example, besides the English language, was 'the most enduring heritage' of the British in India[3]; arguably most people might have expected it to be parliamentary government, educational or legal systems, or the pragmatic legacy of builders and engineers. If India was the 'Jewel in the Crown' of the British Empire, however, the Dominion of Canada became not only the largest member of the Imperial Club but the one with the most numerous sporting ties with Mother England during Victoria's reign. This was due in large measure to the office of governor-general of Canada. While industrialization, urbanization, new technology and modes of transport generally affected the development of nineteenth-century sport in similar ways in several countries, including Canada, the viceregal patronage of sport in this northern Dominion must be considered as a unique contribution both to the growth of sport within Canada itself, and to the spread of international sport in the English-speaking world. How many people in today's Commonwealth are aware of the fact that 'the oldest series of international matches' in cricket, begun in 1844, is between Canada and the USA?[4] Canadian governors-general used sport to unify the young country from within, and to consolidate its links with the Empire. Although a book could be written to justify this statement, perhaps enough evidence can be supplied in a brief chapter to sustain conviction.

A governor or governor-general has served as the resident representative of the Crown in Canada since the beginning of European settlement. Often regarded as a British institution, the office has developed with Canada's evolution from colony to nation, and was actually inaugurated in New France when Samuel de Champlain became governor in 1627. The office may therefore be divided into three periods:

1. *French Regime* (New France), with 18 governors from Samuel de Champlain (1627–29; 1633–35) to Marquis de Vaudreil-Cavagnal (1755–60).
2. *British Regime* (British North America), with 22 governors from James Murray (1764–68) to Viscount Monck (1861–67).
3. *Post-Confederation* (Dominion of Canada), with 23 governors from Viscount Monck (1867–68) to Jeanne Sauvé (1984–9).

Initially, governors-general represented imperial governments and were responsible to various colonial ministers. After Confederation they governed internally according to the wishes of the Canadian Prime Minister, but until the First World War they were still obliged to acknowledge British policy in external relations. They became the sovereign's personal representatives with the Statute of Westminster of 1931; until George VI formally delegated, in 1947, all the sovereign's authority in Canada to the governor-general. Vincent Massey became the first Canadian to be appointed governor-general in 1952, and since then a tradition of alternating anglophone and francophone governors-general has evolved. The 60th holder of this prestigious office, the Rt. Hon. Jeanne Sauvé, was the first woman to be appointed.[5]

I

We are concerned here with the first part of the post-Confederation period, from the time when the Dominion of Canada was created in 1867 until almost the outbreak of the First World War: to be exact, to the year 1909 when Earl Grey donated a trophy for the Canadian Football Championship. This represents the most significant period for sport as an imperial 'cultural bond'. During this 42-year span the various contributions of the first nine governors-general (see Table 1) became increasingly important in this respect. Earl Grey's action, in fact, may be seen as the culmination of a consistent viceregal policy in which sport played a major role, both internally and externally.

While the change in status and role alone of the governor-general at Confederation may justify it as a starting point, it must be admitted that the impact of the first two post-Confederation governors Viscount Monck and Sir John Young (Baron Lisgar, 1869–72) in terms of any sporting contribution was almost negligible, unlike the next seven Excellencies in office. To be sure, both were acknowledged diplomats who made their mark. Monck had been an astute governor-general of British North America since 1861, and was in fact deliberately rewarded by the extension

TABLE 1

THE GOVERNORS-GENERAL OF CANADA, 1867–1911

1867–68	Sir Charles Stanley, 4th Viscount Monck
1868–72	Sir John Young, Baron Lisgar
1872–78	Frederick Temple Hamilton-Temple-Blackwood, 1st Marquis of Dufferin and Ava
1878–83	John Douglas Sutherland Campbell, Marquis of Lorne
1883–88	Henry Charles Keith Petty-Fitzmaurice, 5th Marquis of Lansdowne
1888–93	Frederick Arthur Stanley, Baron Stanley of Preston
1893–98	John Campbell Hamilton-Gordon, Earl and later 1st Marquis of Aberdeen
1898–1904	Gilbert John Murray-Kynnymod Elliott, 4th Earl of Minto
1904–11	Albert Henry George, 4th Earl of Grey

of his term so that he might be the first governor-general of the new Dominion. Lisgar was greatly admired by Prime Minister John A. Macdonald and among his other contributions, he helped to diffuse tensions created by the Red River Rebellion and the Fenian Raids. Yet during Monck's brief tenure there occurred one significant event with social ramifications for the future. Rideau Hall in Ottawa was purchased during his term to serve as the official viceregal residence; and during Confederation year, Monck set aside some land on the west side of Rideau Hall for cricket.[6] In years to come this was transformed into a veritable playground-of-sorts for the leisure amusements of its inhabitants. Indeed, our thesis really begins with the appointment of the Earl of Dufferin (1872–78), who shortly after his arrival in Canada had a curling rink built at his own expense at Rideau Hall.[7]

The historian of that Hall informs us that despite the many political difficulties during his tenure (especially the Pacific Scandal which forced the resignation of Prime Minister Macdonald), the curling rink 'never lacked for use',[8] and Dufferin formed a Viceregal Curling Club which played often and well. The wife of this handsome and elegant diplomat, the Marchioness of Dufferin and Ava, kept a diary, later published as *My Canadian Journal*, which provides a fascinating account of the viceregal couple's experiences and travels in Canada, and demonstrated fully their fondness for sport. In it, for example, she describes the opening (on St. Andrew's Day) of 'our new curling rink' stating that 'it is quite close to the Skating Rink and the tobogganing hill is on the other side'; and goes on to document through many references their sporting participation and achievements. The entry for 11 February 1874, proudly records that she was elected a member of the viceregal rink, being also, she believed, 'the first wife of a Governor-General who has ever skated here'. Lady Dufferin consistently recorded her husband's social endeavours under the abbreviation of 'D', especially his prowess at curling, such as in this entry for 10 March 1874:

There was tremendous excitement in the curling rink today – D

12. The Earl of Dufferin – with snowshoes

13. Lord Dufferin and party curling at Rideau Hall, Ottawa

playing another opponent, Mr. Russell for 'the horns'. The game was very interesting. They had to make 21 points and five times during the course of the game they were tied, D winning finally by one – a very honourable and unexpected victory, as Mr. Russell is 'skip' of the Ottawa club.

Although references to curling and skating may predominate in this prestigious eyewitness account – a reflection of the Canadian winter climate as well as of their Excellencies' sporting preferences – Her Lady-ship's diary is a valuable source of information for other contemporary sports (as will be seen).[9] More needs to be said about Dufferin's passion for curling first, however, for it was his active example in the Scottish game which really set the pattern for future viceregal patronage of sport in Canada.

It would be surprising indeed if curling – 'Scotland's ain game' to many chroniclers[10] – had not thrived in Canada, given the ubiquitous and powerful Scottish presence allied to the Canadian climate and geography. Before Dufferin's arrival Scots had settled throughout the country, from Nova Scotia on the east coast to what had been 'New Caledonia' (in British Columbia,) on the west coast, with numerous Scottish place names in every province in between. More importantly, they predominated in govern-ment, the fur trade, banking, education, in businesses such as the Hudson's Bay Company and Canadian Pacific Railway (CPR), and so were an Establishment group well situated to indulge their favourite pastimes.[11] Pierre Berton, one of Canada's ablest and most prolific historians, has written of 'the dominance of the Scot in pioneer Canada … the Irish outnumbered them, as did the English, but the Scots ran the country'.[12] In many respects, nineteenth-century Canada really was a 'New Scotland'. For transplanted Scottish devotees of curling – the sport codified in their homeland where the Grand Caledonian Curling Club (formed in 1838) became the arbiter of the sport – the Canadian environment provided them with innumerable frozen lakes and rivers upon which to enjoy 'the roarin' game' for several months a year. And when the weather was too cold to enjoy the sport outdoors, curlers in Canada constructed enclosed rinks to prolong their enjoyment, a significant development in the evolution of the sport.

While there is no reason to doubt that Dufferin's enthusiasm for curling was spontaneous and genuine, if he had wanted to choose an appropriate sport in Canada as a social vehicle for deliberate diplomacy, he could hardly have selected better. The sport had democratic traditions and an etiquette suitable for participation by all classes, even nobility, and later by both sexes. Its Scottish pedigree was advantageous to its growth and offered an affectionate link with the 'old country', while at the same time it offered new Canadians of every background a chance to flex their athletic muscles during the long winter months. Consistent viceregal patronage then added a lustre to the sport which served to increase its status even more.[13]

The Viceregal Curling Club entertained various opponents often at Rideau Hall, with considerable success, and His Excellency also participated in bonspiels in other parts of Canada during his extensive travels. It was Dufferin who instituted the Governor-General's Prize, which became one of Canada's most coveted curling trophies, and was first awarded in 1880. Before this he had awarded and donated a number of other curling medals and prizes over the years. On his departure from Canada, the curling clubs of Quebec presented him with a picture of a Canadian curling match, which featured 'faithful portraits of many of Canada's keenest curlers, and some of His Excellency's most attached friends'. In fact, so enamoured of curling was his Lordship that in his next post as British Ambassador to Russia, he endeavoured 'to establish a curling rink at St. Petersburg on the Canadian principle'. Without doubt he was an 'avid curler' and 'gave a most decided impetus to Scotland's ain game', to the extent that it became one of Canada's own games as well.[14]

Dufferin's contribution to curling alone would assure his place as an active and significant patron of Canadian sport; in fact, he contributed in a similar way to several sports. He and his wife became very proficient at skating, and demonstrated their skill often at winter carnivals, pageants, costume balls at the Victoria Rink, Montreal, and elsewhere; although one doubts the claim that 'both found time to skate every winter day'.[15] Not surprisingly perhaps, skating was another winter sport for which Dufferin awarded a number of medals and prizes. The popular sport of snowshoeing too, met with his favour. This activity had been adapted from the Indian and was necessary for survival to earlier hunters and trappers. Snowshoe clubs now held competitive races over various distances (and even over hurdles on occasion), as well as enjoying longer distance treks across the countryside, preferably on a moonlit night. Lady Dufferin described such a scene in her diary:

> They wore white blanket coats, tight leggings and red caps, and the sight really was very picturesque and very Canadian. The bright night, the snow covered ground, hundreds of sleighs and thousands of tinkling bells, the torches and the gaiety of the whole scene was delightful.[16]

In January 1873, the first Montreal Snowshoe Carnival was held in honour of the governor-general; and on 8 March the same year, Dufferin presented a gold medal at the first Ottawa Snowshoe Carnival. The viceregal couple also found time for the recreational winter pastime of tobogganing, enjoying excursions to the famous beauty spot of Montmorency Falls for this purpose. At home in Ottawa, Dufferin increased the length and height of the toboggan run at Rideau Hall, much to the delight of both hosts and visitors who participated 'in every sort of way, double and singly, standing, sitting and lying'. Although obviously blessed with considerable leisure time in which to do so, the Dufferins unquestionably set an important example to all of actively enjoying the long Canadian winter.[17]

A perennial theme in emergent Canadian nationalism has been 'the idea that Canada's unique character was derived from the northern location, her severe winters and her heritage of "northern races"'. The northern climate was seen as a challenge to which Canadians necessarily responded, with a subsequent beneficent and unique effect upon their character. It was an idea promoted by several prominent figures. George Parkin, Principal of Upper Canada College in the 1890s, pronounced the Canadian climate to be 'one of our greatest blessings'. William Hales Kingston developed the theme further, maintaining that it produced 'a hardy, long-lived, intelligent people' in a disease-free country.[18] And even George Beers, the Father of Lacrosse (a summer game) was 'probably the greatest public relations man ever for the Canadian Winter in this respect' because of his frequent allusions to the character-building effect of sport on ice and snow.[19]

The thesis of alleged superiority of 'hardy northern races' has since been challenged in this century, being seen to possess an unfortunate racist aspect. But its emergence may be understood in the pioneering context of the building of a young northern nation, newly independent of the Mother Country and anxious to assert itself, and adjacent to the larger and more powerful United States of America. But certainly Lord and Lady Dufferin contributed to this complimentary self-image by their consistent and vigorous endorsement and enjoyment of the Canadian winter, a viceregal example which could not fail to be noted and emulated. Perhaps, too, His Excellency even played a part in initiating the over-enthusiastic rhetoric of others after him, when he exclaimed that 'A constitution nursed upon the oxygen of our bright winter atmosphere makes its owner feel as though he could toss about the pine trees in glee'.[20]

However, Governor-General Dufferin lent his active support to summer sports as well, cricket being one of them. One of his predecessors in office, the Duke of Richmond, had played cricket at Kingston in Upper Canada in 1819; and the first tour of British North America by an English cricket team took place in 1859. As *Sport Canadiana* stated:

> This was a significant event, the first time that a team from another continent had visited Canada for sports competition of any kind. Canadian teams each fielded 22 players, against the English XI.[21]

This international series may have been a precocious event, but cricket was firmly established as one of Canada's most popular pastimes during the 1850s. In 1857, Canada had defeated the United States in an international match at Toronto; and in 1858, *The Canadian Cricketer's Guide* was published, with full instructions for playing 'the truly British game'.[22] A second visit by an English side occurred in 1868, when Willsher and Freeman's XI played in Montreal; but the capital city of Ottawa did not play sporting host to an England cricket team until 1872 – but this was Fitzgerald's Gentlemen of England XI, which included the legendary Dr. W.G. Grace. Happily, Lord Dufferin's term of office had begun by this time, and throughout his tenure he was an active supporter of the Ottawa

Cricket Club. One letter to the governor-general from the Club, written in 1874, thanks him for his presentation of a medal,[23] and another just before his departure in 1878 thanks him for his 'past kindness and patronage'.[24]

Such viceregal support for cricket was only to be expected perhaps, since cricket was by now being widely regarded as the imperial game which helped to join the Mother Country and its colonies in friendly competition. It was also in 1878, for example (when the Australian cricketers were touring England) that Edward Thring, headmaster of Uppingham School, wrote a letter to George Parkin, declaring that cricket was more than 'a mere game', it was a link of Empire, 'the greatest bond of the English-speaking race'.[25] Canada certainly played its part in cementing the cricketing bond during the second half of the nineteenth century. Between 1859 and 1891, cricketers from other parts of the Empire – English, Australian, Irish and West Indian – had toured parts of Canada on at least eleven occasions; and Canadian cricketers had toured England twice, in 1880 and 1887.[26] Yet there were circumstances which mitigated against the continued growth of the imperial game in the Dominion, not the least of which was the Canadian climate. A small population, large distances to travel for competition, and the fact that most of the international contests were embarrassingly one-sided in the visitors' favour, were also impediments to progress. And there was the new factor of a natural and rising Canadian nationalism at work, represented in sport by the evolution of lacrosse and ice-hockey.

By Confederation, indigenous lacrosse was already challenging cricket for supremacy as a popular sport in Canada, having been developed from an Indian game, the most commonly used term for which was 'baggataway'. As indicated earlier, Montreal dentist George Beers was the individual most responsible for the codification and promotion of lacrosse. Author of *Lacrosse: The National Game of Canada*, published in 1869,[27] this 'muscular Christian' was an ardent Canadian nationalist, but loyal to the 'old country'. He was the leader of the two successful tours of Britain by Canadian lacrosse teams in 1876 and 1883, both of which were designed to foster goodwill between the young Dominion and the hosts. During the first tour, matches were played in Belfast, Dublin, Glasgow, Edinburgh, Newcastle, Manchester, Sheffield, Birmingham, Bristol and London. Banquet speeches following these games stressed the social links and unity of Empire. A cable was received in Ottawa on 27 June 1876, by Governor-General Dufferin, which read:[28]

> The Canadians and Indians played their game of lacrosse before me here yesterday.
>
>   The Queen
> 19 Windsor

As a patron of the game in Canada and a facilitator of the tour[29] Dufferin was no doubt gratified to receive Queen Victoria's signal. During his term, he and his wife attended many lacrosse matches. As early as 10 October

1872, Lady Dufferin had written in her diary: 'It is almost the national game here ... The ball is caught on a racket and thrown from one side to the other. It is very pretty and amusing to watch'.[30]

Another sport patronized to a certain extent by her husband was rugby football, which Her Ladyship apparently found less amusing to watch. One entry in her diary refers to a game in Quebec City between the 'Dufferin Club' and B-Battery of the Citadel garrison, in which she complains: 'The soldiers were somewhat rough and one gentleman had his nose broken', before adding that 'the Dufferin Club won'.[31] Although Lord Dufferin as usual awarded some medals in this sport, we shall see that it was one of his successors who donated the football trophy which subsequently obtained considerable fame and significance.

It was the continued presence of a considerable number of soldiers in military garrisons across Canada, of course, which fostered interest in the sport of rifle-shooting. Many shooting clubs were in existence before Dufferin's arrival; in fact, a Dominion of Canada Rifle Association was formed in 1868. The National Rifle Association in England had been formed earlier, in 1860, and 'its annual matches became a magnet for the best marksmen of the British Empire'. A team from the Ontario Rifle Association of Canada first competed there in 1871. The following year at Bisley, a Canadian team actually won the Kolapore Cup, one of the Empire's highest riflery awards. These annual meets were described as 'great imperial occasions, drawing marksmen from many corners of the British Empire'.[32] Dufferin's arrival in Canada coincided with the impressive Canadian victory of 1872, and not surprisingly perhaps His Lordship soon began his enthusiastic and consistent patronage of rifle-shooting. In his book: *Canada Under the Administration of the Earl of Dufferin*, George Stewart calculates that Dufferin awarded no fewer than four gold medals, 22 silver medals and 17 bronze medals for shooting during his term of office.[33] And the ebullient Lady Dufferin claimed to have scored a bull's eye one year, when Their Excellencies opened the Dominion Rifle Match ceremonies, and to have received an engraved silver tablet for the feat.[34]

Lawn tennis was another sport which spread quickly from England; it is believed that the sport 'was first introduced to Canada in the Toronto area about 1874'.[35] Here again, Their Excellencies at Rideau Hall lost little time in becoming actively involved and added to the already resort-like status of their official residence by having a tennis court built, which was later used as a supper room for large parties as well. However, their participation seems to have been confined to social occasions in Ottawa, and this is one sport for which there is no record of Dufferin awarding any medals.[36] This was probably due to the fact that the sport was still very much in its infancy during his term of office from 1872 to 1878. His successor, the Marquis of Lorne, was later able to donate a governor-general's prize for the sport, an incentive which was becoming ever more customary in Canadian sport. (A similar comment applies to ice-hockey, also still being developed and first codified and given its modern form by a group of McGill University students at Montreal in 1875.)[37] Before Lorne appeared on the scene, however, Dufferin had also awarded medals for quoits, swimming and yachting;[38] and especially for another sport in which young Canada was gaining an international reputation, that of rowing.

Rowing races and regattas were popular all over the English-speaking world in the nineteenth century, and by Confederation in 1867, Canadian oarsmen had already enjoyed considerable success against American rivals. But it was the startling victory of four rowers from St. John, New Brunswick, at Paris in that year – they were renowned forever afterwards as 'The Paris Crew' – which really confirmed an international status in the sport for Canada, a reputation that it upheld for the rest of the century and beyond.[39] Much of this status was garnered by one individual who began his unique career shortly before Dufferin took office. It was in 1871 that Ned Hanlan, 'The Boy in Blue', won the first of literally hundreds of races. In his ten-year heyday, between 1874 and 1884, he took part in some 350 races and lost no more than half a dozen, regularly beating American, Australian and British champions. The historian Pierre Berton has written: 'He was to sculling what Roger Bannister was to the mile run ... when Hanlan rowed, the world turned out to watch'.[40] Aided by the increase in leisure time, the rapid development of railways and steamboats, concessions and sponsorship by the railway companies, and an opportunity to indulge their passion for gambling as well as nationalism, these crowds numbered between ten and twenty thousand.

The Dufferins were often among the spectators at these well-attended rowing meets. A regatta in the viceregal family's honour was organized by the Toronto Rowing Club in 1873; and His Lordship was so taken with a rowing exhibition in the St. John harbour, New Brunswick, that he offered a gold medal to be rowed for on some future occasion. In 1875, Hanlan won the governor-general's medal in a two-mile race at Toronto, defeating Louden and Douglas. 'D. again went to the regatta to give away the medals won' wrote the busy Lady Dufferin in her diary;[41] and another chronicler recorded of His Excellency that 'in his earlier days, he had been interested in boating contests, and although he could not claim to have gained excellence in the use of the oar, still he had an eye for a good stroke'.[42] In her thesis on the governors-general, McLaughlin has maintained that Hanlan, in particular, was the tremendous drawing card and stated: 'Riding on the crest of this popularity, Lord Dufferin offered several medals to rowing championships being sponsored by clubs in Ontario, Quebec and the Maritimes'.[43]

Dufferin himself enjoyed great popularity during his term of office, and most Canadians were genuinely sorry to see him leave. This handsome, eloquent Irish aristocrat had travelled widely in office, actively pursuing his official duties, and proved to be a great ambassador. As Drummond Black later observed in 1903: 'no governor was ever a greater social success and that after all has now become almost the chief thing'.[44] In correspondence with his successor, Lord Lorne, Dufferin had written:

I have myself done something during the last six years towards

consolidating the various elements of which the Canadian Community is composed as well as towards creating a more intimate
union between the Colony and the Mother country. ....[45]

As seen, his active patronage of all kinds of sport – whether of British origin
or Canadian extraction and invention – was a crucial ingredient in the
diplomatic process. It could be argued in one sense that his timing was
fortunate. In the series *Canada's Illustrated Heritage*, which presents a volume
for each decade, the author of 'Sporting Times' for the years from 1870 to
1880, states:

> The age of innocence was a decade of firsts in Canadian sports – first
> world champion oarsman, first organized hockey game, first inter-
> national and intercollegiate football games, first North American golf
> club, first bicycle club and first tennis tournament. And newspapers,
> scrambling to cover the scene, first established the post of 'sporting
> editor'.[46]

To which could be added that Dufferin was the first governor-general to
encourage sport vigorously in Canada, through both patronage and participation, to such an extent that he established a tradition which actually
became regarded as part of the expectations of his office. As one observer
put it: 'Vice-regal patronage of Canadian sport would become customary
practice for his successors in office.'[47]

II

The next governor-general, Canada's fourth, was 33-year-old John
Douglas Sutherland Campbell, Marquis of Lorne, who was married to
Princess Louise, the fourth daughter of Queen Victoria. He was a Scot, son
and heir of the eighth Duke of Argyll, and like his predecessor took both an
official and personal interest in the sport of curling. Soon after taking office
he offered a Silver Cup 'to be played for all the regularly organized Curling
Clubs of the Dominion who desire to enter into the competition'.[48] This was
soon altered to two Silver Cups, one for clubs using granite stones and one
for clubs using iron ones, which were first awarded in 1881. Silver medals
were also awarded to individual curlers. The rink at Rideau Hall never
lacked for use in the meantime, as Lorne acted as skip for the Viceregal
Curling Club on many occasions, and won praise for his curling ability.[49]

It was also in the summer of 1881 that the governor-general made his
well-remembered cross-country tour of the Dominion, travelling from
Halifax to Portage La Prairie (then the end-of-line) by train. By this time in
office, Lorne was persuaded that Canada should be more appreciated in
the Mother Country. He deplored the lack of favourable publicity, and
wanted the British countrymen to come out in greater numbers both as

settlers and as tourists. To this end, English reporters joined the tour at His
Excellency's expense, a junket which was later described as a 'huge
success':

> The English newspapermen were dazzled by the energy, variety and
> vastness of the Canadian scene. The clear waters of Lake Superior,
> the rugged Lakehead wilderness, the Indians, frontier Winnipeg, the
> steamer trip down the Saskatchewan, and the fabulous Rockies were
> a stunning delight to the newsmen. They wrote reams of copy, all of it
> lavish in its praise of Canada.[50]

Apparently, this favourable publicity – 'serialized descriptions of cross-
Canada journeys appeared in dozens of English papers' – had the desired
effect, as the numbers of settlers and visitors from Britain did increase
significantly in the following years.[51]

This campaign for more British emigration to Canada was a serious
business to Lorne, as two other events alone demonstrate. He assisted
enthusiastically in the arrangements made for the tour of Britain by the
Canadian lacrosse team of 1883; for by arrangement with the Dominion
Government, tour members acted as 'emigration agents' to attract settlers
to the Canadian West, and over 500,000 copies of the *Canadian Illustrated
News* were distributed at matches, together with 'sundry other publications
on Canada'.[52] This scheme undoubtedly represented imperial sporting
links in a unique and pragmatic way, which appears to be without
precedent elsewhere. Lorne's practical inclinations in this area were
further demonstrated even after his tour of duty at Rideau Hall. He wrote a
travel guide to Canada, with 'hints to intending emigrants', which was
published in England in 1886.[53]

During his tour of duty Lorne was actively involved in other sports
besides curling and lacrosse. When they were not travelling elsewhere, the
sporting facilities at their official residence were enjoyed to the full by the
viceregal couple. In *Picturesque Canada*, an illustrated survey of 'the country
as it was and is' published in 1882, there is a delightful picture of the
Marquis and Princess skating outdoors at Government House.[54] Tobogganing was another winter pastime which appealed to them, also. In the
summer, Rideau Hall continued to play host to numerous cricket matches
during Lorne's term; and in 1880, a Mr. A. Browning of Montreal scored
204 runs there, then the highest individual total in Canadian cricket. Lorne
took a keen interest in the game, and occasionally took to the field himself.
In a letter to his father dated 30 April 1879, he wrote: 'We are to have a first
cricket match on Saturday and I am to command an eleven of senators and
M.P.'s and be as autocratic as I choose for the day!'[55]

The Ottawa Lawn Tennis Club was formed in 1881, and officially
opened on 16 June 1882. The governor-general agreed to be the club's
patron and offered prizes for a ladies' tournament, 'open to the Dominion'.
It is interesting to note that Drill Hall in Ottawa was used for the purpose,
thus becoming the first indoor tennis court in Canada.[56]

With a surname like Campbell it is not surprising perhaps to find the Marquis also acting as Honorary Patron for the Montreal Caledonian Society, and attending its popular Caledonian Games.[57] And during his famous cross-country tour of 1881, he presented the prizes at the Games of the St. Andrew's Society of Winnipeg.[58] Like his predecessor, Lorne donated prizes for the sport of rifle-shooting; in fact, even money prizes were offered in an attempt to encourage more widespread participation. His Excellency was concerned with both internal and imperial links through the sport, as shown by his remarks in an address to the Dominion Rifle Association:

> ... the association should be recognized as an important adjunct to the means of our country's defence, and as such obtain sufficient support to send annually a representation of Canada's defensive force to England, as well as provide a respectable prize list for the annual competition in Ottawa, such as would encourage riflemen from the most distant parts of the Dominion to come here as competitors.[59]

Such was the prestige associated with Dominion Rifle Association competition, that an imposing awards ceremony was instituted in the Senate Chamber in Ottawa.

Like many of those in office before and after him, Lorne was also an outdoors 'sportsman' in the hunting and fishing sense, seeking such recreations as a form of relaxation from official duties. He made frequent expeditions to the Grand Cascapedia, which he described as the most beautiful river he had seen, and visitations by him and his successors established its reputation as 'the queen of all Canadian salmon fisheries'.[60] As skilful a hunter as he was an angler, he is credited in one account of a duck-hunting trip to Long Point, Lake Eric, with bagging 115 ducks.[61]

Much credit accrued to Lord Lorne as a patron of the Arts while in Canada – he was instrumental in the founding of both The Royal Canadian Academy of Arts in 1880 (and the National Gallery of Canada) and the Royal Society in 1882[62] – and he will undoubtedly be well-remembered for his cultural role in the young country. As a patron of sport to follow in Dufferin's enthusiastic footsteps, he deserves much credit as well, for there is no doubt that he helped to establish further the viceregal sporting tradition in the Dominion, and to foster its imperial connections. He left his mark, and Canada left its mark upon Lorne. This is clearly evident in the books he wrote afterwards: *Memories of Canada and Scotland* (1884); *Imperial Federation* (1885); *Canadian Pictures* (1885); *Passages from the Past* (2 vols., 1907); and *Yesterday and Today in Canada* (1910).

III

The man who succeeded Lorne was Henry Charles Keith Petty-Fitzmaurice, fifth Marquis of Lansdowne, an Irishman educated at Eton and Balliol College, Oxford. A liberal who served as Under-Secretary of

State for India in 1880, he broke with Gladstone over Home Rule for Ireland and his appointment as governor-general of Canada was regarded as a kind of political exile in London. *Punch* carried a cartoon of Lansdowne on skis, 'in his new Canadian costume adapted to remaining for some time out in the cold'.[63]

Inevitably, Lansdowne did spend a great deal of his time outdoors during the Canadian winter, but never on skis. Like his predecessors he was a serious patron of curling, and he became a respected participant under the tutelage of his military secretary, Lord Melgund (later the Earl of Minto, and governor-general himself from 1898 to 1904). Skating and tobogganing parties continued to be regular social occasions at Rideau Hall; and the governor-general and Lady Lansdowne were hosts to a French-Canadian Snowshoe Club in 1884, and patrons of the Frontenac Snowshoe Club in Ottawa. The viceregal pair also enjoyed themselves immensely at the Montreal Winter Carnival.[64] It is written of Lansdowne that he 'seemed to regard his Canadian years as a respite from the more arduous duties of British public life'.[65] In this respect, and notwithstanding *Punch's* satire, winter sports in Canada definitely provided an unusual and stimulating change.

But it is probable that the most refreshing respite of all was provided in summer, salmon-fishing on the Grand Cascapedia and Restigouche rivers. As noted in the accurate witticism of Anthony Kirk-Greene:

> Fishing was more a private sport, more a personal recreation than a public duty. The Marquis of Lansdowne was only one of a line of Viceroy anglers; there were, if I may be allowed the conceit, many more angling Viceroys! The number of colonial governors who chose to enter 'fishing' against their recreation in *Who's Who* is legion.[66]

Lansdowne would certainly qualify as a candidate to head that 'line of Viceroy anglers'. It is recorded that in four Canadian summers, he caught no fewer than 1,245 salmon.[67]

Another joy in summer for Governor-General Lansdowne, and much more so this time than for this predecessors, was cricket. In his history of the game in the Ottawa area, Napier has called the Lansdowne years 'a golden era' of cricket, describing His Excellency as 'himself no mean player' who did much to popularize the sport. In 1885, Lansdowne was top scorer for the Government House XI versus the Members of Parliament and Senators' team; and during his term he welcomed to Ottawa cricket teams from other parts of Canada, the United States, and the West Indies.[68]

Lansdowne continued the strong viceregal support for the sport of rifle-shooting, and accepted the position of Patron of the Dominion Rifle Association during his first year of office. At the annual meeting of the Association on 15 March 1888, just before his Excellency's departure from Canada, Lansdowne was thanked for his generous contribution of $500 towards the previous year's prize money, the gifts of silver and bronze medals to the Provincial Associations, and his parting gift of $250 for a trophy to be known as the Lansdowne Cup, awarded for Association competition in the 'Lansdowne Match'.[69]

It is interesting to note, too, that although the Montreal Golf Club was the first to be formed in Canada, in 1873, it was later during Lansdowne's term of office that permission was granted for the Club to affix the adjective 'Royal' to its title. This request was acceded to, through the governor-general's office, by Queen Victoria.[70]

IV

Lansdowne's successor, Baron Stanley of Preston, was at Rideau Hall 'when sport figured more prominently than ever before'[71], but curling was featured less, and the Scottish Reverend Kerr does not deign to mention His Lordship in his mammoth account of curling's progress in the Dominion[72]. Yet he continued the viceregal patronage of other sports in the usual ways. Lord Stanley contributed $500 to each year's prize list of the Dominion Rifle Association, and presented medals to the Provincial associations. He also enthusiastically supported the Rideau Hall Cricket XI, and facilitated the reconstruction of the Ottawa cricket pavilion after it had been destroyed by fire. Lord Stanley was particularly instrumental in bringing about the presentation of the Queen's Cup for Yachting in 1891, thanking Her Majesty in a telegram for her gracious support; and the Royal Victoria Yacht Club was formed in the following year. And His Excellency naturally hosted various winter parties at Rideau Hall, especially some notable skating carnivals.[73]

Despite all this enthusiastic sporting sponsorship, Stanley's biographer in *The Canadian Encyclopedia* informs us that he was 'a publicly shy and politically careful governor-general', and a strong advocate of closer ties between Britain and Canada. He also understates in a casual way why Stanley is the one governor-general in the nineteenth century that most Canadians are familiar with: 'He is primarily remembered for his donation in 1893 of the STANLEY CUP, designed to determine a Canadian hockey champion in a fair and uniform manner'.[74] This now qualifies as the oldest trophy competed for by professional athletes in North America. Donated by Governor-General Stanley in 1893 for presentation to the amateur hockey champions, it was first awarded to Montreal Amateur Athletic Association; and except for the 1918–19 season (owing to an influenza epidemic), it has been presented every year since.

It is difficult to exaggerate the importance of ice-hockey in Canadian society, since no other sport so closely aligns itself with the Canadian psyche. In *Colombo's Canadian Quotations*, for example, there are no fewer than 47 entries for 'hockey' (the prefix 'ice' is considered superfluous in Canada) – more than the total number included for all of the other twelve sports listed in the Index. If statistics must be regarded with suspicion, however, and quality affirmed above mere quantity, then the *message* of many of these quotations culled from a wide spectrum of observers and participants, also confirms the singular status of hockey in Canada. To Ralph Allen in 1965 hockey represented 'the only true Canadian invention'; while the President of Brock University believed that a Canadian victory over a hockey team from the USSR 'probably did more to create a Canadian identity ... than did ten years of Canada Council fellowships'. To another observer hockey is 'the Canadian metaphor', which captures 'the essence of the Canadian experience in the New World ... The dance of life'. Small wonder, then, the affectionate references to the Stanley Cup as 'Lord Stanley's Mug', or the semi-serious allusions to 'the Holy Grail of Hockey'.[75] Ice-hockey is the Canadian game, and the fact that its most revered trophy was conceived of and awarded by an aristocratic English governor-general in the previous century is an indication that viceregal patronage was a living, changing and meaningful process. Stanley surely deserves credit for accurately measuring the sporting pulse of the nation in the early 1890s, with regard to the status and future of this indigenous and rapidly developing sport.

V

Lord Stanley's enduring donation was by way of a timely parting gift to the Canadian people, and he was succeeded in 1893 by John Campbell Hamilton-Gordon, Earl and later first Marquis of Aberdeen. Although he proved to be an able and popular governor-general during his five-year term, his wife is probably better remembered today. Lady Aberdeen was an aristocrat, but also an energetic and democratic 'busybody' possessed of a strong social conscience. She particularly involved herself in women's issues, and immediately helped to form the Canadian branch of the National Council of Women. Despite fierce opposition from the Canadian medical establishment, she also created the Victorian Order of Nurses. This irrepressible feminist faithfully kept a diary (even on the days she gave birth) and her *Canadian Journal* has been described by historians as 'the most important single manuscript' of the 1893–98 period.[76] Specifically, the historian of Rideau Hall calls it 'the best social portrait of Canada in its time'.[77]

Certainly the viceregal social traditions were well maintained at Rideau Hall by the Earl and his conscientious wife. By now the facilities there for winter sports included 'three high toboggan slides, two open-air rinks for skating and ice hockey, another indoor rink for curling matches; and all around the Rideau and Rockcliffe woods for snowshoeing and skiing'.[78] That indoor curling rink particularly enjoyed a return to favour as His Excellency was described as 'an ardent Scottish patriot, who had been a curler from his youth onwards', and who, both as patron and participant, soon demonstrated that he had 'a first-rate knowledge of the fine points of the game'.[79] The Ontario Curling Association especially benefited from Aberdeen's active involvement, as he formulated policy and rule changes and instituted a trophy in 1894 to be awarded to the winner of competitions held within its jurisdictions.[80]

14. The Canadian lacrosse team at Kennington Oval, London, 1876

15. His Excellency Lord Stanley's team for a cricket match v. Members of Parliament at Rideau Hall, c. 1890

The following year, in 1895, this Edinburgh-born governor-general also instituted a Canadian trophy for golf, another imported sport from the land of his birth. This again demonstrated the sure viceregal touch for astutely identifying with a sporting trend at an appropriate time, as 'Golf's popularity was rapidly increasing in Canada and during the 1890's clubs were established in many more major towns'.[81] The Aberdeen Cup was awarded for the Amateur Golf Championship of Canada, and was first competed for in 1895 at the Ottawa Golf Club, when Scotsman Tom Harley of Kingston was the winner. The competition was held under the auspices of the Canadian Golf Association which had been formed only the year before, in 1894. Later – and in keeping with similar status-seeking precedents already mentioned which indicate the significance of such affiliation with the Mother Country – both the CGA and the OGC had the prefix 'Royal' added to their titles.[82]

Although these were the only new sporting trophies donated by Lord Aberdeen during his five-year term, he was also assiduous in cultivating those sporting traditions established by his predecessors in office, and like them he often travelled widely to give his support. Winter sports were participated in beyond Rideau Hall, for example, as the viceregal family sometimes spent Christmas holidays at Montreal where they 'enjoyed snowshoeing, tobogganing, skating, curling, hockey, etc., and especially the storming of an ice castle by members of the various snowshoe clubs'.[83] Aberdeen continued the practice of officially supporting the goals and activities of the Dominion Rifle Association and regularly attended its competitions. The large cash donation received from His Excellency was divided into three prizes, each eagerly competed for, as indicated in the Minutes of the Association: 'There is no higher ambition on the part of riflemen at the annual meeting than to be partakers in the Governor-General's bounty'.[84] His Excellency was certainly amenable to numerous requests for his name to be listed as 'Patron' for various clubs and sports, whether it be the Aberdeen Hockey Club, the Scottish Athletic Football Club, the Montreal Junior and Juvenile Football League, the Capital Lacrosse Club, or the Dominion Chess Championship. All governors-general were approached in this manner, of course, but Aberdeen seems to have been particularly agreeable towards the practice. Perhaps his wife's zeal as a social crusader influenced him somewhat, as he was also involved in the affairs of the Boys' Brigade and the Young Men's Christian Association.[85]

This Scot also kept up the cricketing tradition established at Government House; and even assisted the Ottawa Cricket Club in the alleviation of some financial difficulties by allowing the grounds to be used further for other sports, such as tennis, bowls and quoits, giving as his reason that he wanted 'to see cricket flourish'.[86] In 1896, Aberdeen was entreated by the President of the Vancouver Yacht Club to use his good influences with the Queen to obtain permission for the use of the word 'Royal' in the club's title, a request subsequently granted after the customary formalities.[87] All things considered and despite having some difficult acts to follow, in terms of viceregal sporting patronage, Lord Aberdeen acquitted himself very well. His tenure in this respect was marked by a sensible blend of both the innovative and traditional roles.

VI

At this point it may be appropriate to record a sentiment voiced on behalf of the Ontario Curling Association, just before Lord Aberdeen's departure from Canada: 'It is possible that you may be requested to use your efforts in influencing a visit of Scottish curlers to Canada'.[88] In fact, the word 'definite' could have been used instead of 'possible'. As early as 1858, curlers in Upper Canada had sent a challenge to the Royal Caledonian Curling Club in Scotland, which evoked no response. Scots in Canada were naturally proud of the sport's tremendous progress, and several other invitations for a Scottish curling team to visit the Dominion were issued over the years, none of which was accepted. They especially requested the departing governors-general to do whatever they could to bring about a Scottish tour upon their arrival back in Britain. Dufferin, Lorne, Lansdowne and Aberdeen faithfully passed on these wishes to the RCCC, without success. The invitations became more challenging, more personal, and more urgent, until the pride and curiosity of the Royal Club was stretched to the limit. Eventually the long-awaited tour became a reality, taking place during the term of the next governor-general, the Earl of Minto.[89] In terms of sport as an imperial bond between the two nations, this tour represented a unique example in British Empire history.

This bond was explicit in correspondence between A. Davidson Smith of the RCCC in Edinburgh, and Governor-General Minto, dated 25 April 1902, regarding the proposed tour of Canada by a Scottish Curling team:

> As your Lordship may be aware this proposal has been often raised before and hitherto the difficulties have appeared so considerable that no definite steps have resulted. It is now strongly felt that in view of His Majesty the King's approaching Coronation and other recent events, together with the strong Imperial feeling as to the desirability and necessity of cementing the ties that unite the Mother Country with her Colonies, that the auspicious time has arrived when such a proposal should take effect.[90]

Indeed, with Minto's help and encouragement from other notable figures such as Lord Elgin and Lord Strathcona – and after suitable financial arrangements were completed – the touring Scottish team of 24 curlers arrived in Halifax, Nova Scotia, on 20 December 1902.

The tour was a great success. At the first rink the tourists entered in Halifax, the welcoming address was given by the eloquent Reverend W.T. Herridge who stated his convictions that:

> They felt as much as their Scottish brethren did that they were part of

the British Empire, with their own part to play in the modelling of its destiny. He [the preacher] was convinced that the visit of the Scottish Curling Team would help to cement still more closely the bonds which united them, and that every interchange of a similar kind would strengthen the true Imperialistic sentiment, and make them quick to discern our essential unity.[91]

Such sentiments became commonplace as the team progressed from Halifax to St. John (New Brunswick), and then to Quebec City, Montreal, Ottawa, Peterborough, Lindsay, Toronto, Hamilton, Guelph, Stratford, St. Thomas, Windsor and Winnipeg. Everywhere their hosts pledged their loyalty to the British Crown, to Scotland, 'the auld mither', while also praising Canada and taking pride in the term 'Canadians'. One of the happiest outcomes is that it inspired the Reverend Kerr, Captain of the Scottish team, to produce his comprehensive *Curling in Canada and the United States* (787 pp.), an unsurpassed record of the sport's development up to 1903, especially with its profuse and valuable photographs. On page vi just before the Preface four quotes are reprinted, two of which emphasize the imperialistic theme. A Report of the Ontario Curling Association ends with the hope: 'May the enthusiasm that has been kindled bear fruit on both sides of the Atlantic by drawing not only the curlers, but the people generally of the Motherland and Young Canada closer together'. Below this appears a verse by Tennyson:

> Shall we not through good and ill
> Cleave to one another still?
> Britain's myriad voices call,
> 'Sons, be welded each and all,
> Into one imperial whole
> One with Britain, heart and soul!
> One life, one flag, one fleet, one throne!'
> Britons, hold your own.

And the book was dedicated, not surprisingly, to the Earl of Minto and Lady Minto.

Somewhat paradoxically, in view of these bonding and loyalist sentiments, Minto's term as governor-general was marked by controversy and political strife, and his support for Joseph Chamberlain's imperial preference campaign caused tension with Prime Minister Laurier, whose ambitions were for a more independent Canada.[92] However, there was a positive side, as reported in the *Canadian Encyclopedia*, for Minto also 'attempted to forge closer ties between French and English Canadians, preserve the written and material record of Canada's past, promote sports (the Minto Cup in lacrosse) and protect Canada's northern miners and native peoples from the neglect and mismanagement of government'.[93] As indicated, his promotion of sports was regarded as significant legacy and extended well beyond viceregal facilitation of the 1902–03 Curling Tour.

The Minto Cup was donated to be emblematic of the national senior lacrosse championship of the Dominion. The first game played for the Cup was between the Ottawa Capitals and the Cornwall Club in Ottawa in September 1901, and was also notable in being witnessed by visiting British royalty:

> A match that will long be remembered in the annals of Canada's national game was that played on the varsity oval here this afternoon before Their Royal Highnesses, the Duke and Duchess of Cornwall and York, for possession of the trophy donated by the Governor-General and known as the Minto Cup. The match was not only noted for the presence of Royalty, but as a clean, manly exposition of scientific and cleverly played lacrosse.[94]

Once again, by the award of another national trophy for an indigenous and popular sport, a governor-general had diplomatically identified with Canadian aspirations in a timely fashion.

The winter sport of ice-skating, long a favourite pastime at Rideau Hall as already noted, was also becoming more popular and widespread as the number of rinks increased and better skates were mass-produced. Lord and Lady Minto were both excellent skaters, they had the rink at Government House improved, and they hosted numerous skating parties. In fact, both donated prizes for men's and women's figure skating, and before leaving Canada Their Excellencies founded the Minto Skating Club at Ottawa in 1903. This has prospered since, and produced some of Canada's finest skaters (such as Barbara Ann Scott, the 1948 Olympic and World Champion).[95]

VII

It was stated earlier that Lord Stanley may be 'the one governor-general in the nineteenth century that most Canadians are familiar with' because of his donation of the Stanley Cup for ice-hockey. The rival candidate for the twentieth century might well be Minto's successor, Lord Grey, and for a similar reason. Grey's biography in the *Canadian Encyclopedia* actually states that he is 'perhaps best remembered as donor of the Grey Cup for football supremacy'. Albert Henry George, fourth Earl Grey and a man of considerable energy and charm, would have preferred to have been remembered for the music and drama festivals that he inaugurated, or as as keen imperialist who attempted 'to forge stronger links of empire'.[96] But when he presented a Challenge Cup for the amateur rugby football championship of Canada in 1909, he knew not what he had wrought. He may have been simply following the example of his predecessors, but the trophy bearing his name became a Canadian symbol and tradition far beyond whatever His Lordship may have envisaged.

Originally presented by the Canadian Rugby Union, since 1966 the Cup has been awarded by the Canadian Football League (CFL). In the early years (1909–24) amateur university teams were invariably Grey Cup champions; from 1925 to 1945, the representatives from city leagues were supreme, until the professional teams that later comprised the CFL began to dominate. In 1948 'the Calgary Stampeders and their supporters transformed the Grey Cup game into a week-long carnival of festivities, a national celebration, and the most watched sporting event in Canada'.[97] Writing in 1959, social historian Miriam Chapin in her book, *Contemporary Canada*, provided a graphic description of the significance of the Grey Cup celebration in Canadian society at that time, which is worth quoting:

> In the final week of each November, thousands of people travel to some Canadian city, even from Montreal to Vancouver, on pilgrimage. Each spends several hundred dollars on the trip. They go to observe two dozen young men push and batter each other over a muddy field marked with white lines, as they struggle for possession of a bag of wind. Those who cannot leave home sit by their television sets, taut and intent. The net gate at the Grey Cup, Canada's playoff football game, may be a quarter of a million dollars. Enough money probably changes hands to finance the Colombo Plan. A brewery firm pays a huge sum for the television rights.[98]

Since those words were written, of course, the statistics pertaining to the Grey Cup have become even more impressive. And Chapin did not exaggerate, for in 1962, Parliament decreed that both major Canadian television networks (CBC and CTV) must make the television transmission of the game available to the other so that all regions could see it. The reason given, which would have gladdened Lord Grey's heart, was that the Grey Cup final was 'an instrument of national unity'.[99]

Since Dufferin's day, of course, sport had been promoted by governors-general to foster a sense of national unity in the young Dominion, although none could have foreseen the future spectacular roles of the Grey Cup and the Stanley Cup in this respect. Although his donation to football over-shadowed his other contributions, however, it should be recorded that Earl Grey was also active in other sporting areas. Symbolically, his first duty in office in Ottawa late in 1904 was facing-off the puck in a hockey match between Ottawa and Dawson City.[100] An eloquent and witty speaker, he was in demand as Patron of several sport associations, such as the Ontario Curling Association or the Royal Canadian Yacht Club.[101] But it was his timely sponsorship of football that has set him apart, and this act may be regarded here as an appropriate climax of viceregal patronage of Canadian sport. One can certainly look beyond Grey to his immediate successor and find the Duke of Connaught, governor-general from 1911 to 1916, award-ing a similar trophy for the association football (soccer) championship of Canada – and assiduously supporting other sports as well[102] – but the impact was less; and much of Connaught's energy, and Canada's atten-tion, was inevitably taken up with the war effort. The period from Dufferin the instigator to the donation of the Grey Cup in 1909 really represented the golden age of viceregal patronage of Canadian sport. A report in the *Ottawa Journal* for 6 May 1909 stated: 'Not since the Earl of Dufferin have we had so popular a Governor-General as Earl Grey', and Their Excellencies' enthusiastic and sensible promotion of sport was in large measure responsible for that popularity.

As J.A. Mangan has correctly stated: 'John Bull's imperialism, Canuck independence, Yankee hegemony were the three potent forces affecting the evolution of games in the Canadian ',[103] a statement also applicable to the wider context of Canadian sport as a whole. The great skill of John Bull's seven aristocrats discussed in detail here – Dufferin, Lorne, Lansdowne, Stanley, Aberdeen, Minto, and Grey – lay in their diplomatic handling of these forces while in office. Although American influence could usually be politely regretted and resisted (but not always successfully), and in the same English language, the tension between loyalty to the Crown on one hand and the independent aspirations of a growing young Dominion on the other required a more delicate balancing act. The governors-general recognized sport as a pragmatic vehicle for the relief of such tension. Old British and new Canadian sports were all stimulated in Canada through sincere and serious viceregal support. The governor-general's office was used to facilitate several sporting tours of both countries as a desirable cultural and imperial bond, many more than took place between Britain and any other former colony during the same period.

In fact, given the Canadian pedigree in this relationship, it should not be regarded as surprising that when an 'Inter-Empire Sports Meeting' was held in London in 1911 as part of the Festival of Empire to celebrate the coronation of George V, that Canada emerged as overall winner of the Earl of Lonsdale Cup; or that the first British Empire (now Commonwealth) Games were held in Hamilton, Ontario, in 1930.[104] Dufferin and his successors had helped in a unique way to lay a sure foundation for such future Canadian initiatives within the British imperial family. Anthony Kirk-Greene has expressed the belief that '... when we finally learn what "they" thought of "us", the sporting enthusiasms of His Excellency and so many of his officials will have played a positive part in the shaping of our imperial image and reputation at the personal level.'[105] The evidence from Canada certainly confirms this sentiment, and the governors-general who represented the Crown from Confederation to the First World War may rest assured of a favourable verdict. Their Excellencies' consistent and astute patronage still endures in many tangible forms which have become an integral part of Canadian culture. It is one aspect of the British legacy in Canada which is remembered with gratitude.

NOTES

1. J.B. Sykes (ed.), *The Concise Oxford Dictionary of Current English* (London, 1980), p. 539.
2. See, in particular, J.A. Mangan, *The Games Ethic and Imperialism* (New York, 1986).

3. L. Collins and D. Lapierre, *Freedom at Midnight* (New York, 1975), p. 15.
4. R. Bowen, *Cricket: A History of its Growth and Development Throughout the World* (London, 1970), p. 272.
5. J. Monet, 'Governor General', in *The Canadian Encyclopedia*, Vol. II (Edmonton, 1985), pp. 757–8.
6. Alistair Napier, 'Ottawa Cricket, 1840–1960' (Ottawa: Public Archives, M31, H21, Public Records).
7. J. Cowan, *Canada's Governor-General: Lord Monck to General Vanier* (Toronto, 1965), *passim*. It is noteworthy that Monck and Lisgar are not elaborated upon in McLaughlin's thesis beyond this brief sentence: 'Following a tradition set by Lord Monck, Lord Dufferin was actively involved in the Ottawa Cricket Club' (p.17); see M.K. McLaughlin, 'Vice-Regal Patronage of Canadian Sport, 1867 to 1916' (unpublished MA thesis, University of Alberta, 1981).
8. R.H. Hubbard, *Rideau Hall: An Illustrated History of Government House, Ottawa* (Ottawa, n.d.), p. 33.
9. Marchioness of Dufferin, *My Canadian Journal, 1872–78* (London, 1891), *passim*.
10. See for example, W.A. Creelman, *Curling, Past and Present* (Toronto, 1950); R.S. Fittis, *Sports and Pastimes of Scotland* (Paisley, 1891); J. Kerr, *History of Curling* (Edinburgh, 1890); and D.B. Smith, *Curling: An Illustrated History* (Edinburgh, 1981).
11. There are more books on the Scots in Canada than any other ethnic group in the Dominion; for a list of 46 such works see Appendix A (pp.91–3) of G. Redmond, *Sport and Ethnic Groups in Canada* (Ottawa, 1978).
12. P. Berton, *The National Dream: The Great Railway, 1871–1881* (Toronto, 1970), pp. 319–20.
13. G. Redmond, *The Sporting Scots of Nineteenth-Century Canada* (Toronto, 1982), pp. 35–8, 104–58.
14. Kerr, *History of Curling*, pp. 149–50, 320.
15. R. Collins, *The Age of Innocence, 1870–1880: Canada's Illustrated Heritage* (Toronto, 1877) pp. 13, 15.
16. Marchioness of Dufferin, *My Canadian Journal*, p. 62.
17. McLaughlin. Vice-Regal Patronage', pp. 27–34.
18. C. Berger, 'The True North Strong and Free', in P. Russell (ed.), *Nationalism in Canada* (Toronto, 1966), pp. 6–22.
19. G. Redmond, 'Diffusion in the Dominion: in Canada, to 1914', in *Proceedings of the 1982 Annual Conference of the History of Education Society of Great Britain* (1983), pp. 108–9.
20. W. Leggo, *History of the Administration of the Earl of Dufferin in Canada* (Montreal, 1878), p. 599.
21. B. Schrodt, G. Redmond and R. Baka, *Sport Canadiana* (Edmonton, 1980), p. 47.
22. S.F. Wise and D. Fisher, *Canada's Sporting Heroes* (Don Mills, 1874), p. 10. For details of the 1859 tour, see W.F. Lillywhite, *The English Cricketers' Trip to Canada and the United States* (London, 1860).
23. Letter to Lord Dufferin (Ottawa: Public Archives, RG7 G18, Vol. 72, Public Records).
24. Letter to Lord Dufferin (Ottawa: Public Archives, RG7 G18, Vol. 32B, Public Records).
25. As quoted in D. Brown, 'Canadian Imperialism and Sporting Exchanges: The Nineteenth-Century Experience of Cricket and Lacrosse', *Canadian Journal of History of Sport*, XVIII (1987), 55–66.
26. A.E. Cox, 'A History of Sports in Canada, 1868–1900' (unpublished Ph. D. thesis, University of Alberta, 1969), pp. 70–94, 428–36; G.G.S. Lindsey, 'Cricket in Canada', *The Dominion Illustrated Monthly* (1892 and 1973), a series of four articles: I, 432–41, 495–508, 609–19; and II, 160–7. See also J.E. Hall and R.O. McCulloch, *Sixty Years of Canadian Cricket* (Toronto, 1895).
27. W.G. Beers, *Lacrosse: The National Game of Canada* (Montreal, 1869)
28. *Correspondence of Lord Dufferin* (Ottawa: Public Archives, RG7 G13, Vol. 12F, Public Records).
29. McLaughlin, 'Vice-Regal Patronage', pp. 17–19, 214.
30. Marchioness of Dufferin, *My Canadian Journal*, p. 42.
31. Ibid., p. 147.
32. Wise and Fisher, *Canada's Sporting Heroes*, pp. 177–8.

33. G. Stewart, *Canada Under the Administration of the Earl of Dufferin* (Toronto, 1878), p. 690.
34. Marchioness of Dufferin, *My Canadian Journal*, p. 199.
35. N. Howell and M.L. Howell, *Sports and Games in Canadian Life: 1700 to the Present* (Toronto, 1969), p. 116.
36. McLaughlin, 'Vice-Regal Patronage', p. 20, 185–7.
37. E.M. Orlick, 'McGill Contributions to the Origins of Ice-Hockey', *McGill News*, Winter 1943, 13–17.
38. McLaughlin, 'Vice-Regal Patronage', pp. 185–7, 231–14.
39. Wise and Fisher, *Canada's Sporting Heroes*, pp. 82–5, 100–5, 112–14.
40. Pierre Berton, *My Country: The Remarkable Past* (Toronto, 1976), pp. 197–211.
41. Marchioness of Dufferin, *My Canadian Journal*, p. 243.
42. Stewart, *Canada Under Dufferin*, p. 267.
43. McLaughlin, 'Vice-Regal Patronage', p. 23.
44. C.E. Drummond Black, *The Marquess of Dufferin and Ava* (London, 1903), p. *xx*.
45. *Correspondence from Lord Dufferin to Lord Lorne, Quebec, 12 August 1878* (Ottawa: Public Archives, MG27 I E4 A-716), p. 303.
46. R. Collins, 'The Age of Innocence, 1870–1880', in *Canada's Illustrated Heritage* (Toronto, 1977), p. 21.
47. McLaughlin, 'Vice-Regal Patronage', p. 34.
48. *Office of the Governor-General* (Ottawa: Public Archives, Public Records RC7 G21, Volume 401).
49. *Ottawa Citizen*, 19 April 1880.
50. J. Batten, 'Canada Moves Westward, 1880–1890', in *Canada's Illustrated Heritage* (Toronto, 1977), pp. 115–57.
51. Ibid., p. 117
52. McLaughlin, 'Vice-Regal Patronage', p. 55; D.L. Morrow, 'The Great Canadian Lacrosse Tours of 1876 and 1883', in *Proceedings of the 5th Canadian Symposium on the History of Sport and Physical Education, University of Toronto, 1982*, pp. 11–22.
53. The Marquis of Lorne, *Canadian Life and Scenery: With Hints to Intending Emigrants and Settlers* (London, 1886).
54. Batten, 'Canada Moves', p. 110.
55. *Lorne Papers, Copies of Family Letters, 1878–1885* (Ottawa: Public Archives, MG27 I B6).
56. *Ottawa Daily Citizen*, 17 June 1882.
57. *Papers of the Montreal Amateur Athletic Association* (Ottawa: Public Archives, MG28 I 128 Vol. 15), p. 334.
58. *Constitution of the St. Andrew's Society of Winnipeg* (Winnipeg, 1886), p. 13.
59. As quoted in McLaughlin, 'Vice-Regal Patronage', p. 52.
60. W.S. McNutt, *Days of Lorne* (Fredericton, 1955), p. 206.
61. *Kingston Whig Standard*, 5 Oct. 1880.
62. Batten, 'Canada Moves', p. 94, 116.
63. A.H.W. Kirk-Greene, 'The Governors-General of Canada, 1867–1952: A Collective Profile', *Journal of Canadian Studies*, 16 (1964), 35–55.
64. H.W. Becket, *Record of Winter Sports* (Montreal, 1884), p. 20, 52.
65. *The Canadian Encyclopedia* (1985), p. 977.
66. A.H.W. Kirk-Greene, 'Imperial Sidelight or Spotlight?: Sport and His Excellency in the British Empire', in *Proceedings of the XIth HISPA International Congress* (Glasgow, 1985), pp. 1–11. See also Kirk-Greene's chapter in this volume.
67. Cowan, *Canada's Governor-General*, p. 48.
68. *Ottawa Cricket, 1840–1960* (Ottawa: Public Archives, MG31 H 21), p. 2.
69. *Governor-General's Civil Secretary's Correspondence* (Ottawa: Public Archives, RG7 G21), 15 March 1888.
70. McLaughlin, 'Vice-Regal Patronage', p. 217.
71. Hubbard, *Rideau Hall*, pp. 75–84.
72. J. Kerr, *Curling in Canada and the United States* (Edinburgh, 1904).
73. McLaughlin, 'Vice-Regal Patronage', pp. 70–73.
74. *The Canadian Encyclopedia* (1985), p. 1752.
75. J.R. Colombo (ed.), *Colombo's Canadian Quotation* (Edmonton, 1974), *passim*.

76. J. Callwood, 'The Naughty Nineties, 1890–1900', in *Canada's Illustrated Heritage* (Toronto, 1977), pp. 119–23.
77. Hubbard, *Rideau Hall*, p. 80.
78. Ibid, p. 84.
79. J.S. Stevenson, *Curling in Ontario, 1846–1946* (Toronto, 1950), p. 92.
80. McLaughlin, 'Vice-Regal Patronage', pp. 86–9.
81. Howell and Howell, *Sports and Games*, p. 104.
82. *Canadian Encyclopedia* (1985), pp. 750–51.
83. Cowan, *Canada's Governor-General*, p. 67.
84. *Governor-General's Civil Secretary's Correspondence* (Ottawa: Public Archives, RG7 G21 volume 1, Public Records, Minutes of the Dominion Rifle Association).
85. McLaughlin, 'Vice-Regal Patronage', pp. 96–7.
86. *Papers of Governor-General Aberdeen: Haddo House Records* (Ottawa: Public Archives, MG27 I B5, A-825).
87. *Correspondence of Governor-General Aberdeen* (Ottawa: Public Archives MG27 I B5).
88. *Correspondence of Governor-General Aberdeen* (Ottawa: Public Archives MG27 I B5, Letters from the Ontario Curling Association).
89. Redmond, *The Sporting Scots*, pp. 141–9.
90. *Correspondence of Governor-General Minto* (Ottawa: Public Archives, MG27 II B1).
91. Kerr, *History of Curling*, p. 243.
92. A. Philips, 'Into the 20th Century, 1900–1910', in *Canada's Illustrated Heritage* (Toronto, 1977), pp. 25–9.
93. *Canadian Encyclopedia* (1985) p. 1144.
94. *Manitoba Morning Free Press*, 21 Sept. 1901.
95. McLaughlin, 'Vice-Regal Patronage', pp. 105–8.
96. *Canadian Encyclopedia* (1985), p. 774.
97. Ibid.
98. M. Chapin, *Contemporary Canada* (Toronto, 1959), pp. 226–7.
99. *Canadian Encyclopedia* (1985), p. 774.
100. Hubbard, *Rideau Hall*, p. 115.
101. McLaughlin, 'Vice-Regal Patronage', pp. 122–4.
102. Ibid., pp. 127–33.
103. Mangan, *Games Ethic*, p. 165.
104. For the most comprehensive treatment of these 1911 and 1930 events, see K.E. Moore, 'The Concept of British Empire Games: An Analysis of its Origin and Evolution from 1891 to 1930' (unpublished Ph.D. thesis, University of Queensland, 1986).
105. Kirk-Greene, 'Imperial Sidelight or Spotlight?', p. 11.

CHAPTER NINE

Badge of Office: Sport and His Excellency in the British Empire

ANTHONY KIRK-GREENE

In any anatomy of the cultural bond as an imperial phenomenon, it is prudent to approach the concept with chronological care. During the period of colonial overrule, cultural manifestations were expectedly at their most vigorous: in work patterns and leisure habits, in dress and speech, and throughout much imitated social behaviour. This was the moment of the cultural bond as cultural impact. On the other hand, during the post-colonial era the cultural bond tends to become looser and far more selective. This is the time of the cultural legacy. Historically, such a heritage tends to crystallize in two post-imperial areas. These are institutions and language. Catholicism, the art of the *siesta*, and Spanish as a national language in most of Latin America; Parliament, Clubs and the continuity no longer of driving on the left but of English in higher education throughout most of former anglophone Asia; a presidential system, cuisine rather than cooking, and the very *timbre* of martial music in much of francophone Africa; and the whole range of the artefacts of the Coca-Cola culture in the Philippines, Panama and Puerto Rico, all underline the essence of the respective culture legacies.

Culture impositions, however, need cultural agents. Frequently the most formative of these are not so much the official as the informal influences. A conspicuous example of such an agency is the lasting impact of the one-time ruling power's national sport: cricket in the Caribbean and on the Indian sub-continent, rugger in Australia, New Zealand and South Africa, baseball in the Philippines and latter-day Japan, polo in the Argentine; and, seemingly, football the ex-colonial world over. In keeping with the thrust of the whole volume, of sport as a manifestation of the imperial contact, this chapter exemplifies a certain category of agents of imperialism: the governing elite who, always unofficially and often uncon-sciously, influenced colonial society by their incidental commitment to and amateur love of the practice of sport.

As an enquiry into the social and intellectual history of sport in its colonial setting, this study also takes the argument a step further. When we come to the cultural *legacy* as a follow-up to the cultural *impact*, the matter of memory remains paramount. One of the considerations to exercise the study of the post-imperial age, and one which will likely continue to do so for several generations to come, is to understand exactly how 'they' saw 'us'. How much more is there to the history of the British abroad than the 'mad dogs and Englishmen out in the midday sun' syndrome? Were yesterday's rulers, plumed proconsuls and field administrators, missionaries and box-wallahs alike, respected, ignored, feared or just figures of fun? What exactly were the features that characterized, and on occasion immortalized, for better or for worse, the received image of the alien governing class? If *we* thought we knew what we were doing, was it necessarily the same as *they* thought we were doing? This study concludes that, for many of Britain's governing elite, it may well be that in the long run they are more vividly remembered for having made their mark not through public acts and official achievements but through their private enthusiasms and personal attributes. Such a premise is demonstrably evident in the influence of the sporting record of Britain's imperial elite.

I

Writing in his diary, Edward Atiyah, a young Syrian brought up in the Anglo-Egyptian Sudan who became one of the British Administration's most trusted go-betweens, recalls his childhood image of British officialdom in Khartoum as a perpetual procession of 'tall commanding figures, riding out to play polo on their well-trained ponies'.[1] Ahmadu Bello, first and last Premier of Northern Nigeria, remembers the pride with which his house at Katsina College won the cricket trophy, and how one of the British teachers immortalized himself in the memory of several generations of Nigerian students because he introduced the game of Eton fives (albeit played with a tennis ball).[2] Ham Mukasa, secretary and companion to Apolo Kagwa, the Chief Minister of Buganda, on his visit to England to attend the coronation of King Edward VII in 1902, records in his diary of their wonderment at the traditional British deck sports: 'One would not have believed', he concluded, 'that such things could be done on a ship'.[3]

The common theme in these influential impressions is the significant sporting image of the ruler in the mind and memory of the ruled. Today, a quarter of a century beyond the close of the colonial era and nearly twice that period since the end of the Raj, we are still a long way from grasping how Asians and Africans perceived the *dramatis personae* of Empire. The probability is that the received image was often widely different from the one projected and believed in by the governing elite themselves. That was more akin to, say, the Edgar Wallace definition of Commissioner Sanders acting out his role as King of the Great River, 'a slim and dapper figure in spotless white ... sitting crosslegged on his canvas chair, chewing an unsmoked cigar and drawing little patterns with his ebony stick in the sand', his eyes 'cold and prohibitive', and whose voice, when he spoke as Keeper of the King's Peace, had 'the quality of an ice-cold razor';[4] or, in later years, the Kiplingesque imagery of the grave and serious-minded District Officer as *man bap*, the father and mother of his people, the Plato model of the 'Guardians', who in the day's work assumed the White Man's Burden: able, alert, and more than just a little aloof.

The closer one analyses the sociology of Britain's overseas administrators, their family and class provenance, their educational patterns and performance, their traditional values and their Service ethos, the more one becomes aware of the influence of the argument that in any examination of who the imperialists were (a necessary priority towards sensing what imperialism was in practice if not always in theory) an important key is to be found in understanding the role and relevance of sport in the making of our-man-on-the-imperial-spot, that typical middle-to-upper-class District Commissioner who was the backbone of the Indian Civil, the Sudan Political and the Colonial Administrative Services. J.A. Mangan in his *Athleticism in the Victorian and Edwardian Public School* (Cambridge, 1981), and Peter Parker in *The Old Lie: The Great War and the Public School Ethos* (Constable, 1987), have compellingly scrutinized the critical cult of sport in the formative years of those members of Britain's youth who were destined (and the word is not used lightly) for a career of public service overseas, in the army or administration. Reinforced by Henrika Kuklick's anatomy of 'The Imperial Bureaucrat', Robert Heussler's and Richard Symonds' accounts of the educational influence of Oxford on the formation of colonial administrators, and most recently by two tentative identikits of the District Commissioner in the Sudan,[5] the positive link between sport and service in the British Empire is being progressively and persuasively constructed. Pursuing the transformation of the schoolboy Victor Ludorum and yesterday's hero of Bigside into a fully-fledged colonial administrator, the concept of a veritable 'athletocracy' has now been developed to account for the striking preference attaching to the athletic imperative in the selection of Britain's career administrators overseas.[6]

But all the analyses have so far focused on the colonial cadet, the Service greenhorn or griffin at the bottom of the administrative ladder. The present study advances this line of enquiry to the topmost level of Britain's ruling elite in Asia and Africa, whether Dominion, Colony or Protectorate, namely the Viceroys, Governors-General and Colonial Governors, by concentrating on the incidence of sport in their careers. On the wider canvas, one might ask whether the sporting attributes of His Excellency provide just a small social sidelight on Britain's imperial history or whether they furnish something of an imperial spotlight, too. The present approach not only seeks to determine how conspicuous the athletic factor frequently was in the make-up of His Excellency – to the extent of its being interpreted as a potential badge of office – but also asks why it may have been considered an advantage and what it meant to his performance in his relations *vis-à-vis* both his staff and his subjects. Underlying the whole analysis is the single question of how far the sporting factor may have contributed to His Excellency's reputation in post-colonial retrospect: how he is recalled, or whether he is remembered at all. 'Whatever reputation on other counts I may have gained here', confided Sir Hesketh Bell to his diary as he looked back on his Uganda days, 'I shall always be remembered as "The Governor Who Rode On An Elephant"'.[7]

When Lord Curzon heard of the appointment of the Earl of Minto to succeed him as Viceroy of India in 1905, he expostulated 'Isn't that the gentleman who jumps hedges?'[8] For Minto had made his name as an outstanding gentleman jockey, riding under the name of 'Mr. Rolly' and in 1874 winning the Grand Steeplechase of Paris. He was the only Viceroy who could claim to have ridden in the Grand National. Racing may be the sport of kings but it did not quite fit with the Curzonian expectations of viceregal dignity. For it should not be forgotten that, as the sovereign's personal representative, a governor-general took precedence over all save his own Royalty and, in his own domain, exacted the courtesy bow from even a visiting British Prime Minister.[9] On this point of punctilio, it was Governor-General Byng – the man who not only told His Majesty, on learning that in his new job in Canada he would be just like a king in his kingdom, replied 'No, Sir, I shall just be Byng in my Byngdom', but who also described his role of governor-general as being 'a governor who doesn't govern and a general who cannot generalize ... with my better half as a governess-general' – who had no hesitation in sending for [sic] the Prince of Wales, then on a royal visit to Canada, after the Prince had monopolized a certain Ottawa lady at the Government House ball and not returned to Rideau Hall till dawn – and then warned [sic again] H.R.H. never to come back to Canada so long as he was Governor-General: 'in flouting the authority of the Governor-General he had technically disobeyed the King'.[10] So much for the authority of Government House. No wonder that the same heir to the throne, on subsequently having a mere colonial governor presented to him on another of his overseas tours, is said to have whispered to his equerry, 'Now I know what it is like meeting royalty'. Devotion to horsemanship was not unique among sporting proconsuls. At least two Governors of Lower Canada were killed when out fox-hunting, Sydenham in a riding accident and Richmond after being bitten by a fox. Several Viceroys – among them the successive Irwin and Willingdon – were proud to be Master of Hounds.[11] The last of the Viceroys, Earl Mountbatten, was a polo player of international class and wrote one of the classic books on the sport. Few colonial governors on an official tour of the Northern Nigerian emirates, where the local aristocracy were practically brought up on horseback, would forgo the thrill of riding in a caparisoned cavalcade of pomp and pageantry to the palace when paying the necessary courtesy call on the chief, impressively escorted by members of his personal staff, similarly accountred and mounted though by no means always comparably happy or confident in the saddle. Curzon, one hardly need add, preferred to ride in princely processions on an elephant, and it was in the viceregal howdah that Lord Hardinge was badly wounded by a bomb in an assassination attempt during his state entry into Delhi in 1912.

Shooting and fishing were the other components in the established trinity of British aristocratic and upper-class social accomplishments. Even with his withered hand, Linlithgow was an extremely good shot, as well as a fine golfer whose handicap was down to four. Few governors-general of India escaped the viceregal tiger hunt. Lord Lansdowne, one of the no fewer than four Governors-General of Canada who went on to be appointed to that supreme eminence of Britain's overseas ruling elite, the Viceroyalty of India (at least two others entertained high hopes of such preferment), considered the hunting of tigers a very second-best sport after experiencing Canada's superb salmon-fishing. Innumerable are the photographs of the Lat (Lord) Sahib standing triumphantly beside the corpse of his statutory tiger or behind several hundred brace of duck shot on the jheel by His Excellency's party before breakfast.[12] Describing such a traditional proconsular breakfast in his days in Aden, Lord Belhaven talks of 'roast teal with an orange sauce and a flask of chilled Orvieto, and the memory of early dawn by the delta, the sky astir with wings'.[13] For Archer, too, passing through Cairo on his way to take up his post as Governor-General of the Sudan, the customary Friday duck shoot at Ekiad was to him, as the personal guest of Lord Allenby, British High Commissioner to Egypt, 'a day after my own heart'.[14] La vie coloniale was well worth living when it had such pleasures. Fishing was a more private sport, a personal recreation rather than a public requirement. The Marquis of Lansdowne was only one of a line of Viceroy anglers; there were, if I may be allowed the conceit, many more angling Viceroys! The number of colonial governors who chose to enter 'fishing' against their recreation in Who's Who is legion. The triple 'hunting/shooting/fishing' expectations of His Excellency were demanding enough for Sir Frederick Burrows, one-time President of the National Union of Railwaymen who in 1946 was appointed to the Governorship of Bengal by an innovative Labour government, to comment that his own socio-sporting graces were limited to shuntin', hootin' and whistlin'.

So far the data presented have been in line with the distinction made by a pioneer Commissioner in Uganda, who declared 'for me, sport in Africa must mean game, not games'.[15] But besides a gentleman's sports, there were the so-called 'manly' sports. His typical Excellency seems to have excelled at many of these, too. For instance, Sir Charles Arden-Clarke, Governor of Sarawak and then the last – and enormously popular – Colonial Service Governor of the Gold Coast, had once been an Army heavyweight boxing champion. Rufus Isaacs, afterwards Marquis of Reading and Viceroy of India, was a self-taught and successful boxer, who a little more than 100 years ago made his debut by knocking out the fo'castle bully of a Glasgow cargo boat. Sir Gawain Bell, the last British Governor of Northern Nigeria and before that Political Agent in Kuwait, was a rifle-shooting Blue, while Sir Harold MacMichael, Civil Secretary of the Sudan and then High Commissioner in Palestine, had gained a Blue for fencing. None of these sporting skills could presumably be invoked in dealing with what one proconsul generically termed 'native races and their rulers' (rephrased by another, more athletic, as 'native rulers and their races'), though colonial folklore tells of how now and again a frustrated District Commissioner was momentarily tempted to throw a straight left at the nose of a particularly irritating agitator or hints at how a governor at end of his tether secretly dreamed of the pleasure of transfixing the heart of some vexatious nationalist with a blade of murderous steel or scoring a Bisley-like bullseye through the brain.

Walking and climbing are recreations as much as sports, and the proverbially remote outposts of Empire often gave His Excellency superb opportunities to indulge in these manifestions of rugged manliness. Notable among Government House walkers and climbers was Canada's Governor-General Lord Tweedsmuir, better known as John Buchan.[16] No reader of *Sick Heart River* can escape the authentic voice of climbing in the Canadian mountains, just as nobody who reads the Richard Hannay novels can fail to sense the romance of tramping in the Scottish Borders. The energetic Sir Richard Turnbull, Governor of Tanganyika, whose warm relationship with the nationalist leader Julius Nyerere became a byword in the Colonial Office (in contrast to that between Nyerere and the preceding governor, Sir Edward Twining, whose hobbies were the less athletic ones of identifying crown jewels and conducting the police band at Government House receptions), used to make a point of taking what Americans call 'R. and R.' breaks by pitting his wits against the challenge of his home-made assault-course in the Pugu hills. This was the Turnbull who, as his subordinates described him on his previous incarnation as a Provincial Commissioner of Kenya's rugged N.F.D., 'strode along in seven-league boots, 4½ or 5 miles an hour, counting thirty miles a day a very modest day's march', and whose time for the ascent of the steep rocky hill outside Lodwar was never beaten, even if he was once driven to dispute the starting point.[17] And when his duties were too onerous to allow him to leave Dar es Salaam, he could often be seen pedalling his bicycle through that humid city, a notable example of commoner's exercise if not of standard Excellency conduct!

A mountaineer of international repute was Sir Edward Windley, Governor of the Gambia. But no colonial governor ever excelled the mountaineering record of Sir Percy Wyn-Harris (who also ended up as Governor of the Gambia, scarcely noted for its mountainous terrain). As a young official in Kenya, he earned the honour of a place on the Everest expedition of 1933 and again of 1936 – it can be no coincidence that in 1933 three out of the twelve expedition members were imperial administrators, including the leader himself, Hugh Ruttledge. Uniquely, Wyn-Harris claims an entry in the annals of world-class mountaineering as well as in the register of Britain's African governors. For good measure, on retiring from Government House, Bathurst, he set sail in his own 12-ton yacht on a seven-year navigation of the world. Jogging may well be a post-colonial sport, but 80 years ago Sir Percy Girouard, one of the only two Canadians who, unusually, became the governor of a British colony in Africa, used to run around Nairobi every day before settling down to the cares of Government House. One morning, very soon after his arrival as the new Governor of British East Africa (as Kenya was then known), he overtook another runner. 'Morning', he panted to the colonial official whom he half recognized. The recognition was not mutual, for when His Excellency challengingly repeated the greeting all he received in return was 'B – off, you bloody settler!'[18]

In the data marshalled on the making of an 'athletocracy', it is a proven capacity for team games which seems to have dominated the selection of the District Officer.[19] There is an element here of the time-honoured prescription for Britain's youth, from the proverbial playing fields of the nineteenth-century Eton and muscular Christianity of Arnold, Thring *et al.*, through the turn-of-the-century 'cold baths and cricket' curriculum of training for Empire, to the mid-twentieth century ukase fictionally uttered by the martinet West African Frontier Force Brigadier to his astonished National Service ADC: 'Every young man should learn to drive, swim, dance, play at least one game concerning a ball, and go for seventy hours without sleep'.[20] To a considerable extent this apparent athletic imperative reflected the inclinations ('hunches', he called them) of Sir Ralph Furse, who between 1910 and 1950 was responsible at the Colonial Office for Colonial Service recruitment. Appropriately, he is often described as the father of the modern Colonial Service. Furse's *beau idéal* was what one colonial governor summed up as a good Second and a Blue. 'He wanted men who had been prefects', records another, ' ... who had learned at school the elements of leadership and to carry a little responsibility and at the university learned to be detached and self-reliant'.[21] In detecting these qualities, team-games – particularly the captaincy of a team – constituted for Furse a positive pointer. To borrow the words of Margery Perham, godmother to Furse's fatherhood of the Colonial Service, 'It was in the confident, athletic and privileged class that the necessary combination of qualities could most often be found'.[22] It is to Furse that we owe a memorable definition of what he believed to have been the benefits conferred by the British Empire: 'The abolition of slavery ... the long campaign against disease and want ... the example of justice and fair play ... [and] the introduction of cricket ...'.[23]

As the pre-1914 pioneering days, when colonial governorships frequently went to outsiders (mostly military men, with just now and again a politician or Home civil servant) gradually gave way to the inter- and post-war period, the majority of colonial governorships began to be filled by men who had themselves been recruited into the Colonial Administrative Service. This meant that they had, as it were, come up from the ranks – the real and only way, in the eyes of many[24] – as District Officers and Provincial Commissioners. Naturally, these new-styled governors reflected the recruiting bias of Furse and his colleagues, with high marks for high-fliers who could display above-average achievements in team games. In the words of the College Bursar's rueful comment to the Senior Tutor as he faced up to the likely outcome of his son's Tripos results: 'He's thought to stand a chance of the Colonial Service if he can scrape a Third, though I can't see why our colonies should need third-class men with a capacity for organized sports'.[25]

This emphasis on the importance and validity of team-games in the making of the overseas administrator was at its most conspicuous in the selection of the Sudan Political Service. Robert Collins has usefully rationalized it like this:

The fact that most members played games and participated in sports gave them a similarity of outlook which was clearly reflected in their handling of administrative matters. The *esprit de corps* which bolstered the provincial polo team was equally applicable in organizing an African road gang or supervising the construction of a bridge.[26]

The ambitious Governor of British Somaliland, who went on to become, however briefly and ingloriously, Governor-General of the Sudan, was likewise in no two minds. 'For Native Administration', Sir Geoffrey Archer wrote, 'the qualities of scholarship and academic attainment are not to be prized so highly as the leadership of men. Brilliance in debate can hardly equal the initial advantage gained in youth by having led in the field a body of well trained and disciplined young men of similar age.'[27]

There was, too, the sheer necessity of being physically fit enough to undertake day after day of arduous trekking, on horse or foot, and to survive the health hazards: 'to climb the hillsides to villages on or near the top called for good wind and stout thighs', emerges the verdict of a latterday District Officer.[28] Out of the 300 graduates appointed to the Sudan Political Service in its 56 years of existence, no fewer than 93 – one out of every three – had gained Blues or the equivalent by playing one team game or another for his university. And these men were amateurs, often with a First or a good Second Class honours degree, not the holders of athletic scholarship awards so dear to the ranking of many American universities. A few, for good measure, were double Blues, and at least one was a triple Blue. Several were international players. As one of them observed, looking round his compartment in 'The Desert Express', the boat-train from Wadi Halfa to Khartoum, as it brought in the latest cadet entry, 'I think we had been chosen mainly because we were athletes'.[29] Out of his seven-man group, one had captained not only Oxford at rugby football but Scotland too; another had captained Cambridge at cricket; and four others were either Blues or county colours – or both. Not that such laurels were all that rare in the Sudan Service: a couple of years later, the new entry of four was made up of one cricket Blue, one hockey Blue and two oarsmen – one of whom went on to row in the 1912 Olympics. Small wonder that the Sudan earned the nickname of 'The Land of Blacks ruled by Blues'. The almighty Civil Secretaries in Khartoum included Sir Harold MacMichael, who had fenced for Cambridge as well as collecting a First in Classics, Sir Angus Gillan, who rowed for Britain in the Olympics, and Sir James Robertson, who had played rugger for Oxford. Messrs Wilson and Laurie, though not achieving quite the administrative eminence of some of their peers (one became Deputy Governor, the other retired early), surpassed them all by winning the Coxwainless Pairs in the Olympic Games of 1948 – Wilson still recovering from a spear wound inflicted a few months earlier by a dissatisfied litigant upcountry.

Examples of the athletically gifted District Officer of the 1920s and 1930s who progressed to become the colonial governor of the 1950s and 1960s are numerous. The researcher has only to consult the recreations listed in the 'Who's Who' of British colonial governors[30] or the obituaries published in *The Times* to be aware of the validity of this particular connection between proconsular eminence and sporting distinction. Out of a corpus of 150 British governors of the African colonies between 1900 and 1965, more than half opted to give prominence to the pursuit of sporting activities. Often these amounted to two or three sports per governor. In statistical terms, of Britain's African governors who labelled their recreational interests as sporting, 40 per cent named golf (why else, one wonders, should Sir Reginald Wingate, the 'Master' and longest serving Governor-General of Sudan, have chosen to retire to Dunbar?), 27 per cent listed fishing and 22 per cent shooting. Then come tennis (12 per cent), cricket and riding (5 per cent each). Miscellaneous sports include swimming, sailing, mountaineering, squash, polo, hunting, with one listed as flying and two (in Africa, remember!) as skiing.

The range of proconsular sporting activities knew no bounds, the ingenuity no limits. That 'most energetic of men',[31] the Honourable John Fremantle, one of the early Nigerian Residents and later Private Secretary to the Governor-General of Canada and Acting Lieutenant-Governor of Northern Nigeria, quickly commandeered a disused bungalow in Bauchi Province and built a squash court out of its ruined walls. The first thing his neighbour, the new Resident of the desert-like Bornu Province, did in 1910 was to found the Lake Chad Polo Club; and, there not being enough Europeans in this outpost of Empire, he conscripted some of the Mounted Infantry native NCOs.[32] In Kenya they went one better; up in the sand-and-scrub Northern Frontier District the Provincial Commissioner established the Royal Wajir Yacht Club, unique among the yacht clubs of the world in that there was no water within 100 miles. Its 'sole nautical manoeuvre was splicing the main brace'.[33] No wonder that, in Lord Cromer's judgement on the making of modern Egypt, just about the first things the British built in their colonies were racecourses and golf courses.[34] In Kenya the huge range of sporting activities was part of the attraction to the settler society (Lord Cranworth chose for his history of the colony the title *Profit and Sport in British East Africa*): to quote an old-timer's ditty about the social life to be found in pre-war Nairobi:

> Are you fond of your sport
> Or a glass of old port ...
> Would you sooner have cricket or tennis ...
> Play your bridge or sing solo,
> Or show off your prowess at polo?[35]

Characteristic sporting entries in *Who's Who* are, for example, those of the last two Governors of Uganda, Sir Frederick Crawford and Sir Walter Coutts, both noting 'golf and fishing', or again of Sir Philip Mitchell, Governor of Kenya, Sir Shenton Thomas, Governor of the Gold Coast and then of sad Singapore in 1942, and of Sir Glyn Jones of Nyasaland, respectively listing 'golf, shooting, fishing', 'cricket, tennis, golf', and 'shooting, fishing, golf, tennis'. Less typical, perhaps, yet by no means uncommon, are the sporting declarations of such Excellencies as Sir Robert Coryndon and Sir Frederick Jackson, both Governors of an earlier Uganda, with their 'big game hunting', or Their Excellencies Harry Cordeaux, Edward Denham and Edward Garraway, content with their all-embracing entry of 'field sports' or simply 'outdoor recreations'. One, kept anonymous here because of his rather pretentious entry, has declared 'gentle swimming and rough shooting'. Perhaps Sir Godfrey Lagden, Resident Commissioner in Basutoland, summed it up when he put down '*all* games and sports'. Among Sir Bernard Bourdillon's proudest moments was winning the Captain's Plate at the Entebbe golf club when Governor of Uganda. One of the first things Sir Charles Arden-Clarke did on assuming the governorship of Sarawak in 1946 was to repair the tennis-court after the savage ravages of the Japanese occupation and fix up a badminton court.[36] *Pari passu*, one of the first things the British Consul-General-elect, Trevor Mound, hoped to do when in 1985 the Foreign Office announced the reopening of its Shanghai post after almost 20 years of the cultural revolution, was to resurrect the FO cricket roller rusting among the camphor trees at the old consulate on the Bund.[37]

Not surprisingly, cricket is a continuing theme in the story of British imperialism. Sir Geoffrey Colby, Governor of Nyasaland, is reputed to have kept the mystified members of his Executive Council waiting for half an hour in order to listen to the closing overs of the Test match 5000 miles away, while a senior civil servant in the Western Pacific, P.A. Snow, made his name among the locals no less by administration than by writing the standard history of cricket in the region. In Fiji, the first Governor, Arthur Hamilton (later the first Baron Stanmore), had no hesitation in assuring the Colonial Office that the decrease in head-hunting following the island's cession in 1874 was thanks to the civilizing effect of cricket as introduced by the Royal Navy.[38] Sir Gordon Guggisberg, Governor of the Gold Coast, had captained the Royal Engineers' cricket XI as well as being acknowledged as 'a fine player of polo, racquets, golf and football'.[39] His love of cricket, described as 'powerful and lifelong', is encapsulated in the not necessarily apocryphal Accra story that on being required to sign the indent for the following year's cadet entry, he bore in mind the local needs of the Gold Coast in its annual match against Nigeria and requested the Secretary of State to assign to the colony three new Assistant District Commissioners, one of whom should be a reliable slow left-hand bowler.[40] Further East, another Governor zealous for the reputation of his civil service watched a visiting ship's doctor hit a century against the Singapore Cricket Club and then offered him an immediate job as Government Medical Officer, with the explanation 'You're the sort of man we want in the Malayan Service'.[41] Sir Alan Burns, also Governor of the Gold Coast, rarely allowed any engagement in his retirement to interfere with watching cricket at Lord's, while Sir James Robertson, old Sudan hand who went on to become Governor-General of Nigeria, used to tell how he once declined to sail on the date booked by his employers because it clashed with the Calcutta Cup at Murrayfield.

There is evidence that even the 25-hour-a-day workaholic Lord Lugard, colonial Excellency *par excellence* and first Governor-General of Nigeria, took to the tennis court on at least one occasion. His doctor had ordered him to take more exercise and suggested an hour's tennis. At five o'clock Lugard summoned his Private Secretary and two officials to play on the Government House court. Punctually at six, he put down his racket in the middle of a game and went back to his office.[42] Elsewhere among Excellencies, Charles Bruton, Resident Commissioner of Swaziland, had played cricket for Gloucestershire; Vice-Admiral Sir Peveril William Powlett, Governor of Southern Rhodesia, had played rugger for England; and the unusual Sir Arnold Hodson, Governor of the Gold Coast, had been Vice-President of the National Rifle Association besides writing and producing a pantomime for Government House (some saw no need for any new script here). Lord Willingdon, captain of cricket at Eton and Cambridge, 'a deft fives player, a good shot and a keen rider to hounds',[43] is believed to have improved his chances of being nominated Viceroy of India when King George V's Private Secretary was instructed to remind the Cabinet that Willingdon had often played tennis with His Majesty. By and large, as illustrated by three successive Residents of Zanzibar, Sir Vincent Glenday, Sir John Rankine and Sir Arthur Mooring, their combined interests of fishing, shooting, sailing, golf, squash and tennis underline the point made in a recent study of the sociology of colonial governors, that their choice of sporting hobbies perforce lent itself more easily to the individualistic and often restricted facilities of recreational life in the colonies than to a replay of the team games enthusiasm of their schooldays.[44]

In the social roll-call of the British Empire a notable number of Excellencies furnish a formidable record of administrative distinction combined with sporting success. David Cecil, sixth Marquis of Exeter, was Governor of Bermuda at the end of the Second World War. Better known as Lord Burghley, he was three times Cambridge winner of the Oxford and Cambridge hurdles races, both 120 and 220 yards, winner of eight British athletic championships in a single year, medallist in the Olympic Games hurdles in 1928 and 1932, President of the Amateur Athletic Association and Chairman of the British Olympic Association for over 30 years. At the same time, Lord Porritt, who became Governor-General of New Zealand from 1967 to 1972, was breaking similar records for Oxford: holder of the 100 yards record in the inter-varsity athletic competition, Olympic Games finalist at Paris in 1924 and captain of the New Zealand Olympic team in 1924 and 1928, and Vice-President of The British Empire and Commonwealth Games Federation. New Zealand seems to breed a special relationship with sport. When Viscount Cobham (Charles John, yet another member of the remarkable Lyttelton family of noted athletes), K.G., P.C., G.C.M.G., G.C.V.O., was appointed its Governor-General in 1957, he took with him a long record of cricket honours at Eton, Cambridge and Worcestershire, as well as having been vice-captain of the MCC tour to New Zealand in 1935 and ending up as President of the MCC. Canada, too, came within an ace of rivalling this Dominion record, if only William

16. The tennis court at
    Government House,
    Grenada

17. Colonial
    administrators at
    play: Kuala Lumpur v
    Kuala Kubu, 1903

NIGERIA vs. GOLD COAST—1939

"At Kumasi ; won by Gold Coast by 58 runs"

GOLD COAST

P. H. Fitzgerald (Capt) b Wrench	15 — b Butler	5
W. E. M. Logan hit wkt. b Wood	13 — c Wrench b Butler	8
C. D. A. Pullan c Laing b Price	28 — c Ruffet b Wood	38
P. J. McCosh b Butler	21 — c and b Cohen	19
B. de L. Inniss b Wrench	9 — b Wrench	43
Capt W. H. L. Gordon l.b.w. b Wrench	7 — c and b Stewart	68
Capt P. M. Hughes not out	51 — c Wrench b Cohen	48
J. Casley b Price	6 — c Stewart b Wrench	31
N. Bradley c Moull b Stewart	18 — b Wrench	17
B. T. Steemson b Wrench	1 — c Ruffet b Wrench	4
J. M. Perkins l.b.w. b Wood	2 — not out	1
Extras	5	13
Total	176	295

NIGERIA

D. G. Stewart b Perkins	19 — c and b Inniss	16
W. M. Wood c Hughes b Pullan	48 — c sub b Inniss	54
A. N. Cohen c Logan b Inniss	7 — Hughes b Inniss	38
F. K. Butler (Capt) c Hughes b Casley	35 — c Hughes b Inniss	39
P. W. Price c Gordon b Casley	16 — l.b.w. b Inniss	19
H. L. Noble b Perkins	3 — c McCosh b Perkins	13
P. F. Mason run out	7 — c McCosh b Casley	17
Capt. G. Laing c and b Perkins	6 — l.b.w. c Casley	15
W. H. L. Moull l.b.w. b Logan	1 — c Gordon b Logan	7
H. D. Wrench not out	5 — not out	2
T. P. Ruffet b Pullan	17 — b Inniss	6
Extras	13	7
Total	177	236

Nigeria Bowling

	Overs	Mdns	Runs	Wkts	Overs	Mdns	Runs	Wkts
Noble	3	1	6	0	4	0	22	0
Stewart	18	5	46	1	14	2	64	1
Wood	20.4	2	44	2	15	4	49	1
Wrench	13	0	39	4	21	6	64	4
Butler	6	0	19	1	13	5	40	2
Moull	2	0	7	0	—	—	—	—
Price	4	1	10	2	4	2	12	0

Gold Coast Bowling

	Overs	Mdns	Runs	Wkts	Overs	Mdns	Runs	Wkts
Pullan	20.2	5	52	2	11	0	60	0
Casley	10	4	26	2	6	1	7	2
Perkins	10	1	33	3	22	4	42	1
Inniss	6	0	19	1	29.1	9	68	6
Logan	10	1	34	1	19	4	48	1
Bradley	—	—	—		1	0	4	0

Umpires .. F. L. Hamilton and J. S. Page.

18. Memento of a match between Nigeria and the Gold Coast, 1939

Henry Grenfell (Lord Desborough) had not turned down the governor-generalship when it was offered to him in 1921. Athlete, oarsman, swimmer and mountaineer, who 'in the field of sport and athletics, by land and by water, held a place unrivalled by any of his contemporaries', Desborough's sporting achievements occupy a whole column in the *DNB*, inspiring his memoralist to conclude with the sportsman's inspiration that 'only a happy and resolute nature could have made so much out of the hours of each day'.[45] Regrettably, Lord Desborough turned down Ottawa for family reasons: instead, Canada got the rhyming, worthy but unathletic Lord Bessborough, Chairman of Cheltenham Ladies' College and of the Hotels and Restaurants Association.

Then there is the fourth Lord Harris (George Robert Canning) who is officially registered as 'cricketer and administrator'.[46] The former fame refers to his captaincy of the Eton, Oxford, Kent and England XIs, the latter label relates to a long family connection with the British administration of India culminating in his own appointment to the governorship of Bombay in 1890. Again, there is the colourful Sir Hugh Boustead, *inter alia* British Agent of the East Aden Protectorate and Political Agent in Abu Dhabi. He had been British Army lightweight boxing champion, a member of the 1933 Mount Everest expedition, and had captained the British Olympic team in the modern pentathlon. Although not literally one of the Empire's favoured men-on-the-spot, Joseph Chamberlain, when Secretary of State for the Colonies at the turn of the century, was enthusiastic enough to construct a mechanical device for playing after-dinner cricket indoors at his house at Highbury, thereby doubtless endearing himself to his colonial officialdom.[47] He was succeeded in 1903 by another member of the ultra-sporting Lyttelton family, Alfred – father of Oliver, later Lord Chandos, himself a golfing Blue, who was to succeed to the same honourable post in 1951. Alfred Lyttelton's career is relevant enough to the British Empire (he looked on his office as being that of 'Captain of the Colonial Office XI') and distinguished enough in his athletic accomplishments to earn a place in this double pantheon of sportsman-administrators. For all his multiple careers of distinction, it is held that in his case 'neither the lawyer nor the statesman had ever reached the first rank so indisputably as the cricketer', in which role he displayed a style described by no less a connoisseur than W.G. Grace as 'the champagne of cricket'.[48] He was mortally struck down while playing cricket, having just scored 89 at the age of 56. On the day of his funeral, which fortuitously coincided with the Oxford–Cambridge match at Lord's, play was suspended for one minute's silence.

A third principal category of sport remains: manly or individual; team or organized; and now games, pastimes and hobbies. While it is the athletic make-up of a Viceroy and Governor which has provided the burden of our enquiry, to ignore these indoor skills would be to betray the common understanding of what is meant by 'games'. For instance, their West African Excellencies Sir Hugh Clifford, Sir Bernard Bourdillon and Sir Arthur Richards, all one-time incumbents of Government House, Lagos; Sir Hilary Blood of the Gambia; and Sir Alan Burns of Christiansborg

Castle, Accra, were all noted bridge players (the last-named was Bridge correspondent of the *Daily Telegraph*) – often to the chagrin of their fatigued Private Secretaries. A billiard table was as much a standard item of Government House equipment as the cypher office or His Excellency's wine cellar. Just as martial India is generally recognized as 'The Cradle of Polo'[49] so the origin of the game of snooker has been attributed to the messes and clubs of British India.[50] On tour in Eastern Nigeria, the Governor, Sir Bernard Bourdillon, promised the snooker buffs of the African Club at Enugu a new set of billiard-balls, since age had confusingly turned theirs all into the same colour. Although there are no records of any Scrabble, Ludo or Monopoly champion from Government House, in at least one colony a form of Snakes and Ladders was popular among junior officers, with a dramatic leap up the ladder for him who sycophantically complimented the Governor's wife on her hat and a deadly snake for the cadet who had the temerity to ask His Excellency's daughter for a second dance at the Government House Christmas Ball. There was, too, a widespread belief among the cadet entry in one of the provinces of Northern Nigeria in the early 1950s that their Resident was in the habit of basing his confidential reports of their career prospects on how well or how weakly they scored at the Mah Jong evenings innocently organized by his wife.[51]

II

What conclusions can be drawn from the data provided by this extensive examination of Excellencies? One may at once dismiss any belief that in appointing to the plums of British governance overseas the powers that be solemnly asked themselves 'Is this man a good enough athlete to be Governor of Wonderland?' and made their disposition accordingly. For all the attraction of the concept of an 'athletocracy' in the making of Britain's imperial administrators, in no way can the argument be advanced that athleticism *per se* made a good governor. Sporting attributes and Hawks' or Vincent's Club ties may well have been to the advantage of candidates appearing before the Civil Service Commissioners and the Colonial Service Appointments Board, with their undertones of determination, team spirit, leadership, self-reliance, quick thinking and 'character'; but the gap between the two decisions to appoint, as cadet or governor, is likely to have been 20 to 35 years. The later conditions were as different as the earlier circumstances. Nevertheless, in rejecting that kind of rationalization as simplistic or superficial, the question remains whether it can be so easily dismissed from the understandably confused minds of countless Africans and Asians, who often glimpsed only the enthusiasm and energy of the sportsman. It is an image tellingly summed up in Atiyah's enduring memory of tall, commanding officialdom daily riding forth to play polo. The 'average native' then, and the post-imperial observer later on, may quite reasonably be unable to think of any rational explanation of why impeccable athletes should be considered by the British – *only* the British, never the French or Portuguese or Italians – *ipso facto* to make imperial administrators, other than that for the British athleticism was held to be next to godliness. Theirs not to know the direct link between the *rites de passage* of a British public school and the self-discipline of fair play, or recognize the strong connection between the system of school prefects and the principles of indirect rule, where the District Commissioner was the housemaster, the native chiefs the prefects, and their subjects the fifth form riff-raff. In the event, guidance is likely to be found in terms of a straightforward, however informal, specification: 'Will this man, with or without his Blue, make the kind of governor we in Whitehall believe such and such a territory needs today?' As it happened, a sporting prowess often came too.

If this colonial conundrum is answerable at all, it may be susceptible to the most likely degree of resolution when it is considered at two levels. One is that of the colonial people to be ruled or administered by the new Governor. The other is that of his own countrymen with whom His Excellency would, willy-nilly, have to work. Both can be reduced to a matter of public and personal relations, an art which, fundamental to every colonial situation, was consistently at a premium.

Thus, for His Majesty's subjects a sports-gifted governor might with some confidence be assumed to possess the admired and advantageous properties of a real gentleman, a pukka sahib, one who, as the saying went in Africa, was also a 'chief in his own country'. He was therefore worthy to be the sovereign's personal representative. As such, he would be expected to be interested in – even better, to indulge in – the conventional sporting pursuits of the British gentleman: riding and shooting, presenting the winners' Cup at cricket matches, boxing competitions, race or athletic meetings, and maybe instituting a new trophy bearing his own name. A no-show governor would find it that much harder to win hearts and minds – Byng, for instance, was politically shrewd enough never to miss an Ottawa Senators' game whenever they were playing at home, although, outstanding horseman, excellent shot and keen fisherman that he was, he was nevertheless intelligent enough to give up learning to skate in public. At the more sophisticated level, where his political opponents might be fellow-graduates and maybe fellow sportsmen too, such governors could also have recourse to the shared idiom of sports to make a point through a common experience. Sir Richard Turnbull, Governor of Tanganyika during the final years of the transfer of power, was perhaps adopting this line of argument when he said that the kind of colonial administrator who read the *Economist* would not behave in exactly the same way towards the new political class as the man who had stroked the Jesus First Eight.[52] Lord Milverton made his point less ambiguously. Never the most enthusiastically received of Excellencies, 'Old Sinister', as he was nicknamed, none the less got straight through to the West Indians' cricketing hearts when, at a farewell banquet in Jamaica, he referred to the difficulties he had encountered in facing from both ends the hostile bowling of the two nationalist leaders, Messrs Manley and Bustamente. 'Even a Captain – not to mention a Captain-General', he joked, 'is human enough to enjoy hitting the bowling over the pavilion for six, though he knows if he goes on he will do it once too often and be caught out'. He concluded: 'But it's good fun while it lasts'.[53]

As for the perceptions of the local British community, the problem was often lessened if the new incumbent of Government House was a career colonial administrator with previous experience in the same territory. His Excellency's reputation would have preceded him via the bush telegraph – give or take a 50 per cent exaggeration. Every expatriate (not that the term reaches back beyond the decolonizing decades) knew pretty well what to expect when John Lawrence became Viceroy or when Sir Arthur Benson and Sir Bryan Sharwood Smith (the last-named's Hausa nickname of 'Iron Pants' marked his tireless ability – as his superiors saw it – and tiresome habit – as his subordinates felt it – of covering up to 50 miles a day in the saddle) became Governor of Northern Rhodesia and Northern Nigeria respectively, for had he not virtually grown up with them over the past 20 years or more? But in the case of a governor transferred from the outside, the majority kind of appointment in keeping with modern Colonial Office conventions, there was much more of a need to generate the belief that His incoming Excellency was not only a good administrator who would keep or put all to rights, but was also a good man.

Now if the concept of the 'good man' dictated a certain need to appease, if not totally to please, local opinion-nationalist and expatriate alike – about the new governor, it is the image of a 'good chap' which was of concern to HE's colleagues and compatriots. And in establishing that image in the mind of the local British community, there were, *ceteris paribus*, few attributes or reputations of greater advantage in helping the unknown governor to overcome the initial and inevitable suspicion attaching to a new broom than that here was a sportsman. Not necessarily a 'sport' or a 'hail-fellow-well-met' type, but a man who could be relied on to display, in Bombay, Brisbane or Bechuanaland, those self-same qualities which would ensure his ready acceptance in British society back home – qualities virtually guaranteed among Britons by the fact of being a sportsman. What this meant to British society, from Edwardian to early Elizabethan (Mark II), was that, in brief, to be a sportsman constituted a social open-sesame, a warranty, if you like, even more sterling than a public-school accent – for twisters as well as toffs can talk posh – that here was a gentleman who would invariably act with all the modesty, courtesy and care for others implicit in such a status. Here was a major encapsulation of Baron Coubertin's Olympic ideal of men of noble character possessing the spirit of enterprise. The accuracy of the novelist's description of the American Elliot Templeton's immediate acceptance by the stiff society of Edwardian London on the grounds that he was 'well-favoured, bright, a good dancer, a fair shot and a fine tennis-player' or of the new recruit to pre-war Malaya's plantocracy – 'he was ideal planter material – proficient, a good shot and a good sport'[54] – is reinforced by the actuality of those appointed to jobs overseas in the same interwar period, with their shared conviction that prospective employers 'wanted athletic people. ... You ask a chap if he plays games. If he does and he's got a reasonable academic record as well, you're not going to go far wrong, because *chaps who are good at games are usually well-oriented overall* (italics added).[55] It is these hidden assumptions of instant status which make the spoof memoirs of Major the Honourable John William Wentworth Gore, 1st Royal Light Hussars, so revealing and relevant as well as such good reading:

> I am an excellent polo player, standing practically at the top of that particular tree of sport; and again, I am a quite unusually brilliant cricketer. That I do not play in first class cricket is due to long service abroad with my regiment; but now that we are at last quartered in England, I daily expect to be approached by the committee of my county eleven.
>
> I consider myself, not before taking the opinion of my warmest friends, the best racquets player of my day in India; and I have rarely played football (Rugby) without knowing by a strange instinct (born, I feel sure, of truth) that I was the best man on the ground. On the hunting field I am well known as one of the hardest riders across country living ... the trophies of head, horn, and skin at Castle Goreby, our family's country seat, are sufficient guarantees of my prowess with big game in all parts of the world; and when I mention that I have been one of an Arctic Expedition, have climbed to the highest mountain peaks explored by man, voyaged for days in a balloon, dived to a wreck in the complete modern outfit of a professional diver, am as useful on a yacht as any man of my acquaintance, think nothing of scoring a hundred break at billiards, and rarely meet my match at whist, piquet, or poker, it will be admitted that I have not confined my talents, such as they are, to any one particular branch of sport.[56]

To his own countrymen, then, the reputation of His Excellency being a sportsman carried a rather special nuance. Andrew Gilmour of the Malayan Civil Service called it the 'unforced affability' of the gubernatorial cadre.[57] It was calculated to signify to hard-pressed and slightly fearful civil servants that, underneath the plumes and epaulettes, the grey top hat and morning coat, and once reduced to shorts and plimsolls, His Excellency had a less formal side. He knew how to mix and relax, and, given half a chance, he would unbend on the tennis court or in a chukka of polo and enjoy messing about in boats, displaying all the relaxed moments of easy camaraderie and lowered guard which are common to the brotherhood of sportsmen everywhere but which are virtually ruled out by reason of being His Excellency – for, to cite George Orwell's famous dictum about the imperial ruling class, has not 'a sahib got to act like a sahib'?[58] Asides like 'Not nearly as stiff as he seems', 'He's all right once he's off duty', 'Human after all, you know! – why, when he missed that volley at the net, I distinctly heard him exclaim "Hell's bells and damnation" ' – such are the images which could easily be projected by a shared *shikar*, a game of golf or a tennis foursome, allowing His Excellency just to be himself for an hour or two. This was the sporting obverse of the Governor's social coin, the reverse side being such obligations as attending Divine Service on Sundays or making a witty speech at those daunting Caledonian Society dinners on Burns' Night in Ottawa or St. Andrew's Night in Ootacamund – and everyone knows who Glasgow (and seemingly the whole British Empire) belongs to on a Saturday night![59]

In Britain and its Dominions, the heart of the matter lay in being a sportsman and a gentleman, not an athlete. In the context of the social history of sport, it is sometimes forgotten that right up to the 1950s Britain's cricketers were officially divided into 'Gentlemen' and 'Players'. One could tell the difference at once in the elegant cricket columns and commentaries of Neville Cardus, R.C. Robertson-Glasgow, John Arlott and E.W. Swanton,[60] where 'Gentlemen' (the amateurs) were sharply distinguished from 'Players' (the professionals), even when playing in the same County XI, by the simple device of always giving their initials in the batting list: C.B. Fry, D.R. Jardine, R.E.S. Wyatt, G.O. Allen, but plain Sutcliffe, Woolley, Hammond and Ames. Early records are even said to read 'Caught Hill, bowled Jones Esq'. As two leading American historians of the British Empire have observed, 'the worship of the well-born amateur' pervaded every aspect of Victorian and Edwardian life.[61] Since the art of the gentleman was to be good in all things without ever committing the solecism of being too good, *ergo* amateurs were gentlemen, professionals could not be. That national prejudices have not changed all that much is demonstrated by the contemporary novelist Jeffrey Archer, who, describing the contest for Prime Minister in far-off 1990, has no difficulty in asserting that, then as now, 'the British have always preferred good amateurs to preside over over their affairs'.[62] A few years ago, a retired Governor of the Sudan commented to a speaker at a conference on sport and empire: 'Yes, we *were* proud of our sporting prowess, but we were even prouder of our gentlemanly manners. Mike Brearley would have got into the Sudan Political Service, but neither Boycott nor Botham would have stood a chance'. To an older-style Englishman, if not a cricketer *pur sang*, no further explanation was necessary.

Overall, His Excellency's *rôle sportif* may be said to have provided an important contribution to what the Collector in E.M. Forster's *Passage to India* called the 'bridge' party:[63] the need to cross barriers in colonial society, be they those erected by European class or by native caste. It showed, precisely as it was meant to, that beneath the superhuman GCMG (colloquially known in the Service as 'God Calls Me God') there beat a human heart, of one who had himself once been just another muddied oaf or flannelled fool. It also reinforced that almost tangible British respect for the talent of the gifted amateur over the skills of the earnest professional. Here was the typical Briton's typical admiration for the Viceroy who had also been a county cap, for the Governor-General who had once played for Scotland, for the Governor who had twice stroked the Cambridge boat. Nor is this all a reflection of the past, as finished and outmoded as the

British Empire itself. In one of Hugh Maclennan's novels of contemporary Canada, a leading character declares: 'In [North America] people trust an athlete ... Years from now, when I say I was a smooth quarter-back on the Princeton team, people will relax'.[64] Even today, towards the end of the egalitarian and meritocratic second half of the twentieth century, proven fondness of or success in outdoor [*quondam* 'manly'] sports remains a necessary consideration in the selection of Oxford's renowned Rhodes Scholars.[65] It is beyond argument that, in the history of modern imperialism, a sporting record rendered the British colonial governor a markedly distinct and different kind of person from his Latin or Teutonic opposite number in Africa, Asia or the Americas. Reduced to its lowest credit, His Excellency's sporting past at least presumed his continued ability to exhibit Kipling's versified formula of success about walking with kings without losing the common touch. Or, as a more prosaic young administrator expressed his feelings about the warmth of the new Scottish governor after the ways of his stiff and chilly-eyed predecessor, 'Old Sinister', 'You felt that for two pins he would take off his jacket and give you a hand mowing the lawn'.[66]

III

In terms of wider analysis, three major considerations relevant to the history of sport can be identified from these data. One is the vigorous reinforcement of the now widely suspected class undertones attaching to sport in Great Britain, at least up to the end of the Second World War. In their range of sporting prowess, these proconsuls of the British Empire unambiguously reveal not only the public school and Oxbridge origin of their chosen games but also the same upper- to middle-class attitudes and codes integrally associated therewith. Hence, for example, the significance of Sir Frederick Burrows's reinterpretation, quoted above, of the upper-class sporting expectations in the incumbent of Government House. Sport becomes one of the conspicuous hallmarks of the good chap of Empire.

Secondly, there is the characteristic British link between Government House patronage and sport. This is apparent not only in the establishment of, to take the notable example of Canada's Governors-General alone, such long-standing trophies as the Grey or Stanley Cup (however much their players' qualifications may have changed over the years and despite the modern addition of a Beauty Queen contest), but also in the general expectation and exhibition of interest, support and, on frequent occasions, quality performance from Government House in the promotion of sport in its role as the emollient of imperial race relations.[67]

Thirdly, in the continuing and critical post-colonial context of how 'they' saw 'us', the data emphasize the argument that the complexion and interpretation of the imperial administrator in retrospect is going to be forcefully conditioned by 'their' memories of 'our' noonday-mad-dog-English devotion to bat and ball, horse and hound, rifle and saddle. The uniqueness of the phenomenon is underlined by the sharp contrast between the role of sport in the ethos and make-up of the British colonial administrator on the one hand and his colonial counterparts from other European countries on the other.

All three of these influences can in a high degree be traced to the Whitehall perception of what kind of man had the best chance of making a success of imperial governance. In reaching that decision, a sporting record, while in no way a *de rigueur* qualification, more often than not turned out to be a sterling and successful quality. To cite a perception common among those recruited to overseas posts between the wars, 'As long as you could play games and mix with people, that was the sort of person they wanted'.[68] It is clear that the sportsman's badge of office, invisibly yet influentially worn by so surprisingly many of Their Excellencies throughout the Empire, often reflected what was then widely held to represent, in social terms, 'the best of British'.

Finally, one possibly unexpected analytical interpretation begins to take shape from the data marshalled for this study on sport and His Excellency in the British Empire. It used to be part of the imperial myth that Britain's overseas governors were selected for their height: Viceroys the Earl of Halifax and the Marquess of Linlithgow, Governors-General Lord Willingdon of Canada, Sir Stewart Symes of the Sudan and Sir Richard Turnbull of Tanganyika, Governors Sir Bernard Bourdillon of Nigeria and Sir Gerald Reece of Somaliland, all were over six feet tall, nearer seven when they donned their dress helmet topped with its 'gust of plumes'.[69] In the aftermath of this prosopographical presentation, maybe a new myth will take root – as it already has in some minds – that British proconsuls were selected for their sporting distinction.[70] Myth or half-truth, when we finally learn what 'they' thought of 'us', the sporting enthusiasms of His Excellency and of so many of his officials seem destined to play a positive part in the shaping of 'our' image and reputation in 'their' collective memory of the *dramatis personae* of imperialism as 'tall, commanding figures, riding out to play polo'.

NOTES

This study has undergone several revisions and acquired further 'imperial' illustrations since its original presentation as the keynote address to the XI International Congress of the History of Sports and Physical Education (HISPA) held in Glasgow in July 1985 under the title 'Imperial Sidelight or Spotlight?. Parts of it were given as 'Sport and Society in the British Empire: A Profile of the Governing Elite', at a public lecture at the University of Calgary, Canada, in December 1985; in another form, as 'Sport and Race Relations: The Case of the British Colonial Governor', a lecture to mark the retirement of Kenneth Kirkwood from the Chair of Race Relations in the University of Oxford in June 1986; and in yet another form, prepared for a lecture tour in Australia, in August 1988. This version first appeared in *The International Journal of the History of Sport*, Vol. 6, No. 2 (September 1989). My thanks to Dr. J.A. Mangan for having provided the original research opportunity and to Professor William J. Baker for having (unwittingly) given me, in conversation, the idea of the new title.

1. Edward Atiyah, *An Arab Tells His Story* (London, 1946), p.28.
2. Sir Ahmadu Bello, *My Life* (Cambridge, 1962), p. 29. The teacher concerned was S.J. Hogben (see *West Africa*, 10 Sept. 1971, 1009). Similarly, it is generally accepted that it was J.O. Udal of the Sudan Political Service who introduced Winchester football to Gordon College, Khartoum.
3. Ham Mukasa, *Uganda's Katikiro in England* (London, 1904), p.43.
4. Quotations from A.H.M. Kirk–Greene, 'Sanders of the River', *New Society*, 10 November 1977.
5. Henrika Kuklick, *The Imperial Bureaucrat: The Colonial Administrative Service in the Gold Coast 1920–1939* (Stanford, 1979); Robert Heussler, *Yesterday's Rulers: The Making of the British Colonial Service* (Syracuse, 1963); Richard Symonds, *Oxford and Empire: The Last Lost Cause?* (London, 1986); and A.H.M. Kirk–Greene, *The Sudan Political Service: A Preliminary Profile* (Oxford, 1982), especially pp. 5–9 and Table I, and J.A. Mangan's 'Manly Chaps in Control: Blues and Blacks in the Sudan' in his *The Games Ethic and Imperialism* (London, 1986). See also, Robert O. Collins and Francis M. Deng (eds.), *The British in the Sudan, 1898–1956: The Sweetness and the Sorrow* (London, 1984), for the undertones of the supremacy of the athletic imperative, often quite unconscious, in the letters, diaries and memoirs of members of the Sudan civil service. Perhaps only in such a context could a memorandum like that by the Bishop of Egypt and the Sudan, the formidable L.H. Gwynne, be taken seriously: it was headed 'The Value of Games on the Administration'. See also P.J. Rich, *Elixir of Empire* (forthcoming).
6. By A.H.M. Kirk-Greene, 'Imperial Administration and the Athletic Imperative: The Case of the District Officer in Africa', in William J. Baker and J.A Mangan (eds.), *Sport in Africa: Essays in Social History* (New York, 1987).
7. Sir Hesketh Bell, *Glimpses of a Governor's Life* (London, 1946), p.203. Bell's reputation is perhaps more envied than that attributed to H.H. Asquith on his downfall in 1916 by the events of the Dublin rebellion: 'Asquith has fallen off an elephant in the face of the whole British Empire' – quoted in Winston Churchill, *Great Contemporaries* (London, 1941), p.172. In his section on the role of sport in the Indian Civil Service, 'Pigsticking and the Purgation of Lusts', Philip Mason has no trouble in coming to the conclusion that 'The men who hunted most among the civilians were the men who were remembered in their districts' – *The Men Who Ruled India: The Guardians* (London, 1964), p.182. A revealing indicator of gubernatorial (and lesser rank) reputations is to scrutinize the nicknames, both in English and the vernacular, by which they are remembered locally!
8. Quoted in Mark Bence-Jones, *The Viceroys of India* (London, 1982), p.197.
9. Cf. Sir James Robertson's account of Harold Macmillan's punctilious behaviour while staying in Government House, Lagos: *Transition in Africa* (London, 1974), p.236.
10. Jeffery Williams, *Byng of Vimy* (London, 1983), pp.296–7.
11. Viscount Mersey, *The Viceroys and Governors-General of India, 1757–1947* (London, 1949), p.157. For the Canadian fatalities, see A.H.M. Kirk-Greene, 'The Governors-General of Canada, 1867–1952: A Collective Profile', *Journal of Canadian Studies* 12 (1977), 4, 44.
12. Cf. the illustrations in Chapter 7 of Valerie Pakenham, *The Noonday Sun: Edwardians in the Tropics* (London, 1985). Kenneth Rose quotes Curzon's invitation to a friend to come out to India, in which the Viceroy expressed himself as being happy to 'arrange for you to shoot tigers from the back of elephants or elephants from the back of tigers, whichever you prefer': *Curzon: A Very Superior Person* (London, 1969), p.338.
13. Lord Belhaven, *The Uneven Road* (London, 1955), p.161.
14. Sir Geoffrey Archer, *Personal and Historical Memoirs of an East African Administrator* (Edinburgh, 1963), p.220.
15. Lionel Portman, *Station Studies: Being the Jottings of an African Official* (London, 1902), p.333.
16. He was a member of the Alpine Club. Cf. Lord James Douglas Hamilton's address given to the annual dinner of the John Buchan Society, 1984, and reproduced in the *John Buchan Journal*, IV (1984), 20–22.
17. Charles Chenevix Trench, *The Desert's Dusty Face* (Edinburgh, 1964), pp.24 and 72.
18. Elspeth Huxley, *White Man's Country: Lord Delamere and the Making of Kenya*, Vol. I (London, 1935), p.239. Roland Michener, when Governor-General of Canada, initiated

the practice of jogging in the environs of Rideau Hall, to the entertainment of the local press allegedly on account of the clothes His Excellency wore for the exercise. (I am indebted to Professor Steward Davidson of the University of Ottawa for this information.)

19. Kirk-Greene, 'Imperial Administration', pp. 91–100.
20. David Caute, *At Fever Pitch* (London, 1959), p. 109. Earlier the Brigadier had offered this advice to another of his National Service subalterns: 'Always keep your eye on the ball and you won't go far wrong' (p.68).
21. K.G. Bradley, *Once a District Officer* (London, 1966), p. 28.
22. Margery Perham, Introduction to Heussler, *Yesterday's Rulers*, p.xx.
23. Major Sir Ralph Furse, *Aucuparius: Memoirs of a Recruiting Officer* (London, 1962), p. 309. Furse, himself a cricketer and rugger-player of no mean distinction at Balliol College, Oxford, would certainly have warmed to the maxim of my father-in-law, R.J.B. Sellar, skilled Scots spinner of so many period-piece sportsman's yarns in the *Illustrated Sporting and Dramatic News* between the wars, who maintained that as far as expertise was concerned, 'if there's one man more than another who requires a good grip of his subject, it's the fast bowler': R.J.B. Sellar, *Sporting and Dramatic Yarns* (London, 1925), p. 189.
24. Sir Charles Johnston, who unusually came to the colonial governorship of Aden through the Foreign Office, did not hesitate to describe the quintessential DC training and outlook as 'the Ark of the Covenant': *The View from Steamer Point* (London, 1964), p. 191.
25. C.P. Snow, *The Masters* (London, 1951), p. 24.
26. R.O. Collins, 'The Sudan Political Service: A Portrait of the Imperialists', *African Affairs*, 71 (1972), 297.
27. Archer, *Personal Memoirs*, p. 25.
28. Stanhope White, *Dan Bana: The Memoirs of a Nigerian Official* (London, 1966), p.45.
29. H.C. Jackson, *Sudan Days and Ways* (London, 1954), p. 15.
30. A.H.M. Kirk-Greene, *A Biographical Dictionary of the British Colonial Governor* (Brighton and Stanford, 1980).
31. The definition is that of his Colonial Service colleague, A.C.G. Hastings, in his memoir *Nigerian Days* (London, 1925), p. 235.
32. Langa Langa (pseud. H.B. Hermon-Hodge), *Up Against it in Nigeria* (London, 1922), p. 117.
33. Chenevix Trench, *Dusty Face*, p. 36.
34. Quoted in Pakenham, *Noonday Sun*, p. 178. In his autobiographical novel *Empire of the Sun* (London, 1984), J.G. Ballard describes how the British residents of Shanghai prepared themselves for being marched off into internment by the Japanese: 'Having spent the years of peace on the tennis courts and cricket fields of the Far East, they confidently expected to pass the years of war in the same way … [they carried] dozens of tennis racquets hung from suitcase handles, there were cricket bats and fishing nets and even a set of golf clubs' (p.241).
35. 'The Life', quoted *in extenso* in W.D. Downes, *With the Nigerians in German East Africa* (London, 1919), pp. 260–61.
36. David Rooney, *Sir Charles Arden-Clarke* (London, 1982), p.62.
37. *Daily Telegraph*, 23 Jan. 1985.
38. Cf. Michael Fausset in his novelist's portrayal of the Governor of one of the Sudan's provinces, who made 'a gospel of sport' to keep his unruly tribesmen in order: 'Each district has its own inspector, and each district has its own form of sport': *Pilate Pasha* (London, 1939), pp. 35–6. Cricket is said to have been introduced to Samoa by the crew of H.M.S. *Diamond* when she visited the island in 1884. Such was the enthusiasm that the game is reported to have been played with 2–3,000 a side, four or five umpires, and three batsmen at each end: John Aye, *Humour in Sports* (London, n.d., c.1932), p. 17. In South Africa, it is related that F.N. Streatfeild, Resident Magistrate of Kaffirland before the turn of the century, 'taught cricket to the native police' (*Sporting Recollections of an Old'Un*, quoted ibid., p. 276), while in Kashmir, according to Charles Chenevix Trench, where the Maharajah Pratap Singh had been persuaded by the Resident to 'abandon pederasty in favour of cricket' (*Viceroy's Agent*, 1987, p. 174), His Highness went on to top the batting averages year after year, 'largely because whenever he was caught or bowled the umpire

used to call "No ball" ' (ibid.). As for Africa, Edgar Wallace has described the mayhem which ensued when Commissioner Sanders's irrepressible police superintendent, Lieutenant Augustus Tibbetts (alias the egregious Bones), tried to introduce rugger among the Isisi and Akasatan of the Lower Niger: 'The Ball Game', *Sanders* (London, 1926). It was Sir Kenneth Maddocks, former Governor of Fiji, who told me of the subsequently neo-legendary story of Major Ratu Edward Cakobau, MC, OBE, of the Fijian Army. After serving with distinction in Malaya, and earlier on the playing fields of Wadham College, Oxford, he was dining one evening in the mess of the Welch Regiment. A young subaltern asked him whether he could explain why the Fijians were such outstanding rugger players. 'I don't know about the rest', he replied, 'but in my case rugger is in my blood – my great-grandmother ate a Cambridge Blue'.

39. Lord Oliver, in *The Dictionary of National Biography* [DNB], 1922–1930 (Oxford, 1937), p. 369.
40. R.E. Wraith, *Guggisberg* (London, 1967), p. 18. See also K.F. Butler, *Cricket in Nigeria* (Lagos, 1946), p. 4, in which he attributes the organization of the first Inter-Colony match, held in 1926, to Sir Gordon Guggisberg and Sir Shenton Thomas. For the latter's cricketing competence, see also Brian Montgomery, *Shenton of Singapore: Governor and Prisoner of War* (London, 1984), e.g. 'It was not often that a Governor was seen to lead his team onto the ground of the Singapore Cricket Club' (p. 56).
41. Quoted in Charles Allen, *Tales from the South China Seas* (London, 1983), p. 18.
42. Interview with Sir Alan Burns, quoted in Charles Allen (ed.), *Tales from the Dark Continent* (London, 1979), p. 26.
43. Mersey, *Viceroys*, p. 141.
44. Kirk-Greene, *Biographical Dictionary*, p. 32.
45. *DNB, 1941–1950* (Oxford, 1959), p. 328.
46. *The Concise Dictionary of National Biography: An Epitome* (Oxford, 1961), p. 199. Harris reappeared prominently in the 1985 Australian television programme, 'Bodyline', where he was credited with the remark that cricket was one of the principal vehicles of *la mission civilisatrice*.
47. From an entry in the unpublished diary of Sir Hesketh Bell for 1899, quoted in Pakenham, *Noonday Sun*, p. 175. Her Chapter 8 is entitled 'Players'.
48. *DNB, 1912–1921* (Oxford, 1927), pp. 349–50. For the story of the close link between cricket and the Colonial Office, including the setting up of stumps in the State Office once the Secretary of State had gone home for the evening, see Furse, *Aucuparius*, p. 37.
49. See Lord Curzon, *A Viceroy's India: Leaves from Lord Curzon's Notebook* (London, 1926; 1984), pp. 185–92.
50. John Galloway, 'A Man's Game', letter to *Daily Telegraph*, 11 Dec. 1984.
51. There is the comparable outcome of the promotion-ploy of two junior officers, both former Blues, sycophantically to let His Excellency, the Governor-General, then on an official visit to headquarters upcountry, win at tennis. There turned out to be no question of 'letting'; and how mortified they would have been had they known what H.E. wrote about them in his confidential touring notes: 'Two former athletes of distinction evidently gone to seed in the fleshpots of the capital.? Chief Secretary to consider early reposting to bush'.
52. In A.H.M. Kirk-Greene (ed.), *The Transfer of Power: The Colonial Administrator in the Age of Decolonisation* (Oxford, 1979), p. 157.
53. Quoted in R.L. Peel's memoir of Sir Arthur Richards (Cambridge, 1986), p. 87. Captain-General was one of the official titles of the Governor of Jamaica. Ric Sissons' and Brian Stoddart's alluringly titled *Cricket and Empire*, published by Allen & Unwin in 1984, turned out to be something of a damp squib for imperial historians, as all it was concerned with was the captaincy of Douglas Jardine (the *Spartan Cricketer* of Christopher Douglas's 1984 biography) in the controversial Australian Test Series of 1932–33. In the television film 'Bodyline' (see fn. 46), where cricket was described as 'the hallowed game of empire', Jardine's determination to win, allegedly at any cost, was underlined by the comment attributed to one of his masters at Winchester: 'We may win the Ashes but in doing so we may also lose a Dominion'. Yet the attraction of cricket as the supreme cultural bond between Britain and the Empire continues to flourish. In the past few years, a socio-

intellectual study of the game has appeared in Mihir Bose's *A Maidan View: the Magic of Indian Cricket* (London, 1986), which at once recalls C.L.R. James's West Indian interpretation of the place of cricket in the post-colonial countries of the Third World (cf. *TLS*, 5 September 1986, 987); while Stewart Brown published a poem with the unexpected title of 'Cricket at Kano' in his collection *Zinder* (Bridgend, 1986) and Nicholas Best gave his new novel the no less arresting title *Tennis and the Masai* (London, 1986).

54. W. Somerset Maugham, *The Razor's Edge* (London, 1944), p. 5; Noel Barber, *Tanamera* (London, 1981), p. 249.

55. Quoted in Allen, *China Seas*, p. 19.

56. Robert Marshall, *The Haunted Major* (London, 1902), pp. 7–9.

57. Andrew Gilmour, *An Eastern Cadet's Anecdotage* (Singapore, 1974), Chapter 12, 'Games and Hobbies'.

58. George Orwell, 'Shooting an Elephant', in *Collected Essays* (Harmondsworth, 1957), p. 96.

59. As an indication of the endearing eccentricities of the colonial legacy, the toast at the Caledonian Ball held in Khartoum on 2 December 1982 (a quarter of a century after Sudan's independence and 35 years after India's) was proposed by the Indian Ambassador in 68 couplets of hilarious doggerel, e.g.

Of all the imperialists, and there were quite a number,
One from my childhood I do remember.
Linlithgow was a Viceroy, the last but two,
A good man in a War, it's no doubt true,
But independence for India he couldn't contemplate:
When he left the country, none was desolate.

(Copy in writer's possession, supplied by courtesy of His Excellency L.H. Rangarajan).

60. Many of these 'golden oldies' commentators of Test Match reporting are included in the BBC anthology of cricket broadcasting, *Cricket on the Air*, compiled by D.R. Allen, 1985.

61. Lewis H. Gann and Peter Duignan, *The Rulers of British Africa, 1870–1914* (Standford, 1978), p. 5.

62. Jeffrey Archer, *First Among Equals* (London, 1984), p. 40.

63. E.M. Forster, *A Passage to India* (London, 1924), p. 19 and Chapter V, *passim*.

64. Hugh Maclennan, *The Precipice* (Toronto, 1948), p. 79.

65. See A.H.M. Kirk-Greene, 'West Africa's Rhodes Scholars', *West Africa* (1984), 1795–6. With the opening of the Scholarships to women, too, presumably the qualifying 'manly' will have undergone revision.

66. Ian Brook, *The One-Eyed Man is King* (London, 1966), p. 150.

67. Cf. Anthony Kirk-Greene, 'Colonial administration and race relations: some research reflections and directions', in A. Kirk-Greene and J. Stone (eds.), *Ethnicity, Empire and Race Relations*, special issue of *Ethnic and Racial Studies*, Vol. 9, No. 3 (July 1986).

68. Quoted in Allen, *China Seas*, p. 20.

69. The phrase is borrowed from Sir Darrell Bates' biography of Lord Twining of Godalming and Tanganyika (London, 1972).

70. If so, it may prove to have been no bad recipe for the top. 'I'll tell you one thing', came Earl Spencer's impromptu reaction in 1984 when the press asked him what he thought about the birth of his grandson Prince Harry, third in line to the throne of Great Britain, 'I hope he grows up to play cricket for Gloucestershire'.

CHAPTER TEN

'The Warmth of Comradeship': The First British Empire Games and Imperial Solidarity

KATHARINE MOORE

'During the organization period a few of us had the opinion we would be able to put the British Empire games over but few ever dreamed the Empire would rally so strongly. We had our moments of anxiety, but we always had a sensational ace in the hole, loyalty to the British Empire, and we felt that we could wave the good old flag and all would gather round.'[1] Bobby Robinson's summary of the success of the first British Empire Games revealed the degree to which he and other organizers had relied on imperial sentiment to help establish the event. The opening of the Games, on 16 August 1930, was punctuated with reminders of the durability of the British bond through sport. Though modelled fairly closely on the Olympic protocol, the ceremony exuded the characteristics of a family gathering. 'From all corners of the world, competitors have come, eager, of course, to reflect credit on their respective colonies, but proud of the blood ties that bind them in a great entity.[2] It was sport for sport's sake, rivalry in friendly competition that was 'devoid of petty jealousies and sectional prejudices'.[3]

The meaning and significance of the Games to the Empire is the theme of this chapter. The British Empire Games were established after a decade of fundamental political and economic change within the Empire. During the 1920s the trend away from formal political control was increasingly obvious, and can be linked to the rise of informal influences. The founding of the British Empire Games in 1930 may be seen as a prominent example of this shift in emphasis. By the 1920s, 'the Commonwealth had become a political framework within which many diverse forces existed. It was a fragile and problematic coalition of interests which required continuous management'.[4] The decade was characterized by a struggle by members of the Empire to find their own identities, attempting to define their status relative to each other and also to Great Britain. Sport had long been a vehicle through which countries of the Empire had maintained friendly, if competitive, contact, and the appeal of the initiation of its own Games was widespread. But the idea of the promotion of multi-sport competition within the Empire must be traced back further, to 1891, when John Astley Cooper proposed the establishment of a Pan-Britannic Festival to celebrate the industry, culture and athletic prowess of the Anglo-Saxon race.

The British Empire of 1891 was dominated both politically and economically by Great Britain; among the dominions only Canada had achieved internal federation by that date. But the global balance of power was shifting away from Britain by the end of the nineteenth century, and one form of response was an increase in the number of schemes mooted which encouraged even more formal union within the existing Empire. The uniqueness of Cooper's Pan-Britannic Festival proposal lay in the fact it included a major sporting component; indeed, the athletic events soon became the most popular portion and the major focal point for discussion. Despite widespread theoretical approval in the press, it is difficult to judge the degree to which the public supported the idea. The problem of uncertain leadership was a key factor in the eventual demise of the Pan-Britannic Festival concept.

Throughout the three years the Pan-Britannic Festival was actively promoted, from 1891 to 1894, Cooper stressed that he was the originator of the idea, not its practical administrator, but he failed to get his plan adopted by any influential sport governing bodies. The co-operation of the powerful Amateur Athletic Association was essential for success, but Cooper met only indifference and opposition from that group. At the same time colonial support for the idea, especially in Australia, was very pronounced, and it was assumed in the colonies that leadership would come from the well-established sporting bodies in England as well as from the organizer. As the months passed and no detailed plans appeared concerning the actual staging of the Pan-Britannic Festival, enthusiasm for the project waned, and Cooper's novel scheme was joined in the international arena of sport by Baron de Coubertin's intention to 'revive' the ancient Olympic Games. Coubertin was successful, and Cooper and his idea were overwhelmed.

The response both Coubertin and Cooper received concerning their proposed athletic gatherings was promising, yet, in the end, the celebration of the early Olympic Games contributed to the demise of the notion of private competition among Empire members. The desire for a 'family' contest may have still been strong, but there could be no disputing the fact that Coubertin's plans had become reality, and the various countries of the Empire continued to participate individually in the Olympic Games. The 1908 London Games revealed a growing degree of anti-American sentiment, and the coronation of King George V in 1911 provided an occasion for the Empire to gather privately for a festival celebrating its achievements in culture, industry and sport. A link between this festival and Cooper's suggestion is clear.

Although the three-day sporting programme in the Festival of Empire was a relatively minor part of the series of activities which carried on for several months, it did provide an important opportunity for the various colonies to compete with Great Britain in several athletic events. The self-governing 'white' dominions were invited to send male representatives to participate in wrestling, swimming, boxing and athletics. South Africa declined the invitation, but Australasia (Australia and New Zealand) and

Canada joined the United Kingdom in the nine events with the Canadians, perhaps unexpectedly, going on to claim the Lonsdale Cup as overall winners. The physical gathering of these Empire countries also allowed meetings to be held at which the future of sporting affairs was discussed; two trends became apparent as a result. The developing political maturity of the Dominions was reflected in the prominent role played by Richard Coombes of Australia and James Merrick of Canada during the Festival. These two administrators suggested the Empire countries gather in London, train together, and then travel to Stockholm for the 1912 Olympic Games; a stronger leading role in sporting matters was beginning to emanate from the dominions. Coupled with this new-found confidence was the tendency that, as the twentieth century wore on, the desire for less direct control by Britain became more obvious in the aspirations of the various members of the Empire. The emerging role of the Dominions was revealing itself, both in sport and politics, to be one of greater initiative and leadership.

The Great War provided another opportunity for the Dominions to display increasing maturity, and their contribution to the Allied cause was considerable. However, in the post-war world, it was generally assumed that Great Britain still spoke and acted for the whole Empire, and formal independent recognition was not easily obtained. Defining membership entitlement in the League of Nations clearly exposed the ambiguous nature of the Dominions' place in the political world; at the same time, sporting competition was providing an alternative means of creating an identity. But the strength of the sentiment of Empire unity continued to be significant.

The 1920s saw the emergence of a desire in athletics to pit an Empire team against the best in the world – the Americans – and a dual competition was held in London after each of the Olympic Games in that decade. In contrast to the nineteenth century, when other countries measured themselves against England, the shift in world power now caused the Empire to gauge itself against an external sporting standard. There were periodic suggestions during the 1920s about establishing games solely for British Empire competitors, and several sets of regional games had been introduced around the world which served as precedents. The initiative was taken by Canada, and at the 1928 Olympic Games Bobby Robinson, manager of the Canadian athletics team presented specific proposals for a celebration in 1930. Robinson was concerned at the trend in the Olympics of increasing hostility and antagonism among the participants, and believed the family atmosphere he was promoting would provide a more relaxed and happy environment for competition. The story of the events leading to the establishment of the British Empire Games centres on the energy, drive and enthusiasm of Robinson. Originally from Peterborough, Ontario, Robinson came to Hamilton as sports editor of the *Spectator* newspaper. He was a great Imperialist, and a firm believer in the British Empire. The financial backing given by the city of Hamilton, coupled with the drive and determination of Robinson, produced a formidable partnership which carried the British Empire Games through to their successful inauguration.

Forty years after Cooper's suggestion of a Pan-Britannic Festival, the Empire displayed significant changes both internally and externally. Australia, New Zealand and South Africa had joined Canada in gaining self-government, and the Statute of Westminster, passed by the British Parliament in 1931, was designed to withdraw Britain's right to legislate for the dominions without their request and consent. More formal political structures within the Empire were being replaced by less formal influences such as sport, and the establishment of the British Empire Games can be seen as an example of the 'informal Empire'[5] at work. In one respect, sport was not too excessive an obligation for members of the Empire; periodic commitment to an athletic festival was more attractive than an ongoing political alliance or treaty. Regular sporting contact was showing itself to be an increasingly unifying influence within the Empire, and the timing of the inauguration of the British Empire Games indicates a shift from formal to informal control. While contact between Empire countries in single sports such as rugby and cricket had long been an established fact, the appeal of separate multi-sport competition gained ground during the 1920s.

It is more than mere coincidence that the British Empire Games were initiated at the end of a decade of fundamental political evolution within the Empire. R.F. Holland has suggested that 'the thrust of Dominion nationalism in the 1920s was not a crude movement towards secession but an attempt to manoeuvre into a position where commitments to the United Kingdom in diplomatic and military crises became optional rather than obligatory'.[6] The Canadian government exhibited this stance in 1922 during the Chanak incident in Turkey, becoming the first Dominion to refuse automatically to stand by the remainder of the Empire in a serious emergency.[7] The 1923 Imperial Conference was in several important respects influenced by Prime Minister Mackenzie King of Canada; Mansergh has argued that significant change was initiated during the meeting, which would be confirmed by the next gathering in 1926.[8]

An important constitutional change was incorporated in the 1925 Locarno Treaty. Austen Chamberlain, the British Foreign Secretary, negotiated and signed the treaty on behalf of the United Kingdom alone. It was stipulated that no Dominion was bound by the treaty unless its government formally voted for it to be. None did. During the same year the Dominions Office was established, separated from the Colonial Office primarily through the efforts of Leopold Amery, but still dependent on the Colonial Office for its services and resources. The 1926 Imperial Conference reinforced the process of emerging nationalism when South Africa, Canada and the Irish Free State all came to the meeting demanding a constitutional definition of the British Empire and an acknowledgement of their place within it. The Balfour Report, while avoiding a precise definition of Dominion status, declared that Great Britain and the Dominions were autonomous communities, equal in status, which were united by a common allegiance to the Crown and freely associated as members of the British Commonwealth of Nations.[9]

Factors outside the Empire were also contributing to its changing nature. While the quadrennial Olympic Games provided a regular meeting place for the sport administrators of the Empire, there was growing disenchantment with the lack of sportsmanship shown at the Games, and the continuing domination by the Americans in many events made the notion of 'private' competition all the more appealing. By 1930, the Empire was no longer the major force in the world, and the Games could be seen as one step towards re-establishing its sagging prestige. Holland has concluded that 'the imperial rapport of 1926 was gradually undermined in the following four years, and by 1930 a more acute sense of doubt as to the long-term prospects of Commonwealth prevailed than at any time since the War'.[10] The Empire needed the British Empire Games in 1930, and the level of enthusiasm shown by both host and participants indicates the degree to which the idea was seen as a welcome salve for a damaged ego.

In practical terms, financing a team to Hamilton was a major item of concern for all Empire countries, particularly when the 1932 Summer Olympic Games were also to be held in North America. However, the greatest financial commitment of all was required from the city of Hamilton. Bobby Robinson headed the on-site organizing committee, and he first met with city council members in January 1929 when he outlined the full Empire Games project. On top of substantial capital expenditure, Robinson calmly explained that up to $25,000 would be needed to cover operating costs, $5000 of it required immediately. The council unanimously approved the smaller grant,[11] and confirmed the availability of the balance if and when it was needed.[12] This solid financial backing, coupled with Robinson's tireless work, continued to be the key partnership.

In July 1929, the Hamilton Olympic Club welcomed athletes from Oxford and Cambridge, and the English visitors defeated their hosts seven events to five in front of an audience of 5,000 enthusiastic spectators.[13] Evan Hunter, Secretary of the British Olympic Association, accompanied the students to Hamilton as an honorary manager. He was subsequently appointed to the influential post of the honorary secretary of the Council of Great Britain, the newly formed body charged with organizing and funding the teams travelling from the home countries to the British Empire Games.[14]

At the end of 1929 Robinson provided another detailed progress report to the Hamilton City Council. While no mention was made of the collapse of the American stock market and its wider implications for world economics, finance was a major concern of the meeting. But instead of questioning its considerable investment the committee resolved to send representatives to England early in 1930 to finalize arrangements there, and also approved in principle the idea of offering financial assistance to Empire countries with great distances to travel to Canada.[15] Both decisions proved to be crucial for the successful launching of the British Empire Games in Hamilton.

By March 1930 Robinson was able to confirm that the positive response of Empire countries had removed 'all doubt as to the extent and ultimate success of the British Empire Games';[16] his own commitment to the idea had been a major force in soliciting the favourable reaction. He had travelled to England earlier in the year in order to convince home country officials that the Games were worth supporting. For Empire countries further afield, a promotional visit by the Games' hosts was not possible, but when doubts about participation began to loom, essential support was offered by the organizing committee. In January 1930 the Amateur Athletic Union of Australia reluctantly voted to decline its British Empire Games invitation largely on financial grounds. Robinson immediately cabled a message offering a $5000 contribution towards team expenses; the decision was quickly reversed and Australia soon confirmed its participation. Similar sums were offered to New Zealand and South Africa, and were gratefully accepted. The promise of free accommodation while in Hamilton enhanced the appeal of the Empire Games as well, and all teams were encouraged to send as many competitors as possible. No record of precisely who was invited to Hamilton has been located, but by June India had declined the offer (at the same time declaring its intention to compete in the Far Eastern Games in Japan), while Australia, New Zealand, South Africa, British Guiana, Scotland, Ireland, Newfoundland, Bermuda, Wales and Canada had all confirmed that their teams would be attending. One country was conspicuous by its lack of response.

The participation of England remained uncertain until July when a radio appeal for funds finally resulted in the necessary £8,000 being raised. The official announcement of the English team, headed by Lord Burghley, the 1928 Olympic 400-metre hurdles champion, was made public on 16 July.[17] Two days later the Australian and New Zealand teams docked in Vancouver, and began their four-day train journey eastward to Hamilton; the last stage of preparations for the Games had begun. The sale of tickets was an important financial contributor to the Games, and the overwhelming response from the public ensured large crowds at all events. As a contemporary author observed the scene in Hamilton, 'from August 16 to August 23 Canada's most sport-minded city will provide the setting for the most comprehensive and inspiring set of athletic tests ever conducted in the particular interest of the British Empire'.[18] The 'great family party'[19] was all set to begin.

An estimated 20,000 spectators packed the Civic Stadium in brilliant sunshine on 16 August to watch the parade of athletes enter the arena behind the Union Jack carried by one member of the Argyll and Sutherland Highlanders of Hamilton. It was a most colourful spectacle, with Newfoundland, the oldest colony (which entered Canadian confederation in 1949), leading the procession dressed in white blazers, followed by Bermuda in royal blue, British Guiana in maroon, Australia in green and gold, New Zealand wearing white, South Africa in black and white, Wales in blue, Ireland in green, Scotland sporting royal blue, England in dark

19. At the opening ceremony of the First British Empire Games, Hamilton, 1930. Left to right: E.W. Beattie, K.C., chairman of the committee for Canada; Viscount Willingdon, Governor General of Canada; R.B. Bennett, K.C., Prime Minister of Canada; G. Howard Ferguson, K.C., Prime Minister of Ontario

20. Lord Willingdon officially opening the Games

blue, and Canada dressed in red uniforms.[20] As each team passed the Governor-General's box, its flag was dipped in salute.

After all teams had marched around the stadium, the 450 athletes and officials gathered in the midfield area while the speeches were made. R.B. Bennett, the newly elected Prime Minister of Canada, referred to the happy occasion of such a family gathering and read messages from King George V, the Prince of Wales, the Duke of Connaught, and Lord Derby. In officially opening the Games Lord Willingdon, the Governor-General, spoke of the high traditions of British sport, and concluded that the 'greatness of the Empire is owing to the fact that every citizen has inborn in him the love of games and sports'.[21] Percy Williams, the Canadian Olympic champion at 100 and 200 metres in 1928, pledged the oath of allegiance on behalf of all competitors; the singing of the national anthem, a 21-gun salute, and the releasing of birds brought the opening ceremony to an end, and the enthusiastic spectators settled back to watch the first events in athletics.

Lord Burghley, the British Olympic champion, ran in the initial race of the Games, a heat of the 440-yards hurdles. But the first final to be contested was the triple jump which was, perhaps fittingly, won by Canadian Gordon Smallacombe. The swimming events, along with diving the only sport open to women, began the same evening in the new Municipal Baths, and Celia Wolstenholme of England lowered her own world record in the 220-yard breaststroke in front of a large and spirited audience. It is not the intention here to discuss athletic performances at the Games; rather, the fact that the Games were established at all and the timing of the event will remain the focus. The successful job of hosting the Games was declared in the foreign press almost immediately, and two comments by English writers are particularly noteworthy reactions concerning the Dominion's maturity as a country in its own right. 'For the first time Canada, which has usually been regarded in this country as circulating within the American orbit, has cut herself loose and given a lead to the Empire that should inspire British sportsmen all around the globe.'[22] The second reporter believed 'that even apart from the influence on imperial sport, the Empire games have given the Dominion its finest advertisement for years'.[23]

No doubt encouraged by the tremendous public response to the Games, the leading administrators of the eleven competing countries met on 20 August to discuss future celebrations. The delegates were unanimously of the opinion that the Games should continue and that a governing British Empire Games Federation be formed. J.F. Wadmore, manager of the England athletics team, was named interim Secretary-Treasurer of the Federation, and other office-bearers were confirmed in 1932 during meetings when the Federation was formally established. The 1934 Games were unanimously awarded to South Africa.

Even before the Games were officially over, their value was being widely praised, and the privilege and obligations of being British were reiterated in the press. The degree of sportsmanship and fair play displayed during the competition was outstanding, perhaps exemplified best in the case of the New Zealand sprinter Allan Elliot, who false-started twice and was disqualified, then reinstated in the 100-yard race in response to the spectators' demand that he at least have a chance to run. He did, and was eliminated from further competition by finishing third in his heat. The rules of British fair play had been adhered to, and the Empire was well-pleased with itself.

In his report to the Amateur Athletic Union of Canada in November 1930, Robinson announced that the entire operation of the Games had resulted in a cash loss of about $4,000, and this deficit was being offset by the presentation to Hamilton of equipment worth more than $8,800 which was to be incorporated into the parks and playgrounds around the city.[24] The organizing committee had spent a staggering $30,000 in subsidizing the countries travelling to the Games, and its total revenue had been $110,839. The Hamilton committee's generous financial commitment to the visiting teams set several precedents which have survived in the Games since 1930, and three are of particular importance. The offer of a travel subsidy made the crucial difference in Australia agreeing to attend the Games, and this gesture was encouraged by the Federation to be a permanent feature of future celebrations. The provision of free accommo-dation for the athletes and officials was another major financial undertak-ing for the organizers, and proved to be a forerunner of the first Olympic Village in 1932. The third factor, of using virtually all volunteer labour to plan, organize and run the Games allowed the project to evolve with a manageable budget and a high degree of commitment from those involved.

The Report of the Council for Great Britain concluded that the success-ful launching of a scheme which called into action so many different and widely scattered units, provided proof of the spirit of friendliness and co-operation found in the British Empire. But apart from sport, the report continued, the meeting had an Imperial value of great significance.[25] Doubt had been expressed in some quarters about the usefulness of international contests, like the Olympics, in promoting understanding in the world. But 'at Hamilton, where Britons alone were concerned, there was a warmth of comradeship, a spirit of cordiality and even self-sacrifice which will assuredly bear fruit among those young men and women of the British race'.[26] The similarity between this feeling and the expressed purpose of Cooper's proposal was more than coincidental; the philosophy behind the Pan-Britannic Festival can be linked directly to the 1911 Festival of Empire and the Hamilton Games. While the concept of sentiment and unity through sport was strong throughout this period, the decline of formal political control within the Empire was coupled with, and replaced by, the emergence of informal influences. The establishment of the British Empire Games may be seen as a clear example of this process.

This forging of a fresh link of Empire came at a time when informal influences were overtaking and replacing formal political agreements. A new vehicle for expressing solidarity had been found which appealed to Empire members, and the response to the initiation of the Games during a time of great economic difficulty confirmed the suitability and necessity of the development. Political domination in the world by Great Britain was a rapidly fading memory, and it was no longer the premier sporting power either. Several factors had combined to allow this new expression of cohesiveness to emerge. Despite the successful performance of Great Britain in the 1924 Olympic Games and the Canadian team at Amsterdam in 1928, there was growing discontent at the attitudes displayed in the world festival, and the value of future participation was openly questioned. Linked with this was the increasing domination by the United States in many events at the Games, an important contributor to the definite wave of anti-American sentiment evident at London in 1908, Paris in 1924, and Amsterdam in 1928. A desire for exclusive Empire athletic competition had been intermittently expressed since 1891, but it took the drive and enthusiasm of Bobby Robinson, coupled with the enormous financial commitment from the city of Hamilton, to initiate the British Empire Games in 1930. At that time the British Empire needed the Games to redefine and reconfirm its unity. Political agreements were losing favour as the various Empire countries matured and blossomed in their own right and increasingly sought independence from the mother country.

The Statute of Westminster (1931) was an act designed to effect certain resolutions agreed at the 1926 and 1930 Imperial Conferences. Concomitantly, multi-sport competition was used to underline and reinforce Empire solidarity at a time when internal and external pressures were calling into question the very future of that Empire. While loyalty to the Crown featured strongly in the Games, athletic competition had more than merely a symbolic importance to the Empire. Sport must be seen as an integral and influential component of the social history of the Empire in the early twentieth century, and the power it wielded is well illustrated by the events leading to the establishment of the British Empire Games in 1930.

NOTES

1. 'Visiting Notables at Monster Banquet Paid Many Worthy Tributes', *Hamilton Spectator*, 25 Aug. 1930, 17.
2. 'To-Day's The Day', *Hamilton Spectator*, 16 Aug. 1930, 6.
3. 'Congratulations', *Hamilton Spectator*, 18 Aug. 1930, 6.
4. R.F. Holland, *Britain and the Commonwealth Alliance 1918–1939* (London, 1981) p. 23.
5. John Gallagher and Ronald Robinson, 'The Imperialism of Free Trade', *The Economic History Review*, Second Series, Vol. VI, No. 1 (1953), 1–15.
6. Holland, op. cit., p. 68.
7. Robert MacGregor Dawson (ed.), *The Development of Dominion Status 1900–1936* (London, 1965), p. 63.
8. Nicholas Mansergh, *The Commonwealth Experience Volume Two: From British to Multi-Racial Commonwealth* (London, 1982) pp. 17–18.
9. K.C. Wheare, *The Statute of Westminster and Dominion Status* (Oxford, 1942), p. 28.
10. Holland, op. cit., p. 87.
11. Minutes of the Municipal Council of the City of Hamilton for the Year 1929. Hamilton (1929), 58.
12. 'British Empire Games Outlined to Members of Council Last Night', *Hamilton Herald*, 12 Jan. 1929, 13.

13. 'The Universities' Tour', *The Times*, 8 July 1929, 6.
14. M.M. Robinson, 'British Empire Games, Canada, 1930: What the City of Hamilton has Undertaken', *British Olympic Journal* (March 1930), 24.
15. 'British Empire Games Committee Conference Was Quite Enthusiastic', *Hamilton Herald*, 18 Dec. 1929, 12.
16. Robinson, op. cit., p. 22.
17. 'Lord Burghley Heads England's Selections', *Hamilton Spectator*, 17 July 1930, 23.
18. H.H. Roxborough, 'An Empire Olympiad', *Maclean's Magazine*, Volume XLIII, No. 15 (1 August 1930), 5.
19. 'To-Day's The Day', op. cit.
20. 'The Empire Games', *The Times* 18 Aug. 1930, 6.
21. 'Most Colourful Scene Canadians Have Been Privileged to View', *Hamilton Spectator*, 18 Aug. 1930, 16.
22. 'Special Writers Send Home Lavish Accounts', *Hamilton Spectator*, 18 Aug. 1930, 16.
24. 'Report of British Empire Games Committee', Minutes of the Forty-Third Annual Meeting of the Amateur Athletic Union of Canada, held at the Hotel Vancouver, Vancouver, B. C., 6, 7, 8 Nov. 1930, 78.
25. 'Report of the Council for Great Britain and Statement of Account', British Empire Games, Canada, 1930 (10 Nov. 1930), 2.
26. Ibid.

21. Percy Williams taking the oath for the countries of the Empire

22. Percy Williams winning the 100 yards final

Teaching the Nations How to Play: Sport and Society in the British Empire and Commonwealth

HAROLD PERKIN

'Let not England forget her precedence of teaching nations how to live.'
– John Milton, *The Doctrine and Discipline of Divorce*

The history of societies is reflected more vividly in the way they spend their leisure than in their politics or their work. Sport in particular is much more than a pastime or recreation. It is an integral part of a society's culture, an expression of its ideal of man (and woman) hood, a pursuit of the ends of life rather than the means, an activity one really wants to do with one's whole self unforced by the constraints of economic necessity or the state. As such the history of sport gives a unique insight into the way a society changes and impacts on other societies it comes into contact with and, conversely, the way those societies react back upon it. In the case of Britain and its Empire in the last hundred years or so, sport played a part in holding the Empire together and also, paradoxically, in emancipating the subject nations from tutelage. Thus it helped the Empire to decolonize on a friendlier basis than any other in the world's history, and so contributed to the transformation of the British Empire into the Commonwealth of Nations.

Every nation thinks itself superior to others in the important things in life. In a marginal note to *Areopagitica*, his unsurpassed argument for freedom of speech, John Milton casually remarked that 'God is English'. For that reason God would naturally 'reveal Himself to His servants, and as His Manner is, first to His Englishmen'. It is not surprising, therefore, that in a later work Milton should naively urge: 'Let not England forget her precedence of teaching nations how to live'. He would have been more prophetic, perhaps, if he had urged his fellow countrymen to teach the nations how to play. Although sports and games are as old as humankind, few would deny that most of the sports and games the world now plays were first organized in their present forms by the British in the nineteenth century: association football, rugby, cricket, tennis, golf, rowing, track and field athletics, and most surprisingly for a country blessed with a mild climate, skiing, which British sportsmen turned from a Scandinavian peasant form of transport into an Alpine winter sport. Even American football derives from rugby, and broke away from the English game only in 1882. The first modern Olympic Games in Athens in 1896, although the brain-child of the French Baron Pierre de Coubertin, were run on the only internationally recognized rules then available, those of the British Amateur Athletic Association. And in 1906 the first international authority in soccer, the Fédération Internationale de Football Associations (FIFA) was supplied by the English Football Association with its first President, in the person of the FA Treasurer, D.B. Woolfall.

This precedence in organized competitive games is all the more surprising since the British had only recently learned to play them themselves. Until the early nineteenth century the British were famous for their *disorganized* games: rowdy, bloodthirsty, cruel sports like bull and bear-baiting, dog- and cock-fighting, rat-killing, bare-fisted prize-fighting, and violent games of football for any number of players *fought* (I use the word advisedly) between the whole populations of villages, or the two ends of the same town such as Derby or Ashbourne. Football at Rugby School before *Tom Brown's Schooldays* might be played between 300 players, and a player might be 'allowed to pick up the ball and run with it, and every adversary could stop him by collaring, hacking over, and charging, or by any other means he pleased'.

The development of team games out of such free-for-alls was due to the demands of the more urbanized and disciplined society which emerged from the first Industrial Revolution, to the consequent need for exercise and relaxation in more confined space and restricted leisure time, and to the 'moral revolution', often called the rise of Victorianism, which suppressed the bloodier and rowdier sports and made way for the 'rational recreation' of the more orderly, civilized world of Victorian Britain.

All classes took part in the new organized games, though some took to organization more readily than others, but the class which mattered most, both to the national and international spread of the games and to the emerging and rapidly enlarging Empire was the class educated at the public schools. These private boarding schools for the wealthy upper and middle classes were, rather absurdly, called 'public' because they replaced the more respectable and traditional system of education by private tutor for the really rich aristocracy and gentry. Their chief value, paradoxically, was economy: they put a quasi-aristocratic education within reach of the middle class by providing dismal fare in Spartan conditions. The games field was a cheaper way of catering for the leisure and exercise of growing boys than the traditional hunting and shooting of young aristocrats, not to mention the drinking, gambling and wenching of the traditional young rake. Demographically, leaving aside Eton, Harrow and Winchester perhaps, they catered more for the upper middle class than for the landed aristocracy and gentry, above all for the sons of the clergy and the higher professions who looked not to business but to professional and government service for their future careers. The small if increasing number of business men's sons who attended them were usually converted by their experience from industrial to professional careers. This confirms, though it does not explain, Martin Wiener's thesis of 'the decline of the industrial spirit', which was really the mirror image of the rise of the public-service ideal.[1]

Organized games were at the heart of the public-service ideal. In their combination of individual prowess and group co-operation for a common purpose they fostered the elite virtues of self-confidence, self-reliance, leadership, team spirit, and loyalty to comrades – all inculcated with brutal, arbitrary and corporal punishment, mostly administered by senior boys, which fostered toughness of character, indifference to hardship, and insensitivity to pain and emotional distress, especially in others. These were the ideal qualities for governing a class-ridden nation in which social control was exercised by a small and mainly amateur ruling class over a mass of underfed and ill-educated workers, still more for a multi-racial empire in which a tiny white minority maintained its ascendancy over a multitude of 'the lesser breeds without the law'. As a later colonial administrator argued:

> My schooling was an excellent preparation for my career in the
> Sudan Political Service. From an early age one was taught to be self-
> reliant and to accept responsibility. The virtues of self-discipline and
> physical fitness, both essential elements in public school training,
> were to prove of inestimable value as also was the exercising which
> one gains from being a house and subsequently a school monitor.[2]

Since the Sudan Political Service was deliberately recruited by Lord Cromer from public-school and Oxbridge athletes, with more 'blues' than brains, it was not surprising that it became the *corps d'élite* of the Colonial Service.[3]

Disciplined sport at school required agreed uniform rules, even for inter-house matches, and inter-school matches extended the need for organization beyond the school walls. Old boys at Oxford and Cambridge who wished to play some kind of football had to agree, for example, on whether or not the ball could be handled. Thus different groups of Cambridge undergraduates in 1848 drew up the rules of both rugby football and what was later to be called soccer. ('Rugger' and 'soccer' were typical examples of public-school slang, for 'rugby' and 'association' respectively – cf. 'brekker' for breakfast.) Finally, in order to play other clubs which were forming outside the schools and universities, the old boys joined together with others to adopt the Cambridge rules, for soccer in 1863 and rugby in 1971, and so founded the Football Association and the Rugby Football Union. In athletics, a Cambridge rowing blue and English national champion walker, John Graham Chambers, founded and drew up the rules of the Amateur Athletic Club in 1866, and went on the next year to draft the Marquess of Queensberry's Rules for boxing. With their self-confidence, drive for leadership, economic resources, and nationwide connections, the old boys of the public schools and Oxbridge were in the best position to organize their favourite sports on a national scale.

Further afield, wherever they went throughout the world, they took their games and their social attitudes with them. Team games like cricket and rugby were ideal for keeping fit and holding the white community together in distant climes, and even where the white rulers were few and far between, tennis, golf, squash or fives were happy substitutes.

But if it had been left only to the old boys within the formal Empire, British games would never have conquered the world. British influence on the world's leisure went far wider than that. We have traditionally thought of the Empire in Britain's century, roughly 1815–1914, in terms both too narrow and too broad: too broad because those red-tinted areas of the map on Mercator's projection which seemed to cover half the world (and *did* cover one quarter of the habitable land by 1900) seemed to suggest an undifferentiated series of British 'possessions' all ruled in much the same way from London; too narrow because there were far larger areas of the world where British influence, economic power and culture (including sport) operated in subtly penetrating ways. We need to see Britain in that century less as a narrowly imperial power and more as an international superpower, its political, economic and cultural tentacles reaching out to most corners of the earth; and the Empire not as a monolith but as part of a continuum in the exercise of British power and influence, from the most directly ruled Crown Colony through shades of increasing self-government up to dominion status, and out beyond the red-tinted areas to places never under the Union Jack where British merchants, bankers, railway and mining engineers, ranchers, oil prospectors, missionaries, schoolmasters, sailors and navvies, and sojourners and settlers of every kind lived and worked.

As Stephen Constantine has suggested, the world from Britain's point of view in its period of hegemony was divided into three concentric circles of influence and trading freedom.[4] In the widest circle, Britain preferred if possible to trade with free self-governing nations who would maintain law and order and freedom of passage for the British merchant and investor at no cost to Britain. Only if countries like China or Japan refused to trade was there a need for political or military intervention, preferably short-lived. The outermost circle therefore consisted of most of the trading world, where British businessmen could operate freely without troubling the home government except in time of war. In some of these countries, for example Argentina, Uruguay and Chile, the British presence was so thick on the ground as almost to make them part of the informal empire. The second circle enclosed the formal Empire. At its outer edge lay the great self-governing dominions which ran practically all their own affairs, except world-wide defence, and maintained the trading system almost unaided: Canada, Australia, New Zealand, and later, South Africa. Then came, for all its dependent status, the Indian Empire, where the white Raj maintained a *de facto* independence in commercial policy. Towards the inner edge lay the countries like Egypt, the Sudan and the Indian principalities, which were technically independent but could not maintain a stable trading ethos without British 'protection'. Finally, the third, innermost circle contained only those colonies which, because they could not guarantee peaceful access for Britain's trade, were simply conquered and subjected to direct British rule. Even there, wherever possible as in the Gold Coast and Nigeria, 'indirect rule' was practised by hard-pressed district officers overseeing the local tribal chiefs. At its core lay the chain of bases, islands and ports around the world which, too small at that time to govern themselves or prevent other great powers from taking them over, safeguarded the trade routes for all the rest.

Looked at from this point of view, the British were everywhere: running cotton mills in Russia, railways and banks in South America, cattle ranches and gold mines in the American Far West, plantations in Ceylon and West Africa, farms in Kenya and Rhodesia, mines in the Transvaal, Malaya and the Andes, and banks, warehouses and factories all over Europe. And wherever two or three Britons were gathered together, to keep fit and while away the time they played the games of home. The English brothers Charnock introduced soccer to Russia among their cotton workers at Zuyevo. A Mr. Nicholson of Thomas Cook's in Vienna joined Lord Rothschild's gardeners in the First Vienna Football Club, and Jimmy Hogan coached the Austrian *Wunderteam* and later the Hungarian national soccer team. In Argentina members of the British colony at Buenos Aires competed for Sir Thomas Lipton's soccer trophy. In Brazil Charles Miller, of English parentage and Southampton United, organized soccer matches among the British gas engineers, railway men and bank clerks of Sao Paolo. In Japan an English teacher named Johns demonstrated soccer at Kogakuryo School in 1874, and Professor Clark of Keio University and a Japanese Cambridge graduate named Tanaka introduced rugby in 1899. English businessmen taught the Danes and Dutch to play cricket, and English and Welsh wine merchants at Bordeaux and Perpignan taught the French how to play rugby. The first tour by an English cricket XI was, surprisingly, to Canada and the United States in 1859, where Anglo-Saxon immigrants played in Toronto, Montreal and Philadelphia.

Within the formal Empire, games were, if anything, easier to organize, since there were often more Britons together and more resources of land and equipment under their control. The first English merchants and administrators in India had tended to 'go native', hunting tiger and playing polo with the Rajahs and taking Indian wives or mistresses, but as their numbers grew and they brought out their own womenfolk they began to import other European comforts, including cricket. The Old Etonians in the East India Company played the local Parsees at cricket as early as 1784, and in 1792 the Calcutta Cricket Club was founded. Cricket was played in Barbados from 1806, in the Cape from 1808, in Ceylon from 1832, in Australia and New Zealand from the 1840s, in Hong Kong from 1851, in Fiji from the 1870s. Rugby was introduced to New Zealand in 1870 by Charles Monro, son of the speaker of the colonial House of Representatives, who had been a student in London; to South Africa by British troops in the Zulu Wars of the 1870s; to Australia by 1875 when the Australian RFU was founded; and to Fiji by British troops in 1884. Track and field athletics were sufficiently advanced in the dominions and colonies for a friendly and unofficial Empire Games to be held after the London Olympic Games of 1908, but not sufficiently advanced to sustain separate regular meetings, which had to wait until the Hamilton Games in Canada in 1930.

The dog which had not barked in the imperial night was, of course, soccer, and that raises an interesting question about sport and society in the Empire as against the world outside. Why did the emerging dominions and major colonies go in for the more 'gentlemanly' sports like cricket and rugby union, while the rest of the world, notably Europe, Russia and South America, so enthusiastically embraced soccer? The answer, at least in part, lies in the different social backgrounds and attitudes of the missionaries of British sport who went to different areas of the world. The old boys from the public schools and Oxbridge who went out to the Empire took not only the games they played at school and college but also their obsession with the distinction between the gentleman amateur and the mercenary profes- sional which they had practised at home. The amateur principle was a defence not only against social pollution by the 'untouchables' of the home country but also against defeat by the highly skilled professionals who emerged from the working class in almost every sport. In athletics the Amateur Athletic Club in 1868 kept out the professional 'pedestrians' who had dominated running earlier in the century by defining an amateur as 'any gentleman who has never competed in open competition, or for public money, or for admission money, and who has never at any period in his life taught or assisted in the pursuit of athletic exercises as a means of livelihood, or is a mechanic, artisan or labourer' (my emphasis).[5] The AAC could not hold this line, but its successor the Amateur Athletic Association, founded in 1880, still upheld the principle of non-payment for any sport, not only athletics. In cricket the amateurs had long sold the pass by employing professionals, especially as bowlers, but the gentlemen remained firmly in charge by insisting on amateur captains of most first- class sides until Len Hutton became captain of England in 1952. Rugby Union has managed to fend off the taint of professionalism down to the present day, and remains 'the No. 1 totally amateur sport', at the cost of expelling the Northern clubs of the professional Rugby League in 1893.[6]

The odd man out among the games taken over by the public schools and organized on a national basis by old boys was, of course, soccer. For twenty years after the founding of the Football Association in 1863 the game was dominated by gentlemen, and the FA Cup (from 1872) was won for the first eleven years by amateur teams like the Wanderers, Oxford University, and the Old Etonians. Then in the famous Cup Final of 1883 a team of working men, Blackburn Olympic, in effect part-time or full-time professionals, beat the holders, the Old Etonians. After a row the following year over the payment of expenses for 'broken time' for working-class players and a threat by the Northern clubs to withdraw (as the Rugby League did nine years later), the FA gave in and from 1885 permitted professionalism. This transformed the game which, despite the survival of first-class amateur clubs like the Corinthians and Queen's Park, became very much a working-class sport. As such it was much less attractive to the public-school men who went out to build the empire. The merchants, engineers and bank clerks who went out to the rest of the world were less commonly public-school boys and rarely Oxbridge graduates, and had less objection to the plebeian and less expensive game. Soccer was easier to organize, and much easier to teach to the locals, who often took it up with enthusiasm.

It would be too simple to claim that cricket and rugby were confined to the empire and soccer to the world. For one thing, there are obvious exceptions, though they tend to 'prove the rule'. The wine merchants who took rugby to France were public-school boys in a traditionally upper-crust trade. C. Aubrey Smith who took cricket to Hollywood had captained England in South Africa in 1889 and remained behind in Johannesburg as a stockbroker before trying his luck in Hollywood in the 1930s with American films, then surprisingly obsessed with tales of the British Empire like *Lives of a Bengal Lancer* and *Sanders of the River*. Some of the British residents in Buenos Aires and Tokyo preferred rugby to soccer and played the amateur game with some skill. The generalization holds good, none the less, that where the public-school boys went in large numbers, inside or outside the Empire, there cricket and rugby prevailed, and where the horny-handed sons of toil, or at least of the counting house, predominated, there soccer fever tended to infect the locals and become endemic.

The clinching thing, of course, was which sport the locals took up in large numbers. Outside the Empire the British residents were comparatively few and conversion to the sport was a matter of spontaneous interest, curiosity and admiration, and soccer seems to have won the popular contest every time. There was a certain zest in beating the arrogant British at their own game, and nationalism undoubtedly played a part, as in Austrian or Spanish soccer or French rugby, but it was not an obsession as it was in the empire. There, beating the mother country became for the expatriates and white settlers a sort of rite of passage, a test of manhood, almost a proof of fitness for home rule. Every cricketing or rugby-playing dominion looks back on its first Test victory over England as its coming of age, and Australia's famous winning of the 'Ashes of English cricket' in 1882 was only the first of such colonial victories. But for the non-white colonies and dominions, when they finally wrested control of their national teams from the settlers and anglophile elites, beating England was a nationalist triumph. When the predominantly black West Indian cricket team – with 'Those two little pals of mine, Ramadhin and Valentine' – finally won a Test series in England in 1950 the triumphalism was understandably boundless. It was all the sweeter for taking over the white man's own game and making him submit.

In some ways this reflects the history of sport in Britain itself. The struggle over amateurism and professionalism was an expression of Victorian class conflict. As Paul Weiss, the American philosopher of sport, has put it, 'By and large the line between amateur and professional is mainly a line between the unpaid members of a privileged class and the paid members of an underprivileged class'. But the existence of conflict does not predetermine the outcome, and each sport found its own solution, whether outright rejection of professionalism, accommodation to it, or compromise. Rugby rejected it, and split into two hostile camps, the mainly middle-class Union and the working-class League. Soccer embraced it, and paid the penalty, no doubt welcome to the working class, of becoming a proletarian sport. Cricket compromised, and perhaps got the best of both worlds until the emergence of the highly paid and mainly middle-class professional superstars of the 1960s and the 'Packer Revolution' of the late 1970s.

In the same way, class as well as race and nationalism played a role in sport in the Empire and Commonwealth. Each sport in each colony and dominion found its own solution to the problem of who best represented the aspirations, political as well as sporting and cultural, of the community – or perhaps, as in the case of South Africa, failed to find it until too late. In the white dominions, always more democratic than the mother country, class differences were less obsessive, and the amateur/professional divide was taken less seriously. They soon found ways, in the interests of technical performance and of beating England, of selecting and funding their best cricket and rugby players from any level of society. In the Indian Empire, cricket was long dominated by Anglophile princes like Ranjitsinjhi and Maharajahs like Pataudi, Porbander, and Vizianagram, and in all four successor states, India, Pakistan, Bangladesh and Ceylon, remains a game of high social status, not readily open to the lower castes and poorer masses. That is not to say, of course, that in those highly stratified societies in which the rich and powerful are still admired and respected sport did not play a part in unifying the nation and paving the way for independence. On the contrary, where democracy was practised in a hierarchical society and equality was not even an ideal, beating the British at sport as in politics was one of the few unifying national objectives. The Indian immigrants who crowded on to the pitch at Edgbaston at the end of India's triumphant Test series in 1986 had more to celebrate than a game of cricket. No multi-racial cricket or rugby could have cured South Africa's problems, though if it had been introduced early enough it might have prevented apartheid.

Nevertheless, the evolution of the British Empire into the Common- wealth of Nations is a unique phenomenon in the history of the world – the only great empire which, after learning a few bloody lessons like the American Revolution and the Boer War, and more recent if lesser ones in Malaya, Kenya, Cyprus, Borneo and Aden, has voluntarily transformed itself into a free and politically equal community of states, which despite immense differences of size, wealth, influence and political attitude, remain on terms of friendship and goodwill. Only a few have fallen away and become irreconcilable – Burma, Ireland, South Yemen, Pakistan, South Africa – and let us hope that recent events will bring a multi-racial South Africa back into friendship. In the maintenance of that friendship and goodwill throughout a difficult and by no means trouble-free transition, sport has played an important psychological part. It helped to foster unity and self-confidence in the old colonies and dominions in their Oedipal, love-hate relation with the mother country, and to smooth the transition from rivalry to independence. Can one imagine any other empire in which the successor states played games against the imperial power? Would the Franks, Vizigoths or Huns have played football with the Romans – except perhaps with their heads?

Although, contrary to their popular self-image, the British have never liked losing, they have always done so (modern soccer hooliganism apart) with more grace than most. At the finish, nothing became the largest empire the world has ever seen than the leaving of it. Losing at organized sports and games prepared the British psychologically, just as winning prepared the colonists, for decolonization and for mutual respect and independence on both sides, and just as winning and losing prepared the British themselves, working-class professionals triumphing over gentlemen amateurs, for a more egalitarian – which is not to say totally equal – society. Thus organized, competitive sport paved the road both from Empire to Commonwealth and from the Victorian 'survival of the fittest' (or 'devil-take-the-hindmost') society to the Welfare State. Let us hope that those who never liked either road, towards decolonization or the Welfare State, and are temporarily in charge of the roadworks, do not manage to break up either of them.

NOTES

1. Martin Wiener, *English Culture and the Decline of the Industrial Spirit, 1850–1980* (Cambridge, 1981).
2. J.A. Mangan, *The Games Ethic and Imperialism* (London, 1986), p.86.
3. Ibid., p. 72.
4. Stephen Constantine, 'Imperialism Re-examined', *Då Och Nu*, Vols. 1–2 (1976), 13–27.
5. Peter Lovesey, *The Official Centenary History of the Amateur Athletic Association* (London, 1979), p. 22.
6. Terry Godwin, *The Guinness Book of Rugby Facts and Feats* (London, 1983), Introduction.
7. Paul A, Weiss, *Sport: A Philosophical Inquiry* (Carbondale, IL, 1969).

Index